Industrial Relations
Under Liberal Democracy

STUDIES IN INDUSTRIAL RELATIONS

Hoyt N. Wheeler and Roy J. Adams, General Editors

INDUSTRIAL RELATIONS
UNDER LIBERAL DEMOCRACY
North America in Comparative Perspective

Roy J. Adams

UNIVERSITY OF SOUTH CAROLINA PRESS

Published in Columbia, South Carolina, by the
University of South Carolina Press

Manufactured in the United States of America

Library of Congress Cataloging-in-Publication Data

Adams, Roy J.
    Industrial relations under liberal democracy : North America in
comparative perspective / Roy J. Adams.
        p.   cm. — (Studies in industrial relations)
    Includes bibliographical references and index.
    Contents: The emergence of modern industrial relations—The
European mainstream—American exceptionalism—Contemporary
collective bargaining—The organized and the unorganized—
Industrial relations and socioeconomic performance—From
confrontation to cooperation: a tale of three countries—
Transcending adversarial industrial relations.
    ISBN 1–57003–019–7
    1. Industrial relations—North America. 2. Industrial relations—
Europe. 3. Comparative management. I. Title. II. Series.
HD6960.5.N7A3 1995
331'.094—dc20   94–18692

CONTENTS

TABLES

PREFACE

This book was written for anyone concerned with relations between labor, management, and the state in North America. My experience is that during the past three decades North Americans concerned with labor-management-government relations have been only mildly interested in comparative work. Research has focused largely on North American problems which, until recently, rarely were set within an international framework. Textbooks also focused almost exclusively on North American institutions and historical developments, although occasionally there was a separate chapter on foreign practices. That separate treatment often made developments outside of North America seem exotic; interesting, perhaps, but of little practical relevance.

In recent years the situation has begun to change. Now there are several notable international projects underway.[1] The change has been brought about in part by growing international competition and in particular due to the observation that the pattern of labor-management-government relations has been critical to the economic success of countries such as Japan and Germany.

In writing this book, my object was to review North American historical developments and contemporary practices to explicitly compare them with developments in other countries that are now advanced, industrialized, liberal democratic nations—that is, other nations that are at roughly the same level of economic and political development as Canada and the United States. My perspective is that North America is both different and not so different at all. Canada and the United States fit squarely within a general liberal democratic pattern of political economic behavior but within that general pattern these countries are exceptional. One major purpose of the book is to explain that exceptionalism within the general pattern of liberal democracy.

Deciding on the structure of this book was difficult. I was born, raised, and educated in the United States but have been living and working in Canada for the past twenty years and am now a citizen of both countries. I wanted to write a book that would be interesting and relevant to both Canadians and Americans. As a result, the final product has a sort of nested box structure. At one level it is a comparison of North America (Canada and the United States taken as a single entity) with, primarily, Europe. At another level, Canadian developments are contrasted with those in the United States. The end product may appear to have an American bias. It was not intentional. However, because Canadians know much more about the United States than vice versa, I have had to devote more space to explaining Canada to Americans than the United States to Canadians.

I have deliberately written the book in plain language and have consciously attempted to minimize the use of jargon. I have also taken the advice of my friend, Joep Bolweg, and have tried to keep the length of the book short thereby making the volume more accessible to those harried by the deluge of contemporary information. As a result, many interesting subjects that might have been included have been sacrificed. I could easily have incorporated much more information on neocorporatism and on workers' participation in enterprise management via works councils and participation on boards of directors. Historians may find my treatment of certain epochs (e.g., industrial relations in the middle ages) blunt instead of nuanced. On the other hand, I hope that I have included enough to enable the reader to appreciate the dominant forces giving rise to modern industrial relations as well as the ways in which North America is different and the reasons for the development of those differences. I hope that the book will whet the reader's appetite for more. For those who find that it is still too long to fit into ever-tightening schedules, the final chapter summarizes the major arguments made in the main text.

This book incorporates a good deal of theory and is intended to be a theoretical contribution to the field of industrial relations. Among the theories embedded in the discourse are those of Marx, the Webbs, Commons, Perlman, Sturmthal, and many others. However, the theories are not, for the most part, discussed as something separate from the phenomena that they were intended to explain. Instead I have made use of them in context. For the most part I have attempted to show what they explain instead of telling what the authors said.

There is also my own theory of the reasons why North America developed differently from Europe. It may be stated in truncated form as follows: in Europe, the labor movement (in the period between about 1880 and 1920) adopted a radical philosophy which called for the overthrow of the capitalist system. In that period it became quite successful in attracting adherents and in mobilizing social protest. The mobilization frightened the political elite and the business elite, who arrived at explicit or implicit accords with labor that produced the industrial relations systems configurations that we find today. In particular, those accords led to the phenomena that Europeans call social partnership. In the United States, labor was unable to pose a threat of the same intensity as European labor and as a result no accord was achieved and labor-management conflict and animosity continued. The result was the system that today is often referred to as adversarialism.

In addition to providing an objective theory, the book also has a normative side to it. A major conclusion is that adversarialism—our culture of conflict—is contrary to ethical, political, and economic objectives that we consider to be important. Our contemporary systems disenfranchise the majority of industrial citizens leaving us far behind the evolution of democratic practice abroad. Our inability to develop institutions capable of containing our propensity for animosity and conflict is jeopardizing our economic future. In the final few chapters, I draw on the international experience to suggest ways that we might be able to move beyond adversarialism towards social partnership.

Several friends and colleagues have helped to prevent me from making too much of a fool of myself by pointing out problems with previous versions of the text. I am particularly indebted to Bernie Adell, Hoyt Wheeler, Trevor Bain, Ron Bean, Kurt Wetzel, Steve Havlovic, John Windmuller, Jonathan Zeitlin, Hans Slomp, and an anonymous reviewer—all of whom read the entire document and provided useful suggestions for improvement. In addition, Walter Galenson, Rudolf Meidner, and Bob Flanagan all read and commented on parts of the book. Several students in my comparative courses also provided me with written comments on parts or all of the draft. I am sure that the book has benefited from the advice that I received but I alone am responsible for the remaining flaws in the text.

Bruce Pearce, at the library of the University of Toronto's Center for Industrial Relations, was very helpful in bringing relevant books and documents to my attention. Although he died before the manuscript was finished, over the years I learned a great deal from Everett Kassalow. He provided me with my initial introduction to the subject as my advisor at the University of Wisconsin's Industrial Relations Research Institute and was continually supportive in the years that followed. A special thank you goes to my wife, Marilyn, who read and commented on the book even though she generally finds industrial relations to be a dreadfully dull subject compared to her passion for epic literature and haute cuisine. She even flattered me on a trip to the United States by telling me she was looking forward to getting back to the manuscript, on the next leg of the journey, to see what happened. To a writer, that is a compliment of the highest order.

INDUSTRIAL RELATIONS
UNDER LIBERAL DEMOCRACY

Chapter 1

THE EMERGENCE OF
MODERN INDUSTRIAL RELATIONS

Modern industrial relations systems first began to take shape during the take off of the industrial revolution in Great Britain between about 1760 and 1830 (Ashton 1964). Compared with the present, it was a period of very little state intervention into employment relations. Employers and employees (then known as masters and servants in the eyes of the law) could agree to essentially any (legal) terms and conditions of employment. Workers were free to move to whatever job provided the best terms and conditions of employment, and employers could hire the person who offered his/her services for the lowest compensation. Either party could end the relationship subject only to reasonable notice, a standard introduced by common law judges (Atiyah 1979; Veneziani 1986). The theory, which provided the base for this system, was that in seeking to maximize their own self interest the parties to the employment relationship were also engaging in activities that would in the aggregate result in the most productive economy. Implicit in this theory (which was just becoming popular at that time) was the proposition that the forces of supply and demand would most efficiently determine wages and other conditions of employment. If labor, management, or the state attempted to interfere with the workings of the market, the inevitable result would be a reduction in wealth and living standards.

This system of employment relations was very different from the ones that had preceded it. Throughout the feudal era, terms and conditions of employment had been highly regulated across Europe. Two ideal types of systems would have been identifiable to the traveller in the years between about 1000 and 1700 A.D. Certainly there were great changes in employment relations over these centuries but the broad pattern of relationships remained sufficiently constant for them to be continuously recognizable (see, e.g., Gregg 1971).

THE RURAL SYSTEM

In the high middle ages, 90 to 95 percent of the population lived in the country and received their living from the land (Pirenne 1937). The main unit of production was the great estate. The center of power and authority was the lord of the manor (a knight, bishop, baron, earl, etc.) who often resided in a walled castle. Estates were subdivided into manors each of which was associated with one or more villages. The land under the jurisdiction of the manor was divided into three parts: (1) the demesne was arable land for the exclusive use of the lord, (2) hides or virgates consisted of sufficient arable land to feed a family as well as a cottage with garden and rights to the commons, and (3) the commons consisted of meadows, marshes, heath, and forest that were considered to be uncultivable. The developed land was divided into several strips and further divided into three fields one of which was always fallow.

There were four principal actors on the estates:

1. The lord who generally held the land in "fief" from another greater lord. In theory the king "owned"[1] the land but in practice the lords controlled it and could generally pass it on to their heirs. As vassals, they owed duties (services) to the higher lord, most notably the duty to supply men at arms in time of war (Duby 1968).
2. Domestic serfs were people directly attached to the lord's household. Among them were servants, artisans, and managers. Bailiffs generally ran the various manor houses and around the manor houses were workshops which produced cloth, ale, and implements required for cultivation.
3. Those who possessed the hides were known as peasants or villeins. They did most of the farming. Feudalism was initially an implicit contract between farmers (peasants) and soldiers. When the Pax Romana of the Roman Empire broke down, in theory peasants agreed to provide soldiers with the necessities of life and the soldiers agreed to protect the peasants from roving bands and other threats to health and security.
4. Cotters were the fourth actor on the medieval estate. These people had no virgate but rather had to make do with a small patch of land in the common for growing vegetables or keeping farm animals. Their income was also supplemented by wages received for their labor, which was often in demand at harvest time.

The relation of the lord to the peasants was a paternal one. "In times of war he defended them against the enemy, and it was clearly to his advantage to do so since he lived by their labor" (Pirenne 1937). In return for protection, the peasants had several obligations to the lord:

1. They had to provide him with part of their produce.
2. They had to work the "demesne" part of the time and provide the lord

with other services as required. Cotters might work for the lord on a casual basis for wages or in-kind payment (e.g., food, clothing).
3. They were often required to grind their grain at the lord's mill and brew ale in his brewery for a fee.
4. They had to pay fees to the lord at special occasions such as when a son took possession of his father's hide or when a member of the family married.

None of the serfs were free to come and go as they chose.[2] By the turn of the tenth century, the custom had taken root that serfs could not leave the estate without the lord's permission. On the other hand, custom forbade the lord to expel a serf from his virgate which the serf had a right to pass on to his progeny. By the high middle ages, the relationship between the lord and serfs had taken on a paternal character with the lord as a father figure and the serfs as his children. They owed him loyalty, love, and obedience. He, in turn, was responsible for their welfare. There were, of course, many irresponsible parents and wayward children.[3]

THE URBAN SYSTEM

After the fall of the Roman Empire, there were few cities of any size in Western Europe. For the most part the medieval manors were self-sustaining although some import and export trade was carried out by travelling merchants.

About 1000 A.D. there was a revival of trade as the forces of Islam were driven back from the Mediterranean and the Norse raiders became settled. With more commerce, traders began to establish bases often on overland or river routes near fortified castles. These new urban centers attracted artisans from the rural areas. Clothmakers who had been scattered over the countryside, for example, found it more convenient to gather in the new centers where they more easily found wool, soap, and dye imported by the merchants. Many of these artisans were sons and daughters of serfs who ran away from the estate and were not pursued vigorously by their lord.

The new urban dwellers initially came under the authority of the lord controlling the castles around which they settled. From him they demanded the freedom to "come and go, to do business, to sell goods" (Pirenne 1937, 39). Freedom was valued primarily because it was seen as necessary in order successfully to carry out trade. Typically it was granted for a price. By the twelfth century, a system of employment relations quite different from that existing in the country had evolved.

Production was carried out primarily by craftspeople working in small household workshops. Among the important urban trades were bakers, butchers, tailors, shoe and boot makers, blacksmiths, carpenters, potters, clothmakers, goldsmiths, and fishers. The medieval craftsworkers combined several functions which are now often separate. He (and sometimes she) was simultaneously:

1. A worker who took part "with his own hands in the more important operations of his craft."
2. A foreperson who superintended "the labors of his journeymen and his apprentices."
3. An employer (a capitalist) "who undertook the responsibilities of production and supplied the capital for materials, food and wages."
4. A merchant who had to secure his/her own raw materials from "the producer in the local market or from neighboring country districts" since there were often no independent wholesalers.
5. A shopkeeper who sold his/her product directly to the consumer. (All quotes from Unwin 1957, 10).

Having a similar community of interest, craftsworkers tended to combine into organizations based on their common skills. By the twelfth century, these guilds had taken on several functions. They ensured that their members produced a product which met certain quality standards; they regulated prices around the concept of the just price; they controlled access to the trade; they regulated wages and conditions of work for journeymen and apprentices; and they functioned as a social club.[4] Guild members attended church together and put on religious plays and parades at festivals. They generally provided for members in troubled times and made sure that deceased members were buried with dignity.

Typically the guilds held a charter from a town authority (usually a lord or a bishop) who granted them a local monopoly in exchange for an annual fee as well as a guarantee of product quality and a just price. Guild regulations were enforced by a council elected by all masters and journeymen.

As on the medieval manor, the relationship of the master to the journeymen and apprentices was a paternal one. In the classic system, both apprentices and journeymen lived in the house of the master and for the most part were considered part of his family. The master was considered to be responsible for both the welfare of his charges and for their conduct. They were expected to obey him with respect not only to the job but also their personal life. Apprentices typically began their training at a young age—seven to twelve years—and thus the acceptance by masters of paternal responsibility was essential.

These systems were not very efficient. They did not elicit maximum productivity. They did, however, a reasonable job of providing for basic needs. The guilds and the manors provided for both the economic and social needs of the producers but the distribution of the product was hardly equitable and exploitation of the weak by the strong was common. In both systems, the producers had a good deal of control over critical decisions. The guilds were self regulating although richer masters dominated decision making and apprentices had little influence. On the medieval farms, villagers were often autonomous in organizing production but had to negotiate the division of the produce with a strong lord who often would impose his will. Custom and practice was a standard which carried considerable force. Even strong lords were wary of going directly against strongly ingrained customs and practices. For the most part, these systems were stable although strikes and riots would occur from time to time.

THE INDUSTRIAL REVOLUTION

The social systems of production described above were destroyed by the forces unleashed by the industrial revolution—a series of economic and social changes which took place over several centuries. The industrial revolution started out slowly then in the seventeenth and eighteenth centuries it gained momentum. It included several elements (Deane 1969):

1. An expanding use of currency rather than barter.
2. The development of improved agricultural and manufacturing technology.
3. A greater ability to transport goods and services (as railroads, steam-powered boats, and canals developed and eventually better roads were built).
4. A large population increase which forced people off the land.
5. The development of the technique of mass production.
6. Concentration of production in urban centers.
7. Development of rational, systematic production in pursuit of profits.

These forces swept away medieval industrial relations. A new belief began to be established that, instead of inevitable cycles of good and bad times, continuous progress was indeed possible. Derived from Calvinism, the Protestant ethic spread throughout society resulting in the widespread adoption of the belief that hard work and frugality would lead not only to worldly success but also to salvation (Weber 1958).

In the countryside during the high middle ages, there was only a limited market for agricultural produce. Population was fairly stable and it was difficult to transport perishable goods successfully. The supply of money was also limited and thus effective demand was not high. As a result, there was little incentive to actively seek higher productivity. If more was produced than was needed it was more likely to rot than to be sold at a profit. The industrial revolution changed this equilibrium. Technological changes accumulated over several centuries to permit higher productivity, and the population began to grow steadily (Ashton 1964). New markets appeared for rural produce. This gave lords strong incentives to renege on promises implicit in custom and practice and to insert their will where custom was ambiguous. The result, especially in Britain, was the enclosure movement in which the peasants were shut off from the common and in other ways driven from the land so that the lord could engage in production for profit. As more goods became available, the preference of lords for money income rather than in-kind income increased and, as a result, fees began to replace feudal duties and sharecropping arrangements. Over time, many peasants were able to accumulate sufficient capital to buy out the lord's interest in the land altogether and thereby become freeholders. On continental Europe, pressure built up in the seventeenth and eighteenth centuries for medieval lords to relinquish their hold on the land and on the peasants. Town burghers were looking for a bigger market in which to sell their wares and kings and princes were interested in creating a larger tax base. As a result in several jurisdictions, laws were passed ending the feudal arrangements (see especially Weber 1966). In France, the Ancien regime was swept away in a single violent upheaval in 1789.

The forces of the industrial revolution also transformed the guild system. As effective demand for manufactured goods increased, some masters began to champ at the bit of guild regulations and sought ways to escape or subvert them. Some moved to the rural areas where guild rules did not apply. There they bought up quantities of raw materials and assigned them to householders for production of items to their specifications (e.g., clothing, shoes). This technique became known as the putting-out system. The masters then flooded not only rural but also urban markets with goods below the quality specifications of the guilds but with a price within reach of a broader consuming public.

The guilds, which had a monopoly in the cities, tried at first to stop this infiltration. In the vanguard of the defense of guild rules were the journeymen and apprentices that had much to lose if their jobs and careers were put in jeopardy by shoddy goods (see especially Leeson 1979). The defense was not so successful and, in fact, the urban masters often joined their rural counterparts to exert pressure for relief from guild restrictions. Many hoped to compete in new markets abroad. By the middle of the eighteenth century the British Parliament was regularly refusing to intervene in upholding guild rules. In 1753, framework knitters appealed to Parliament and were told that rules with respect to entrance to the trade were "injurious and vexatious" and "contrary to the liberty of the subject" (Leeson 1979, 79).

The putting-out system was superseded by the factory system. Factories have existed throughout history and many have been identified in the high middle ages. Most existed under the special privilege of the king or other powerful lord. They were usually opposed by the guilds and were only a minor force until the eighteenth century. In that period, entrepreneurs, who previously may have been successful urban masters, were no longer constrained by strong guilds and began gathering workers into manufactories where they had more control over the production process. Most traditional craftsworkers could not compete effectively against this new form of production. Some of them became entrepreneurs, while others became wage laborers.

As capitalism progressed, constraints on the movement of both goods and labor were removed. Feudal constraints on the freedom of rural workers were removed largely because it was in the interests of the rising middle class. With feudal constraints came obligations to support workers in times of need. But the establishment of freedom of contract instead of feudal obligations meant that the master was no long responsible for the condition of the worker and no long subject to the coercion of custom and tradition. This "made possible the rational division of labor on the basis of technical efficiency alone" and "it created the possibility of exact calculation" (Weber 1966, 137).

By the nineteenth century, what had once been a single class of producers had split into two classes—entrepreneurs and workers. This split was punctuated by rural developments. Many former peasants were heading for the cities looking for work for wages. Those who did so began to compete with the former craftsworkers for the available manufacturing work. New classes began to form. Thus, the stage was set for the development of modern industrial relations.

Medieval practices were never well established in North America. The manorial system was absent except in Quebec where many of its characteristics were retained in what came to be called the Seignorial system. However, contrary to European practice, farmers were not compelled to stay on the land. For the most part, North American farmers were independent entrepreneurs.

In the cities in the sixteenth and seventeenth centuries, craftsworkers did band together into formal or informal societies—although only fragmentary records remain about them (see, e.g., Taft 1964). One of the most famous cases was related by John R. Commons who traced the history of American shoemakers. He found that the Massachusetts Bay Colony granted a guildlike charter to the "Company of Shoomakers" of Boston in 1648. Its main function, like the guilds in Europe, was to ensure quality work in return for a monopoly of production (Commons 1909, reproduced in Larson and Nissen 1987). Never well established, these combinations, like those in Europe, gave way to the burgeoning forces of an expanding market.

LAISSEZ-FAIRE

Until about the middle of the eighteenth century, governments intervened deeply into the workings of the economy. As Pauline Gregg has noted, "the assumption that governments could and should intervene in economic and social affairs was taken for granted from the middle ages to the nineteenth century" (Gregg 1976, 246). There were regulations on production standards, state-approved monopolies, tightly regulated wages, and attempts by the state to export more than was imported. In the late seventeenth century, however, the notion of laissez-faire began to take hold. This doctrine held that the state should stay out of economic life. Market forces should be allowed to work unhindered and if they did the result would be the highest possible production and productivity. It would be as if an invisible hand were moving things about in the most efficacious manner possible. The eighteenth century was the first great modern era of deregulation.

Labor and management were permitted to work out any mutually acceptable arrangement—more or less. Since employers had significantly greater bargaining power than most workers, in fact, they could set terms unilaterally in most cases. Labor is a very perishable commodity. If it is not sold today, it is wasted. Moreover, if the unemployed worker did not accept the terms offered he/she might very well go hungry because there were no state-provided welfare schemes (although churches did provide charity).

Some employers continued the tradition of paternalism by offering employment only to those likely to undertake a long-term commitment to the firm and by ensuring that such employees were taken care of even in bad times. In return, these paternalists expected their workers to conduct their lives, both professional and personal, in a manner consistent with the values of the employer. Commonly, employees were required to attend church and to refrain from various practices (e.g., drinking, smoking, gambling) considered illicit by the employer. They were also cajoled to save as much as possible and to spend wisely.

Other employers embraced the philosophy inherent in the new uncontrolled approach to economic life. They saw their task to be that of organizing production in the most efficient manner. If this meant dismissing workers who were injured or too old to produce effectively—so be it. Under the new rules, which permitted workers to resign their jobs and move to other places of employment as they saw fit, management was no longer ethically responsible for the workers. They were now considered to be adults fully competent to look after their own affairs without the meddling of the employer.

TRADE UNIONS

This new laissez-faire system was a frightening one for the worker. No longer could the guild be counted on for economic assistance in difficult times or for regular social intercourse. No longer could a former peasant count on a place being available on the farm. This was a new individualistic world without security. As one method of filling the void, workers began to form trade unions.[5]

The earliest unions were formed by craftsworkers. Printers were the first craft to form a union in many countries. There were a number of reasons why these better off, more secure, and better paid workers were the first to form defensive organizations. Very generally, unions began to appear when workers began to perceive that their status throughout their working lives was likely to be that of a wage earner (Sidney Webb and Beatrice Webb 1894). In the guilds, the apprentices and the journeymen could reasonably aspire to independent master status and even, "by success in trade, to nobility" (Hibbert 1970, 48). By the early part of the nineteenth century, however, it had become fairly clear that it was not reasonable for most workers to expect that they would some day be able to set up their own shop. A permanent (and large) class of wage earners had come into existence. The route to a better standard of life no longer could be effectively travelled by independent action. Instead, if the lifelong wage earner was to improve his/her conditions of employment, collective action would be necessary.

Although they might not be able individually to follow the traditional route to success, craftsworkers had bargaining power. Should they withdraw their labor in concert it would be very difficult for the employer to replace them. With bargaining power they could effectively impose standards of wages and working conditions which employers would be hard pressed to ignore or subvert. Another reason for the rise of trade unions among craftsworkers was that they were more educated than were the unskilled and thus had more knowledge and more confidence in their ability effectively to confront authority. They were also more able than the unskilled workers to afford union subscriptions.[6]

Guild traditions were also of importance. Within the guilds there had been journeymen's clubs. For the most part these were social organizations. Each had a patron saint and on the saint's day they would celebrate with parties and parades. They also provided mutual assistance to brethren in time of need. During the sixteenth and seventeenth centuries, when the old guild rules were withering, it was the journeymen's clubs that were most active in attempting to maintain the standards in place. In several London trades, for example, it was the workers' clubs rather than the guild hierarchy that organized search parties to root out inferior goods made by nonguild members (Leeson 1979). On the continent, some of these clubs survived and provided the immediate successor to trade unions. In Britain, many of the clubs were outlawed because they had a tendency to challenge the guild hierarchy when rulings went against their members. Even where there was no direct link between the medieval guilds and the budding unions, the tradition of the craft inspired many of the early trade unions to adopt customs, traditions, and symbols from the guilds (Leeson 1979).

The early unions developed naturally out of the meetings of craftsworkers in such venues as taverns where, among other things, they discussed the mysteries of their craft after work. Out of such natural communication, informal groups were formed which by agreement were often transformed into formal organizations. Many of the early unions were set up to provide a form of mutual insurance for their members against death or illness. Burial insurance was very common (Leeson 1979; Webb and Webb 1894).

Most early unions were local, but soon after setting up, contact often would be made with other local organizations and reciprocal arrangements to help brothers and sisters in need would often result. These tramping networks allowed out-of-work craftsworkers to go from one city to another in search of work. On arrival at a new town, the travellers would inquire about the pubs where their crafts typically met. They would usually be assisted in finding work. If no work was available, they would be provided with bed and board for the night and sent on their way the next day. By 1825, there were at least twenty-eight such societies operating in England (Leeson 1979).

Where they were well organized, local craft unions often announced unilaterally the conditions, including wages, under which they would work. Masters or entrepreneurs who refused to abide by the trade rates (known as wage tariffs on the continent) would be "blacked." No member of the craft would accept work with them. In his study of American shoemakers, Commons found this technique being utilized in Philadelphia in the 1790s and in the first years of the nineteenth century. Master shoemakers complained that the workers had adopted "unlawful and arbitrary by-laws, rules and orders" and they had agreed "not to work for any master who should employ any workman violating such rules" (Larson and Nissen 1987, 143).

Collective bargaining during this period was unusual. More often than not, it was the employers who insisted on bargaining instead of acquiescing to unilateral imposition of terms by the craftsworkers (Clegg 1972). Strikes, when they did occur, were typically spontaneous outbreaks against some new employer initiative; protests rather than carefully planned out and executed maneuvers designed to compel a recalcitrant employer to accede to new proposals as a result of a test of strength. These early local unions were very unstable. They would proliferate in good times when they had a high probability of being effective and would disappear in bad times as individual competition for too little work drove out the propensity to act collectively.

Organizations for unskilled and semiskilled workers also appeared in the early part of the nineteenth century. Since these workers could be easily replaced and because the supply of unskilled labor generally exceeded the demand due to rapid population growth and the rural to urban migration, the power of these organizations to win concessions from the employer was slight. Instead, early organizations such as the Chartists in Britain, attempted to convince Parliament to expand the franchise and to introduce policies designed to ameliorate their conditions.[7] What they lacked in skill they made up for in numbers and thus, they hoped, public demonstrations and lobbying might have some effect. The Chartists petitions, however, went unanswered and the movement collapsed. On the continent, workers played a key role in the uprisings of 1848. France briefly put universal male suffrage in place, reduced working hours to 10 per day, organized national workshops to put the unemployed to work, and abolished the Chapelier law which forbade unions. However, conservative forces quickly recovered control of government and overturned all of these reforms (Lorwin 1954; Slomp 1990).

Another type of action taken by workers in protest against the new era was machine breaking. The most famous of these groups was the so-called Luddites who rampaged through England in the early nineteenth century. New technology was seen to be either the direct cause of the deterioration of conditions or at least a hated symbol of the new age. Machine breaking was also common in France, Germany, and other parts of central Europe in the 1830s and 1840s (Slomp 1990, 17).

EMPLOYERS

With several hundred years of largely unchallenged unilateral authority behind them, employers, the successors to the medieval masters and lords, most often opposed vigorously the imposition of employee initiated constraints. Throughout the nineteenth century and, in many countries well into the twentieth century, employers opposed the formation and refused to recognize as legitimate the functions of the trade unions. Traditionally, employers had been paternalistic autocrats. True, the medieval masters had been constrained by guild rules and the medieval lords restricted by rural custom and practice but in neither case were these constraints formally imposed upon them by their subordinates. Indeed, as noted above, independent societies of journeymen and apprentices had been suppressed since at least the fourteenth century. Given the paternalistic legacy, unions were tantamount to a household revolt—children imposing their will on adults.

For those employers who denied the paternalistic tradition, unions were equally egregious (Fox 1985). Under the new laissez-faire philosophy, labor was a commodity to be purchased at the optimal price, to be used as efficiently as possible, and to be discarded when it no longer continued to function at peak performance. Once purchased, labor was owned and ownership, its possessors claimed, allowed one to use it as one saw fit. Unionization was like the revolt of machines or toy soldiers—intolerable.

Employers developed many techniques in opposition to unionization. Most simply, union activists could be sacked and blacklisted. These tactics worked quite well if bargaining power rested on the side of the employer as it most often did. Hearing rumors that trade unionists were active on the shop floor, employers in the nineteenth century often hired spies to root them out so that they could be fired.

Despite the opposition, by the middle to late nineteenth century, national unions with sizable treasuries had begun to appear on the scene. These organizations, referred to as new model unionism in England (to distinguish them from the political, populist movements such as the Chartists which preceded them), were more able to utilize the strike as a systematic tool to bring pressure on recalcitrant employers. In response, employers, where conditions permitted, often hired replacements—strikebreakers who became known in Britain as blacklegs and in North America as scabs. Employers also began, by the late nineteenth century, to make use of the lockout in order to compel their employees to work on their terms instead of those stipulated by the union.

Another tactic used by employers to squash unionism was to require all employees to sign a document, which became part of their individual contract of employment, agreeing as a condition of work not to become a union member. In North America, the document would become known as the "yellow-dog" contract. To head off the organization of their employees by outsiders, many employers took the initiative to set up committees through which their employees could express their wishes and concerns. Typically these committees existed at the will of the employer and could be extended or terminated as he/she saw fit. Independent unions considered these house organizations to be phony or "yellow." They were also referred to as company unions.

THE GOVERNMENT REACTION

At the time the first trade unions began to appear governments were all controlled by a small elite. In 1776, the United States had set up a democratic form of government with enfranchisement based on property ownership. France had its great revolution in 1789 but, after much chaos in the 1790s, Napoleon reestablished an authoritative dictatorship in the early 1800s. In Britain, where the middle class was rapidly on the rise, an elected Parliament had been increasing in power vis-à-vis the monarchy for some time. The first steps had been taken on the road that would lead to the general practice of democracy that we have today—but that future was not clear in the late 1700s. By these governments of the few, unions of workers were considered to be not only a threat to employer authority but also a political threat.

In part in reaction to the French Revolution and in part a culmination of a legislative pattern dating back centuries, Britain in 1799 and 1800 passed laws outlawing worker organizations generally (Jacobs 1986). Over the centuries there had been many laws passed forbidding worker organizations in specific industries but the Combination Acts were the first general prohibition.[8] The British initiative was followed in most other industrializing countries either by the passage of specific statutes or by the interpretation of legal custom and practice. In the United States, for example, the courts ruled in the Philadelphia cordwainer's case in 1806 that trade unions were a monopoly in constraint of trade and were therefore illegal.[9] Even after many countries had legalized unions and collective bargaining, nations starting out on the road to industrialization still resorted to banning these new institutions. For example, Japan in 1900 passed the Public Peace Police Act which had the effect of precluding unions (Shirai and Shimada 1978).

THE LABOR MOVEMENT DEVELOPS

Despite the hostility of the environment, labor organizations still made some progress. Working conditions in the new mills and factories were very poor and they attracted the attention of various reformers. Social disruption resulting from spontaneous strikes and demonstrations added pressure for change. Slowly, across the developing world, two new labor rights were established: the right of association and the right to strike. Britain repealed the Combination Acts in 1824 on the theory they were only causing martyrs and that, if repealed, unions would lose their allure (Pelling 1973, 30). The theory turned out to be faulty when unions did not fade away. Although the mere act of combination was not forbidden after the Acts of 1824/1825, conspiracies in constraint of trade continued to be illegal until 1870. In the United States, Judge Lemuel Shaw of Boston refused to accept the logic of the Philadelphia cordwainer's case regarding another shoemaker case settled in 1842. He reasoned that a combination of workers is not automatically an illegal act. Such an organization should be judged on its actions rather than on its mere existence. A union that engaged in acts otherwise legal was not, by itself, illegal. Because he had a considerable reputation, Shaw's reasoning was widely followed (Chamberlain and Kuhn 1965).

The German antisocialist laws passed in 1878 had the effect of outlawing most unions but those laws were repealed in 1890. In 1791, France had, in the Loi Le Chapelier, made illegal all corporations which stood between the individual and the state. This act was aimed not at trade unions but rather at the medieval guilds which had persisted until that time and in the eyes of the new people's government had acted to the detriment of the individual. For much of the first part of the nineteenth century, however, the Loi Le Chapelier was used, not to the benefit of the common person but rather to suppress unions (Jacobs 1986; Slomp 1990). It was repealed in 1864 but restrictions on unions continued until 1884. Belgium, Spain, and the Austro-Hungarian empire lifted the ban on worker combinations in the 1860s. Australia and Canada, who both had imported British common law (as had the United States), legalized unions and collective bargaining in the 1870s and Japan repealed the Public Peace Police Act in 1925. For the most part the reasoning in these countries was similar to the reasoning behind legalized gambling or legalized prostitution. The conduct was considered by those in power to be reprehensible but, rather than suppress it and have it continue underground, it was better to legalize and control it by regulations.

With these developments, public policy moved from suppression to tolerance. Unions and collective bargaining were not encouraged anywhere in the nineteenth century. Nevertheless, as environmental constraints became less onerous, labor organizations began to develop at an accelerating rate. National unions of crafts first began to appear in the 1850s (Slomp 1990). By the 1860s and 1870s, these national organizations had begun to set up national federations. The first federation to survive—the Trades Union Congress—was set up in the United Kingdom in 1868. Between then and about 1910, national federations came into existence in most Western developing countries.

In this period, socialist political parties were also being formed as political democracy slowly spread through the West. The rising middle class insisted on having a say in the development of policies which affected its interests and some reformers insisted that such rights should be extended to all adults.

In addition to the formation of political parties concerned with the interests of workers, many other worker organizations came into existence: education associations, walking clubs, and chess clubs. By the latter part of the nineteenth century, the Labor Movement in most countries had taken on the character of a broad social movement composed of unions, parties, and cooperatives (Sturmthal 1972).

LABOR'S STRATEGIC CHOICE

As labor movements in various countries took form, each of them was confronted with a choice of ideology and strategy. The early unions had been spontaneous social happenings. They had not, for the most part, thought about their place in the universe. They simply did those things that it seemed sensible for their members to do. At first, national craft unions and then national federations formed; however, labor leaders began to feel a need for a deeper set of principles—a need for a philosophy and for establishing future goals towards which workers could strive. In retrospect, one can see that in that mode they had a menu of strategic choice from which to choose.[10] The menu consisted of a number of ideologies and their associated strategies.

Radicalism

Many thinkers of the nineteenth century, of which Karl Marx was foremost, considered that the political economy of the age was unjust. Capitalism, as it began to be known, was very efficient. By the late 1800s, countries in Europe and North America that had embraced this productive system were growing rapidly. But the fruits of that growth were, in the judgement of the radicals, not being shared equitably. Marx argued that capitalism by its very nature created two classes—capitalists and workers—and that it was the fundamental nature of capitalists to exploit workers in search of profits and growth. Because the interests of the two classes were fundamentally opposed, conflict between them was inevitable. In time, workers would become increasingly aware of the dynamics of this unjust system and eventually would rise up and overthrow it. After the revolution, a socialist caretaker government would reconstruct the economy to ensure production consciously designed to meet the needs of the people. After restructuring, this government would no longer be necessary. It would fade away leaving a just and equitable one-class society.

The Marxist prescription called for trade unions and political parties to work together (under the leadership of the party) to raise the consciousness of the working class as to the exploitative nature of the capitalist system. The long-term objective would be to overthrow capitalism and establish the classless society.

This philosophy had enormous appeal to labor leaders in the second half of the nineteenth century. For centuries, working people had been the most exploited class and the new ideas which made their appearance along with the new technology of the industrial revolution did not relieve this burden. The Protestant ethic, for example, which grew in influence throughout the nineteenth century and continues to have a powerful effect today, held that those who worked hard would prosper and that those who prospered no doubt had been favored by God. Contrarily, those who did not prosper no doubt were not favored by God. By extension, poverty, which throughout most of history had been considered an unfortunate but inevitable phenomenon, now began to be regarded as a self-inflicted evil. A working person, who could hope to rise only to moderate socioeconomic status at best, would now be reviled by society for not being more successful, for not receiving more of God's grace. "Now," according to David Landes, "poverty was a sin and the poor man a victim of his own iniquity" (Landes 1969, 60).

Marxism turned this philosophy around. It held that working people were good not evil and that the future would definitely be theirs as the internal contradictions of capitalism wrenched that system apart. This positive philosophy had great appeal to the budding labor movements. Throughout continental Europe, some version of radical socialism became the guiding ideology of the mainstream labor organizations.

The radical solution called for labor movements composed not only of trade unions but also of other organizations—most notably socialist political parties. In the second half of the nineteenth century, such parties came into existence in most of the industrializing countries. During the 1860s, such a party was formed in Germany. The 1880s saw additional parties formed in France, Belgium, the Netherlands, Australia, and Sweden. An Italian Socialist Party was formed in 1892 (Kendall 1975; Landauer 1959).

Perhaps the critical distinguishing feature of the radicals was their goal to replace the capitalist system with a socialist system. Many, but not all, radicals believed with Marx that the goal could only be accomplished by violent means. In many countries (e.g., Sweden, Germany, Belgium), socialist-labor parties were formed before trade union federations. Where that occurred, the parties tended to function as the central organization for the unions which had embraced socialism. Party leaders generally insisted that political action had precedence over industrial action. As a result, in the 1880s and 1890s, they placed pressure on the trade unionists to lead their members in strikes and demonstrations designed to pressure governments into extending the franchise, improving educational opportunities, and removing legislative practices which hobbled workers. For example, employers were able in many countries to legally apply corporal punishment to workers up until the latter part of the nineteenth century. In some countries, workers were required to carry workbooks in order to get jobs. Employers wielded substantial control of workers with the threat not to sign their workbooks should they leave without performing up to a specified standard (Kendall 1975; Veneziani 1986). Although socialist trade union leaders appreciated the need for a political strategy, they had to answer to the membership who often had modest objectives and who were often not keen to place their employment in jeopardy by engaging in political strikes. Friction over strategy and tactics led to the establishment of trade union federations independent of political parties. Even after independence, however, these two branches of the movement continued to work closely together in most countries (Kassalow 1969, 29–65).

Exceptions to this pattern were Britain where the unions took the initiative to found the Labour Party that only adopted a clear socialist philosophy in 1918 (Flanders 1968, 148), France where the main union federation rejected all ties with a political party in favor of an anarcho-syndicalist strategy of direct action (Lorwin 1954), and the United States where the major union federation settled on the conservative strategy of business unionism. Via the link of international unions, Canada was very much affected by the U.S. choice. Until after World War II, business unionism dominated—indeed, it continues to have a major effect today.

Reform Socialism

Some thinkers of the nineteenth century agreed with Marx that working conditions under capitalism were unacceptable and needed to be changed, but they did not accept Marx's solution to the problem. Instead of revolution, they believed that the conditions of labor could be ameliorated through political action within liberal democracy. Their prescription for labor also called for an alliance between unions and political parties but, instead of revolution, the two wings of the movement should work together to expand democracy and overcome the problems experienced by working people through legislation and industrial agreements. Although unions should do their best to look after the interests of their members on a day-to-day basis, real progress in the conditions of labor would only be made through changes in public policy. This strategy is specifically associated with the Fabian Society in Britain and with the labor leader Eduard Bernstein in Germany.

Although radical strategies originally appealed to many labor movements, over time most have evolved into reform organizations. As a result, reform socialism is the predominant labor movement philosophy today.

Anarcho-Syndicalism

Another strategy available to labor agreed with the radical and reform socialists on the nature of the problem but did not agree with their proposed solutions. The anarcho-syndicalists believed that the solution to labor's problems was direct action (van der Linden 1990). Workers should not put their trust in politicians even if the politicians claimed to be seeking their best interests. Politicians by nature are prone to compromise and susceptible to corruption. They cannot be trusted. The classless society is the aim but the way to achieve it is to organize workers very broadly in trade unions and at the appropriate conjuncture to undertake a general strike. This action would force the collapse of capitalism.[11] After the revolution self-managed corporations could negotiate everything of necessity between themselves.

This philosophy was particularly influential in southern Europe (France, Italy, Spain, and Portugal), although minority federations based on it were formed in other countries. In France, where the form of government had shifted from absolute monarchy to republic to an emperor to the reestablishment of the monarchy to the reestablishment of a republic without noticeable improvement in the conditions of the working class, the idea of working through a political party to achieve real change did not seem the best course of action. Trade unionists were, moreover, disappointed with the performance of socialist deputies in the last two decades of the nineteenth century. As a result, the French Confederation of Labor, in its 1906 Charter of Amiens, adopted a policy of no ties with any political party (Lorwin 1954).

In the United States, this was the philosophy embraced by the Industrial Workers of the World (IWW)—an organization that had considerable impact on U.S. industrial relations in the first two decades of the twentieth century.

Business Unionism[12]

Although major sociopolitical reform seemed to many labor leaders to be the only solution, others did not accept the necessity of such a far-reaching strategy. The latter group of leaders considered their function to be protection of the interests of their own members within capitalist society. Many did not agree that capitalist society was all that bad—it was clearly very efficient and the overall wealth of society was increasing. Workers, moreover, had plural interests. They were concerned not only with labor issues but with a wide range of public policies. The problem was to devise methods whereby workers' interests would be met within the system. The function of unions was to look after their members employment interests primarily by way of directly dealing with employers. From this perspective, the union was considered to be "mainly a bargaining institution" which sought its ends "chiefly through collective bargaining" (Hoxie 1917, 45–46).

Business unionists tended to distrust political action as much as the anarcho-syndicalists. They feared that worker interests would get swamped by the concern of political parties for a much broader array of issues. Business unionists did not consider it to be their role to concern themselves with crime, defense, family relations, and the entire panoply of political policy. Looking after their members employment interests was enough. In fact, their members might find it quite impossible to agree to a common strategy with respect to the spectrum of political issues. So why undertake a futile quest? By and large, what business union leaders wanted from the state was freedom to work out satisfactory arrangements with employers. They did not seek to have the government intervene in the economic system on their behalf. Government neutrality would be sufficient.

Business unionism was to become the dominant philosophy in the United States. Indeed the triumph of this type of unionism is the most critical aspect of American exceptionalism. However, contrary to the impression given by some writers, business unionism was not solely an American phenomenon. It would also play a large part in union development in Canada, Britain, and Japan, and would be a significant substream in many other countries. Indeed, American business unionists drew much of their inspiration from new model unionism which was the British variant of the general phenomenon. On continental Europe, a strain of unionism referred to as liberal had much in common with business unionism. An essential characteristic of both was the acceptance of capitalism. When white-collar workers began to organize en masse from the 1910s onward, pure and simple unionism would be very attractive to many of them (Sturmthal 1966b).

Christian Unionism

The last major choice available to the developing labor movements was Christian unionism. This variant of labor philosophy was initiated by the Catholic Church in response to the inhumanity of liberal economic philosophy and to the antireligious and violent nature of radical socialism. Marx taught that the capitalist class controlled not only the economy but all other societal institutions including education, the press, and the church. Religion, according to Marx, was an opiate. It promised "pie in the sky" rather than salvation on earth. Implicitly, it urged workers to bear their conditions content in the knowledge that after they died they would go to a better life in heaven.

As radical socialism appealed to more workers, it became a threat to the church. In many ways radical socialism was like a competing religious philosophy and the church felt it must counter the threat. Throughout the nineteenth century, local unions which adhered to Christian values were set up at the behest of various bishops (Fogarty 1957). In 1891, however, the pope gave this movement a major boost when he issued the encyclical *Rerum Novarum*. This document contained a far-ranging analysis of the condition of labor in the industrializing nations. It also specifically encouraged workers to form unions based on Christian principles and it urged Christian employers to cooperate with the organizations. Cooperation was the keystone of this approach and strikes were discouraged.

Christian unionism grew rapidly in the first two decades of the twentieth century in those countries where Catholicism was particularly strong—especially France, Germany, Italy, Holland, Belgium, and Austria. It also became an important force in Latin America. In North America, it became important only in the Canadian province of Quebec. It was, however, to remain a minority phenomenon. From the 1930s, Christian unions began the slow process of deconfessionalization—breaking away from formal ties with religious bodies. Successor organizations which continue to exist today are all independent of the Christian churches although many of them are still strongly influenced by Christian social values (Windmuller 1987a).

SUMMARY AND CONCLUSION

Every society has to construct an economic system in order to produce and distribute goods and services. Every society also constructs a social system composed of those engaged in production and distribution—an employment relations system. In the two centuries from 1680 to 1880, the employment relations systems of countries which are now considered advanced liberal democracies were radically transformed. The industrial revolution swept away the institutions associated with the medieval era. Initially the result was an individualistic, capitalistic system with very little formal regulation. That laissez-faire system, however, resulted in considerable insecurity and anxiety. To secure themselves against the vagaries of the market, workers began to form trade unions which persisted against strong employer and government opposition.

During this period, developments in North America fitted squarely within the mainstream. Conclusions drawn from observations made in Europe generally would have been equally valid in North America and vice versa. From about the 1880s, though the path followed by Europeans and North Americans began to diverge significantly. The European path is generally considered to be the mainstream and the American path the exception. In the next two chapters, first the European mainstream and then the American exception will be considered.

Chapter 2

THE EUROPEAN MAINSTREAM

From about the 1880s, the labor movement in Europe began to grow at an accelerated rate. Whereas the movement had initially been one primarily of skilled workers, now increasing numbers of unskilled and semiskilled workers began to form trade unions (Sturmthal 1972; Jacobs 1986). Of particular note were unions in transportation—railroaders and dockers. In 1896, an International Trade Secretariat (ITS) for ship, dock, and river workers was set up primarily at the initiative of British dockworkers. It was the first ITS whose membership was composed primarily of the unskilled. Other ITS's—composed of craftbased organizations such as those for cigar makers, shoemakers, printers, miners, and tailors—had begun to appear since the 1880s (Kendall 1975; Windmuller 1987a).

As the franchise was grudgingly widened, electoral support for socialist and later communist parties grew. Kendall (1975), for example, has estimated that the combined votes for socialist parties in France, Germany, Italy, Britain, Belgium, the Netherlands, and Denmark in the first two decades of the twentieth century increased more than two and one-half fold. Estimated trade union membership increased even more dramatically. There were fewer than three hundred thousand trade union members in Germany in 1890, but by 1920 there were more than seven million. In Britain and France, there were more than five times as many unionists in 1920 as there were in 1890. Equally dramatic increases were experienced in other European countries (see, e.g., Crouch 1993). Industrial conflict also became common in the 1890s and the first few decades of the twentieth century.

This expansion of labor support and militancy put tremendous pressure on governments and on employers to come to grips with labor's concerns. Although in their daily actions labor organizations on continental Europe functioned within in the existing systems, their rhetoric was radical and could not be discounted lightly. By the turn of the twentieth century, it was no longer entirely improbable that the rising labor movement would sweep away capitalism. If they were to survive, the leaders of liberal society would have to devise a strategy or strategies to deal effectively with labor's demands.

GOVERNMENT REACTION TO THE LABOR CHALLENGE

Governments in reaction to this labor challenge took several steps. They expanded the franchise so that by the 1920s adult male suffrage was the standard in most countries (Therborn 1977). They also expanded access to education so that at the basic level it became both free and mandatory (Jarman 1951; Meyer 1965). Most countries passed factory acts limiting the hours for work of women and children. The first steps were taken to create what today we refer to as the welfare state (Hepple 1986a). Labor leaders, who in the 1860s and 1870s were generally considered to be no more than quasi legitimate, were asked to participate in government-organized social schemes (Crouch 1993, chap. 4). In the Allied and neutral countries, this development accelerated during World War I.

In Germany, the dynastic government of Count Bismarck attempted to clip the labor movement in the bud by outlawing unions and socialist political parties while at the same time meeting many of labor's demands by the initiation of a wide-ranging social policy initiative. In 1881 (shortly after the initiation of the Anti-Socialist Act of 1878), a bill providing insurance against industrial accidents was introduced but failed to pass the Reichstag. Two years later, a Sickness Insurance Act did pass. Accident insurance became a reality in 1884 and in 1889 a general old-age insurance scheme came into effect (Köhler, Zacher, and Partington 1982). As a result "German workers . . . were the first to be protected against these hazards of modern industrialism" (Pinson 1954, 246). More social security measures came into existence in the 1890s and the first decade of the twentieth century. There was factory legislation regulating the conditions of labor, restrictions on the hours of work for women and children, and the establishment of state-operated labor exchanges. Unemployment insurance did not become general until the 1920s, but several cities set up municipal schemes beginning in the 1890s. There were also municipal initiatives on "such matters as housing, public works, the relief of migratory workers, and health" (Pinson 1954, 246). The combination of these measures made Germany "the model for advanced social legislation before World War I" (Pinson 1954, 246).

Although extensive, the German strategy did not meet its prime objective of undercutting support for the labor movement. Instead, labor organizations maintained a clandestine existence throughout the 1880s. When the antisocialist laws were repealed in 1890, the reemergent organizations attracted a large following. By the 1910s, the German labor movement was one of the better established in the world (Kendall 1975; Crouch 1993).

Similar, if less dramatic, initiatives were also unsuccessful in undercutting labor organizations in other continental countries. Indeed, the initiatives may very well have led workers to believe that tangible benefits could be had by supporting the labor movement. These policies did, however, have the effect of moderating the objectives and activities of the movement. As the franchise was expanded more socialist members were elected to European parliaments. As they achieved policy victories, they became less enamored of revolution (Kassalow 1969). In 1918, the government of Kaiser Wilhelm collapsed in Germany and it was replaced by the Social Democrats (SDP) whose mandate it was to bring about an end to the world war. Despite a platform calling for revolutionary change, the SDP did not attempt to put the Marxist vision into practice. It did introduce a number of new institutions—such as statutory works councils which had to be established in all firms of any size and the provision of worker representatives on corporate boards of directors.[1] These institutions infused German capitalism with some aspects of social democracy, but they did not destroy it.

By 1940, socialist parties had shared power or had formed governments in many European countries. Only in Russia, however, did a newly installed leftist regime set out to destroy capitalism and replace it with a radically different political economy (Filtzer 1986; Grancelli 1988, 1992). In October 1917, the Bolshevik Party seized power. In the next year, in the midst of a civil war, the party introduced a labor code which established a minimum wage and the right of every Russian worker to a suitable job (as well as an obligation to work). It also quickly nationalized a large part of Russian industry. However, when the civil war ended, a limited form of free enterprise was permitted under the New Economic Policy and some Western analysts interpreted this move as an indication that "the Russian black sheep was in the process of returning to the capitalist fold" (Knapton and Derry 1966, 205). In the late 1920s, however, the Soviets initiated a series of five-year plans and seriously began the collectivization of agriculture. By about the mid-1930s, the economic system had been thoroughly transformed. The Communist Party completely controlled the state and the state assumed control of practically the entire economy. Instead of entrepreneurs or agents of entrepreneurs, industrial managers had become more similar to government bureaucrats in the West.

After a debate in the 1920s about their proper role under communism, trade unions became, to a large extent, part of the governmental apparatus. They were not permitted to engage in free collective bargaining but union leaders were included on the committees that developed the plan. At the local level it became the job of the unions to cooperate with management to achieve higher productivity and efficiency, but also to oversee the implementation of social and labor legislation and to help solve worker grievances. Unions were conceived of as transmission belts between the masses and the Communist Party. Although communication was supposed to flow in both directions, most of the traffic was downward. By allowing the unions to administer various social schemes, the party ensured that labor organizations would have a large membership.

In practice, the effectiveness of unions as agents of workers' interests varied. In high priority factories with relatively abundant funds for social consumption, the unions were often effective. On the other hand, in low priority organizations they generally had little power and often became no more than an "appendage of the administration" (Grancelli 1992, 389).

EMPLOYERS REACT—THE SCANDINAVIAN STRATEGY

In addition to various direct measures to meet the labor challenge, governments in Europe also put pressure on employers to reach an accommodation with this new social dynamo. In most cases, industry did not need to be pushed very hard because business leaders were beginning to realize that this new beast was not likely to be destroyed. Instead, it would be necessary to reach accommodation with the unions or else it was possible that the radicals would manage to achieve their objective of a new economic and political system. The classic European strategy for dealing with the trade unions was worked out in Scandinavia (Johnston 1962; Galenson 1952). The Swedish developments on this subject were exemplary.[2]

In 1898, the Swedish socialist unions set up their own central federation of labor known generally by its Swedish initials—LO. Working in tandem with the Social Democratic Party (which had been formed in 1889 and had initially acted as a central organization for many of the early trade unions) in 1902, LO leadership took its members out on a strike to back the expansion of the franchise. The conflict affected the entire country—no less than 150,000 workers, a very large percent of the contemporary labor force, took part (Carlson 1969, 26). This strike convinced employers that they had to organize themselves in order to protect their interests and find a strategy capable of ameliorating the trade unions. As a direct consequence of the strike, the Swedish Employers Federation (SAF) was formed and shortly thereafter, emulating developments in Denmark several years earlier, it initiated talks with the LO towards establishing a stable relationship.

In 1906, the LO and the SAF signed an agreement, known as the December Compromise, in which the employers recognized the legitimate right of the unions to represent the interests of not only of their own members, but also that of the working class as a whole. In return, the employers insisted that the unions recognize the legitimate right of management to hire and fire workers according to the needs of the enterprise and to organize and direct the production process. The LO and SAF also agreed that their constituent unions and associations would meet on a regular basis to establish general terms and conditions of employment on a multi-employer, industrial basis. This pattern of negotiations satisfied employer interests because they wanted to defend control over production at the enterprise and plant level against union advances. These business leaders were prepared to agree to minimum wages for all employees of specified classes, to periodic general wage adjustments, and to maximum hours but they were unwilling to accept any interference with their exercise of authority at the point of production.

The LO agreed to SAF's conditions for general recognition because its prime objective as a socialist federation was generally to improve the conditions of the working class, not to maximize conditions of particular workers on a plant-by-plant basis. The LO was not happy about the employer insistence on maintaining the rights to hire, fire, and direct work, but it considered that concession to be worth the achievement of a practical means to improve the conditions of Swedish workers. In fact, although the rights won by the SAF formally continued in existence until repealed by legislation in the 1970s, over the decades the unions would slowly whittle away the authority which the federation had hoped to preserve intact. The unions would also manage to establish networks of shop-floor representatives despite the employer objective of minimizing union influence at the point of production (Kjellberg 1992).

In general outline, the Scandinavian pattern was repeated in several other countries. In Germany, for example, when World War I was concluded the socialist government convened a meeting of employer and union representatives which resulted in an agreement (Legien-Stinnes Accord) very similar to the one in Sweden (Taft 1952; Berghahn and Karsten 1987). The employers recognized the right of the unions to represent the interests of workers and to negotiate collective agreements at a multi-employer level, but they insisted on the maintenance of authority at the plant level. The Social Democratic government would not, however, accept an arrangement which excluded workers' participation at the level of the enterprise. The compromise was the establishment, by statute, of works councils elected by all employees at the plant and enterprise level. Employers were required to consult with these councils on a range of issues considered to be essential to employee welfare.

The German and Swedish developments are variants of a general employer strategy for dealing with the labor challenge. The strategy called for: (a) the formation by employers of organizations to look after their interests as a whole, (b) the recognition of the unions as the spokespersons for the interests of workers generally (not just of their own members), (c) insistence on multi-employer bargaining (rather than bargaining on an employer by employer or plant-by-plant basis), and (d) insistence on the maintenance of authority at the enterprise level. This strategy was adopted to some degree in most European countries. The broad recognition agreements reached with unions became known as basic agreements.

THE DEVELOPMENT OF COLLECTIVE BARGAINING

Today the phrase "unions and collective bargaining" seems to be as unitary as "knife and fork" or "husband and wife" but, in fact, collective bargaining was as much, if not more so, a management device as a union method. Unions originally dictated terms where they were strong enough. They simply notified employers of union rules (with respect to apprenticeship, for example) and of the rate for the trade and refused to work for employers who did not acquiesce. As a tit-for-tat, employers insisted on negotiations as partial recompense for recognition. Collective bargaining was beneficial to management because by agreeing to it, trade unions recognized the legitimacy of management to carry out its function. Negotiations ending in binding agreements containing no strike clauses (the general employer objective in most bargaining rounds) could prevent the instability brought about by unexpected, unplanned outbreaks.[3] And agreements implying or explicitly containing management's rights clauses protected management from union interference in carrying out its basic functions.

EMPLOYMENT RELATIONS AT THE ENTERPRISE LEVEL

In the medieval era, employment relations at the level of the enterprise were clearly authoritarian. Masters were the lords of their castles—heads of their households. Within guild rules, their authority was all but absolute. With the growth of democracy, however, many considered this to no longer be appropriate. In the large enterprises which began to become prevalent around the turn of the twentieth century, the logic of paternalism no longer seemed compelling. These firms certainly were no longer synonymous with households. Instead, as limited liability corporations and stock ownership spread, there was the beginning of a separation of ownership and control and the emergence of professional managers (Berle and Means 1932). As the idea of universal suffrage began to be widely accepted so did the principle that working people should be able to participate in the making of decisions that had a critical impact on their interests at work. This principle was put into effect in different ways in different countries.

In Germany, the employers fought hard to keep the unions out of the shop even after the Social Democrats took office. The party of the workers was not prepared, however, to permit the employers free reign. The compromise solution was the establishment of statutory works councils (Taft 1952; Adams and Rummel 1977). These groups would be elected by all employees, whether or not they were union supporters. They would have statutory powers both to receive information and to be consulted about many issues, and also to codecide a few issues. The unions were not enthusiastic about these institutions because they feared that the councils might develop into a power base that would split the labor movement. Nevertheless, they accepted them because of their general support for democratic institutions. Employers were also not keen on being compelled to discuss workplace issues with worker representatives. However, employers considered the councils to be more acceptable than shop-floor unions because they were composed of workers from the firm rather than outsiders. Managers everywhere tended to resent and resist interference by outsiders in the affairs of the firm but are generally more open to internal consultation.[4]

Eventually, statutory works councils would be introduced in Holland, France, Austria, Belgium, and Italy (Sturmthal 1964). In Scandinavia, the union federations would negotiate agreements which required the establishment of such councils. The British equivalent to the works council was the shop steward network.

Even in the United States, this option acquired adherents in the years after World War I when the German initiative was being widely discussed (Douglas 1921; Conner 1983). American employers insisted, however, that they did not have to be compelled by government to consult with their employees. They could see what had to be done and would do the right thing without having to be forced to do so. During the 1920s, thousands of employee representation plans were set up until by the mid-1930s nearly as many workers were represented by them as by trade unions (Chamberlain and Kuhn 1965, 44). American unions were not at all happy about this turn of events. They considered these company unions to be phony, employer-dominated and employer-controlled organizations. When the United States passed major labor legislation in the 1930s, at the insistence of the free unions, company unions were made illegal.

WORLD WAR I AND BEYOND

World War I was an especially turbulent period for labor-management relations. Inflation was high and labor markets were very tight because of the many workers being drafted and sent to the war fronts. As a result, labor had both significant grievances and high bargaining power. Since labor was critical to the war effort, and since it had the capacity severely to hinder the effort, governments attempted to win the cooperation of union leaders. In many countries, union activists who at one point in their career had been considered outlaws, or at least less than fully respectable, were now asked to join the war effort. These actions tended to legitimize trade unions, and the institution which already was closely associated with them, collective bargaining.

During this period, radical leaders had considerable success convincing workers to strike and demonstrate to improve their conditions. In Russia, Soviets composed of workers and soldiers formed the base of the movement which took power in 1917 and established communism as one of the most potent forces of the twentieth century. Radicals were a significant part of the German movement which overthrew the Kaiser. For a few weeks in 1919, it appeared that the very radical Spartacus movement might be able to seize power and establish a German dictatorship of the proletariat (Grebing 1969). Even in staid and conservative Canada the Winnipeg general strike made the government fear that a Canadian version of the events in Russia was about to occur (see, e.g., McNaught and Bercuson 1974). Even though there was little reason to believe that the strike had a radical political intent, eight strike leaders were arrested and six were convicted of seditious conspiracy (Taft 1964, 344). In the United States, the government undertook a campaign against suspected radical activity. Several hundred people were deported and the Industrial Workers of the World was all but destroyed (Taft 1964, 338).

Along side radicalism a more conservative brand of unionism gained its first major momentum in the World War I period. White-collar workers, such as clerks, shop assistants, government bureaucrats, technicians and even professionals, began to organize into unions for the purpose of forwarding their employment interests. Salaried employees up to this point tended to empathize more with the bourgeoisie than with the proletariat. Recognizing that affinity, unionists generally did not make serious efforts to organize white-collar workers. Nevertheless, in the World War I period white-collar workers suffered from many of the same difficulties as blue-collars and in response began to turn to collective action. The unions that did appear generally adopted a pure and simple, nonpolitical strategy.[5] Although they might be convinced to join an organization designed to defend their employment interests, most white-collar workers were not attracted to the revolutionary rhetoric of socialism (Sturmthal 1966b; Kassalow 1969; Adams 1975b).

This period of labor militancy and power came to an end in 1920–1921 as a result of a deep recession. Union membership and strike rates decreased almost everywhere. Radical organizations lost their appeal and many of them faded into history. By this time, however, trade unions were well established. It appeared likely that they would join the ranks of other fundamental modern institutions.

Very shortly, however, that presumption was placed in doubt—fascism made its appearance in Europe. Mussolini, in Italy, was the first to establish it in 1922. By the mid-1930s, he had been joined by Hitler in Germany. Even though the German labor movement was numerically one of the strongest in the world at the time, it was unable to prevent the rise of the fascists (Sturmthal 1944). Looking back on the period after World War II, German unionists decided that the most important reason for their failure to defend democracy against fascist dictatorship was their disunity. Liberal, Christian, and various gradations of socialist unions fought with each other during the Weimar Republic and thus, although numerically strong, they did not provide a united front against fascism. In Spain, a republic was established in the early 1930s but, after a bloody civil war at the end of the decade, Franco was able to establish a long-lasting fascist dictatorship (Lucio 1992). A similar authoritarian, militarist regime was established in Japan in the mid-1930s (Levine 1958).

Fascism was in many ways like Russian communism. Although enterprise for profit was permitted (and indeed fascism is considered by some to be a political mechanism designed to save unstable liberal capitalism from communism), in the fascist countries it was very thoroughly regulated. With respect to employment relations, for example, employers were not permitted to dismiss employees at will. Instead, fascism was paternalistic and populist. It promised, as did Soviet communism, to provide stability and security to the ordinary person in return for discipline and allegiance to a dictatorial leadership. Like Soviet communism, it was totalitarian. The party in power would not permit challenges to its authority. As a result, competing political parties were outlawed as were independent trade unions and free collective bargaining (see, e.g., Pinson 1954).

During World War II, trade union leaders were active members of the underground in most axis countries. As a result, after the war unionists in these countries emerged as heroes. The fascist period was shown to be only a hiatus. When it ended, labor movements reemerged strong and vigorous.

Industrial relations in the Allied countries during the World War II period was, in most critical respects, a repeat of the World War I period. Inflation and tight markets led to the growth of unions numerically and the expansion of union power. Labor leaders were asked to join the war effort and most willingly agreed. In Britain, Ernest Bevin, an up-from-the-ranks union leader, joined the government and became one of its strongest members (see, e.g., Pelling 1973). By the end of World War II, labor leaders in the United States were being referred to as "New Men of Power" (Mills 1948).

CONTEMPORARY INDUSTRIAL RELATIONS IN EUROPE

By the 1950s, industrial relations systems as we know them today had acquired their essential characteristics (Clarke 1993). In Germany and Italy, democracy was reestablished and the institutions which predated fascism were reinstituted. Germany, for example, brought back the works councils and worker's participation on boards of directors that it had initially introduced just after World War I. Once firmly established, institutions have a tendency to persist and to reemerge even after considerable hiatuses (see, e.g., Poole 1993). In order to avoid the interunion battles of the 1920s, union leaders decided to establish a single national federation composed of a small number of industrial unions that would be neutral politically in order to permit participation by unionists of all persuasions. That strategy was not entirely successful. Some white-collar, Christian and public sector unionists decided to stay out of the German Trade Union Federation and to establish their own organizations (Berghahn and Karsten 1987; Markovits 1986). Nevertheless, the federation did emerge as being the overwhelmingly dominant union organization.

Eastern Europe, after World War II, became part of the Soviet orbit and the nations in that part of the world copied the industrial relations institutions pioneered there. Employment relations were tightly controlled by the central government. Only one national union federation, subordinate to the party, would be permitted and its role would be productionist, rather than consumptionist (Héthy 1991).

Portugal and Spain continued, until the 1970s, under fascist dictatorships in which the state tightly controlled all labor-management-government relationships. As in Germany, the prefascist union organizations revived in Spain when the dictatorship ended (Esenwein 1992). In Portugal, however, the free union tradition had been more thoroughly destroyed, and with the reestablishment of political democracy, new union organizations appeared (Raby 1992).

With these exceptions noted, one could broadly depict a European industrial relations system model. It included a major employer confederation that was recognized by society as the definitive vehicle for the expression of employer interests on social matters. For the most part, these organizations had arisen as a response to the challenge posed by labor to the capitalist system early in the twentieth century.[6] Typically the confederation was composed of industry associations that included the large majority of employers.

On the labor side, there was usually a dominant union federation, although in many countries several federations continued to exist. The primary federation almost everywhere adhered to socialist philosophy.[7] Collective bargaining was the major institution for the regulation of wages and other basic conditions of work. Most commonly it took place at the multi-employer level with an employer association on one side of the bargaining table and one or more unions on the other. Collective agreements covered the majority of the work force. Workers were represented on the shop floor by works councils or by shop steward networks, or both. Employers generally did nothing to prevent their employees from becoming trade union members. Like other fundamental civil liberties (e.g., right to free speech, freedom of the press), the right of association was generally respected; but that right also implied that workers could not be compelled to become union members against their interests and thus mandatory union membership was, in many countries, either illegal or considered socially reprehensible (Hanson, Jackson, and Miller 1982; Mitchnick 1987).

Quasi governmental organizations regulating various aspects of the employment relationship such as training, pensions, and job placement typically included representatives from both labor and business.

By the 1960s, most European countries had achieved full employment. In that decade, the war in Vietnam stimulated rapid economic development but also put pressure on prices. Attempting to protect their members from inflation, unions began to demand ever higher wage raises and were increasingly willing to go out on strike in pursuit of them. The result was the initiation of a wage price spiral that placed the health of European economies in jeopardy. Because of the political commitment to full employment, governments could not address this spiral by allowing unemployment to rise. In consequence, many decided to invite labor and management to codecide national socioeconomic policy (Panitch 1977). The result was the onset of a phenomenon dubbed by political scientists as corporatism or neocorporatism, and by industrial relationists as tripartism (Barbash 1972; Goldthorpe 1984; Banting 1986; Crouch 1993). The oil shocks of the 1970s gave further impetus to tripartism, but the Great Recession of the early 1980s resulted in a large rise in unemployment and led to some governments allowing tripartite discussions to whither. Others, however, either formally or informally continued to pursue tripartite consensus (Keller 1991; Thompson 1991; Adams 1992c; Treu 1992b).

Because labor's power was very high during the 1960s and 1970s due to rapid economic growth, full employment, and inflation, the labor movement pushed for additional social protection. As a result, this period saw a rash of social legislation and the rapid expansion of the welfare state.

All of these characteristics may be related back to events which took place between 1880–1920. Why do we find strong, well-organized employer associations in Europe? Because employers felt compelled to unify (despite a propensity to individualism) in order to secure the continued existence of the capitalist system (see, e.g., Adams 1981). Why do we find multi-employer bargaining? Because union and employer organizations agreed to multi-employer bargaining as part of the historic compromises between capital and labor. Why do employers not oppose the unionization of their employees? Because they agreed not to do that as part of the agreements made early in the century and because, with very broad collective bargaining coverage, there is little reason to do so today. Also, the continued viability of Labor/Socialist parties makes that a risky policy. Why do we find labor representatives on quasi governmental agencies? Because the labor movement in Europe was as much political as it was economic. It sought to ensure full participation of workers in all agencies with authority over them. Over the years, those understandings (and the institutions issuing from them) have became part of the custom and tradition of European countries.

Why are unions relatively weak at the shop floor in several countries? Because the employer strategy designed to achieve that end was relatively successful. During the 1920s, German managers maintained a high degree of control within the plant. They were able effectively to keep the unions out of the shop and thereby to negate whatever influence they might have on day-to-day operations. The councils, on the other hand, had to be provided with information and consulted on decisions. In many cases, though, companies actively attempted to marginalize them. The councils were most effective where unions were strongly established.

The German pattern was repeated more or less elsewhere. It was not until the 1970s that labor would make another strong thrust to more firmly establish industrial democracy. The result was the strengthening of the powers of councils and of local union organizations in several countries (see, e.g., Windmuller 1977).

Why, when the original dominant philosophy of labor called for the radical overthrow of the capitalist system, are the unions now willing to work within the system and cooperate with business and government? Reform replaced the revolutionary brand of socialism preached by Marx as well as the anarcho-syndicalist philosophy for a number of reasons. First of all, many of the grievances that had given rise to radicalism were slowly addressed. By the 1920s, the right to vote had been extended to adult males in most of the now-industrialized countries and to women in many nations (Therborn 1977; Hepple 1986b). Today, essentially all adults have the right to vote. One result of the extension of the franchise was the acquisition of political power by socialist/labor parties. In most Western European countries, socialist/labor parties have sometime during the twentieth century either formed the government or taken part in it as part of a coalition. As a result, this branch of the labor movement, which had originally been the most radical branch (in contrast to the more conservative trade unionists), became assimilated into the fabric of society. The socialist/labor parties increasingly became part of the system (Kassalow 1969). Access to education also expanded until free, mandatory, and universal education became the standard. The general work day was reduced from twelve or fourteen hours to eight hours. Many of the social programs that we now associate with the welfare state were introduced between 1880–1920, at least in embryo form, and expanded throughout the twentieth century—especially in the 1960s and 1970s. Egregious symbols of class dominance such as the right of employers to impose corporal punishment and the requirement that all workers carry a workbook were abolished (Veneziani 1986). In short, the labor movement was a large success. Society changed and no longer did radical reform seem imperative.

Radicalism did not entirely disappear, of course. After's Lenin's rise to power in Russia, communism made its appearance on the stage of history. In

France, communism developed as the dominant philosophy in the 1920s supplanting syndicalism (Lorwin 1954). Communism also became the dominant labor movement philosophy in Italy after World War II (Ferner and Hyman 1992a). In several other countries, it had considerable influence on a minority of the movement.

Although the first durable unions everywhere were craft unions, today craft unionism has all but disappeared on continental Europe.[8] How may we account for the transition? The switch was brought about in large part as the result of the embracing of a socialist ideology by union movements. Industrial unionism is more consistent with the egalitarian philosophy of socialism. The transformation was also helped along by employer insistence on industry-wide rather than local bargaining. Generally, employer associations preferred to deal with only one bargaining agent for all of the employees working in the associated firms. As a result, they put pressure on the unions to rationalize their structure in a direction that was coincidentally consistent with the form called for by the ideology. Employer pressure helped labor movements to overcome the resistance of vested craft interests.

Why do we find in many European countries today a strong tendency for governments to involve business and labor in the making of critical socioeconomic decisions? Because when conditions indicated the desirability of adopting that strategy, the institutions necessary for the achievement of effective cooperation were in place as a result of developments early in the century. Today, tripartite cooperation in search of socioeconomic consensus is to be found in many countries (Treu 1992b; Crouch 1993). But in no case was that pattern of behavior indigenous or culturally determined. Instead, in every case adversarial attitudes and propensities had to be overcome.

Chapter 3

AMERICAN EXCEPTIONALISM

Until the last third of the nineteenth century, developments in North America were not so different from those in Europe. The industrial revolution in the United States took off in the 1840s and 1850s (Rostow 1960). Although employment relations were never so regulated by custom and statute in the New World as in the old, nevertheless, the advent of the industrial revolution did see an expansion of impersonal, individualistic employment relations in which the security of the working person was very precarious. As in Europe, North American skilled workers reacted by forming local organizations for defensive purposes. The tactics which these workers used were similar to the tactics described for Europe, as were the countertactics of employers and the state. A good example is provided by John R. Commons' history of the evolution of institutions regulating the employment relations of shoemakers (1909).

As noted in an earlier chapter, in 1648, the Colony of Massachusetts Bay issued a charter to the "Company of Shoomakers" which granted a monopoly of shoemaking in return for a pledge to ensure the production of an adequate supply of good quality merchandise. Within the guild, the three functions of merchant, master, and journeyman were united. By the end of the eighteenth century, however, those functions had begun to separate. In Philadelphia in the 1790s, Commons found that the masters and the journeymen in the shoemaking trade had placed themselves into separate organizations and that the masters were complaining that the workers were arbitrarily adopting by-laws, rules, and orders, and refusing to work for any master who did not honor them. In 1805, a strike broke out and the masters took the journeymen to court on a charge of conspiracy. The court agreed and issued its famous Philadelphia cordwainer's decision stating that unions by their very existence were illegal conspiracies.

Why had the two classes emerged? According to Commons, it was because of the expansion of markets. Masters had begun to "carry their samples to distant markets" and they had begun to stock up on "cheap work sold in the public market." Instead of a standard quality of shoes, several quality gradations appeared and the masters insisted on paying workers "lower rates of wages on work destined for the wider and lower markets." The journeymen, however, resisted these changes and wanted "the same *minimum wage* on work destined for each market" (145).

By 1835, the shoemaking functions had become further separated and the merchant capitalist had appeared. These entrepreneurs had substantial capital and could organize and distribute goods on a large scale. They might use various methods such as putting out raw materials to be assembled in the shops of the craftsworkers, but "more characteristic of his methods, he can employ small contractors, the specialized successors of the master cordwainer, who in turn employ one to a dozen journeymen, and by division of labor and 'team work' introduce the sweating system" (147). In this system, the master becomes a "boss" and profits "are 'sweated' out of labor" (147). This phenomenon of the labor contractor was one found in the evolution of the social relations of production not only in the United States and Europe, but also in Japan and other parts of the world.

Until the 1850s, shoes were manufactured entirely by hand. In that decade and the next, however, new labor-saving machines were introduced. One of those devices, the McKay sole-sewing machine, "did in one hour what the journeyman did in eighty" (151). In that era, several local unions of shoemakers were functioning (Taft 1964, 56), but in the middle of the machine revolution the more broadly based Knights of St. Crispin appeared. This organization of workers intended not to resist the new machines, per se, but rather to oppose "the substitution of 'green hands' for journeymen in the operation of the machines." They engaged in several strikes all of which involved, directly or indirectly, "resistance to wage reductions and refusal to teach 'green hands.'" (152). The Crispins, however, were fighting a losing battle.[1] By the end of the century, shoe workers had experienced not only a loss of skill, but also of status and earning power (Laslett 1970).

It was in the last quarter of the nineteenth century that North American industrial relations took a sharp turn away from the European trajectory. As in Europe, several ideologies competed for allegiance of the budding labor movement. The first union federation of significance to appear was the Knights of Labor. Established in Philadelphia in 1869, this federation wanted to organize all workers, both skilled and unskilled. It sought many political reforms such as equal rights for women, safety regulations, and the establishment of a progressive income tax system. It also encouraged the formation of worker's cooperatives and pushed for the reduction of working hours. Even though negotiating with individual employers was not one of its major goals, many of its constituent assemblies did, in fact, engage in bargaining. Officially, it was opposed to the use of the strike which its most well-known president, Terrance

Powderly, referred to as a relic of barbarism. Ironically, as the result of a victorious strike against a railway owned by Jay Gould, one of the most famous robber barons of the age, the Knights grew rapidly in the 1880s (Dulles and Dubofsky 1984).

The philosophy of the Knights was perhaps more like the English Chartists than anything else. They wanted political reform. They also wanted a return to the age where the working person was his/her own boss. If they had survived, they might have evolved into a reform socialist organization. But, by the end of the 1880s, they had begun to lose many strikes and, in the 1890s, they faded very rapidly. By the 1910s, the Knights had disappeared as a force in the industrial relations system.

The 1860s and 1870s also saw the emergence of national unions of craftsworkers. In 1886, these organizations formed the first union federation to endure in the United States, the American Federation of Labor (AFL). The AFL adopted a set of principles that were to set off the American labor movement as exceptional. The group was established by craft unions and would only admit craft unions into its midst. Each union was to be autonomous in order to set its own internal policies within the overall loose framework of the AFL. There would be only one union for one craft. Dual unions were considered to be a drain on resources and a basis for unproductive interunion rivalry and conflict.

The craft unions in the AFL set as their goal to win the best conditions of work for their respective members. They did not seek to organize the entire labor force and thus could not credibly claim to speak for all workers. Although the merits and problems with socialist philosophy were debated extensively during the 1890s, in the end the Federation rejected socialism. By doing so it accepted the framework of capitalism. The AFL's goal would not be to replace capitalism with another form of economic organization, but rather to get workers the best deal available within the capitalist system.

The AFL was very suspicious of governments and politicians. The craft unions considered that getting involved in politics would dissipate their energies and resources. They believed that they could be more effective regarding their members' interests by focusing their efforts on employers. Collective bargaining rather than revolution or political reform would be the main focus of their activities. Their strategy was very similar to that of the new model unions in Britain: high dues, strong internal organization, and the use of the strike as a last resort weapon when negotiations failed (Slomp 1990, 20). Indeed, many of the emerging American craft unions of the era looked to the British unions for guidance and inspiration.

Because of its wariness of politics, the AFL resolved not to establish or become involved with any political party. It would lobby federal and state lawmakers to refrain from passing laws that would restrict the bargaining efforts of unions and to positively pass laws encouraging bargaining, but the Federation was distrustful of substantive legislation. What the law provided, the law could take away. It was better that government should stay out of industrial relations and allow employers and unions autonomously to work out their own arrangements. This philosophy led the Federation initially to oppose the introduction of unemployment insurance when it was first proposed in the 1930s (Taft 1964, 411–12).[2]

At election time, the policy of the Federation would be to reward friends and punish enemies. In other words, candidates who were likely to vote in ways consistent with the interests of labor would be supported regardless of their party affiliation. This policy was feasible in the United States because of its political tradition of weak party discipline. In Canada where party discipline is strong (a member of Parliament voting contrary to the policy of the caucus might be ostracized from the party and most likely from politics altogether), the approach was never very successful (Horowitz 1968).

As an organization, the AFL made no attempt to organize unskilled workers. Neither would the individual craft unions admit unskilled workers into their ranks. A major strength of unionism, according to the AFL, was in its ability to regulate the supply of labor. Being easily replaced, unskilled workers had inherently little market power and if admitted into craft organizations would only weaken them. The AFL was not opposed to the unionization of the unskilled, but it did little to foster it either.

As in Europe, socialism appealed to some workers. In the late 1870s, a Socialist Labor Party was established and, in 1895 under the leadership of Daniel DeLeon, an immigrant from the Dutch Island of Curaçao, it launched a peak union organization under the name of the Socialist Trades and Labor Alliance (Taft 1964, 280). In 1905, that organization combined with some individual unions and many notable socialist spokespersons to establish the Industrial Workers of the World (IWW). The IWW from the start clearly defined itself as a radical organization. In its preamble it declared that "the working class and the employing class have nothing in common." Initially, it included socialists dedicated to the Marxist strategy of overthrowing the capitalist system under the leadership of a political party. In 1908, however, it dropped all mention of political involvement and followed a strategy very similar to that of the European anarcho-syndicalists. As a result, DeLeon and his followers withdrew.

The IWW was not the only American labor union organization to embrace a radical creed. Several individual unions also accepted socialist ideology in the latter part of the nineteenth century. One of them was the Boot and Shoe Makers Union, the successor of the Knights of St. Crispin. Initially it threw its support behind the Socialist Labor Party of DeLeon, but in the first years of the twentieth century it expanded its membership greatly. As it became more successful in winning collective agreements, its ardor for socialism cooled (Laslett 1970).

Whereas the Socialist Labor Party under DeLeon was hostile to the pure and simple craft unions that were becoming a force in industrial relations (and in 1886 had formed their own American Federation of Labor), the Socialist Party of America which came into existence in 1901 hoped that it "could win the approval of the trade union movement by example and education of the non-Socialists" (Taft 1964, 281). According to Taft, this organization became "after 1901 the representative of socialism in the United States" (1964, 322). Like the socialist parties in Europe, this one also grew substantially in the early years of the twentieth century. In 1912, Eugene V. Debs, the party's candidate for president, polled just over 891,000 votes. That was nearly ten times the number of votes Debs had attracted in 1900, but still it was no more than 6 percent of the vote cast, a much smaller percentage of the vote than socialist parties in Europe were attracting.[3] During this period, the socialists also increased their strength in several individual unions, but they were unable to convince the leadership of the AFL to veer from its nonpolitical strategy of job-conscious unionism.[4]

During his first term of office (1912–1916), Woodrow Wilson passed the Clayton antitrust bill which was designed to make labor immune from antitrust legislation and to curb the use of the injunction against unions. One of its sections proclaimed that "the labor of a human being is not a commodity or an article of commerce" (Taft 1964, 243). Some trade unionists considered the act to be labor's Magna Carta. This initiative and other positive steps taken by the Wilson administration to improve the status of pure and simple trade unions helped to reduce the appeal of socialism. By 1916, the Socialist Party's vote was down significantly and several unions, including the Boot and Shoe Makers, had withdrawn their support. During and just after World War I, the U.S. government launched a "relentless campaign of suppression" against socialists, anarchists and, after the Russian revolution, communists. (Taft 1964, 339). Even though its failure to support the war effort was not popular, the Socialist Party still managed to attract nearly a million votes in 1920. However, the major recession of the early 1920s and the conservative dominance of politics during that time further undermined the power of the broadbased socialist labor movement which declined precipitously (Laslett and Lipset 1974).

The reaction of employers in the United States to socialism was twofold. Most of them zealously opposed it; and because it never became strong enough to pose a serious threat to the survival of liberal capitalism, Americans saw no need to reach a compromise with it. A few business leaders took another tack. They established the National Civic Federation with the objective of "promoting the peaceful adjustment of labor disputes" (Taft 1964, 195). They sought to convince employers to recognize and deal with the pure and simple unions in those situations where they managed to attract a significant following. The role that this organization played was not entirely dissimilar to that played by the Catholic Church in France or in Quebec. The strategy was the same: the way to undermine the attraction to socialism was to foster moderate apolitical unionism (for at least as long as the socialist threat lasted).

The Civic Federation invited participation from, not only businesspersons, but also trade union leaders. Samuel Gompers, the president of the American Federation of Labor, became its first vice president. The Civic Federation was successful in the first few decades of the century in conciliating several labor disputes, but after World War I it became primarily interested in actively combatting communism. It began to lose its credibility and, in 1935, the AFL decided no longer to be associated with it. The federation was never successful in convincing most employers to accept pure and simple unionism. Instead most fought apolitical unionism as hard as they had fought the socialists. The National Association of Manufacturers, for example, "stood for industry's sole and exclusive right to determine both wages and the conditions of employment" (Dulles and Dubofsky 1984, 186).

After World War I, Woodrow Wilson called a national conference of business and labor leaders in hopes of bringing about a general accommodation between labor and business similar to the basic agreements that had been worked out in many continental European countries. The conference, however, was not a success. "When the employer contingent rejected a resolution endorsing to resolution that 'the right of wage earners to organize without discrimination, to bargain collectively, to be represented by representatives of their own choosing in negotiations, and adjustments with employers in respect to wages, hours or work, and relations and conditions of employment is recognized,' the labor group withdrew, and the conference ended" (Taft 1964, 363).

Throughout this period of unrest, the AFL stood firm with its policy of business unionism and by the mid-1920s the ideology and associated strategy of the AFL clearly emerged victorious. In retrospect, it appears as though American workers rejected socialism and chose between either business unionism or the abundance conscious individualism preached by spokespersons for unbound capitalism. Whether it was a real choice or not, the dominance of the bread-and-butter philosophy had profound effects on the evolution of the American industrial relations system. Even though union membership and militancy increased significantly in the United States, just as it did in Europe because of the victory of business unionism, American workers did not pose a serious and credible threat to business as a class.[5] As a result, American employers did not feel compelled to organize in order to defend the capitalist system. Pure and simple unionism accepted the legitimacy of capitalism. It was no threat to the continuation of the system.

Instead of organizing extensively and reaching a general compromise with organized labor, American business remained unorganized. In general, American companies decided that the labor challenge could be met by an individual response rather than a collective one. Since the general propensity of businesspeople is to compete not to cooperate, the relative absence of a superordinate threat allowed this individualism to come to the fore.

For the most part American employers decided to confront unions on a plant-by-plant basis (Adams 1981). Where the unions were strong enough to compel recognition, the result was a mini-accord. Not uncommonly, unions in this situation were able to establish strong shop-floor steward networks to ensure that mutually agreed upon understandings were honored. Collective agreements began to be written down. At first these agreements had only a few clauses, but over time they expanded in size as new issues arose (Chamberlain and Kuhn 1965).

The European employer strategy had been largely successful, at least initially, in neutralizing the influence of unions on day-to-day labor management interaction. Although they would agree to multi-employer contracts regulating wages, hours, and other conditions of employment, their power and authority stayed largely intact inside the plant. In the United States, employers were also relatively successful in remaining entirely free from direct dealings with unions by remaining unorganized. But where the unions were successful in forcing recognition, they also were able generally to insert themselves in the plant where they continually monitored the decisions taken by management. Successful American unions were, as a result, generally more of a burden to employers than were the unions in Europe that were poorly organized on the shop floor. American employers are more intensely anti-union in their behavior than are their counterparts abroad. The success of American unions in influencing the organization of work at the point of production is, no doubt, one important factor.

As noted in the previous chapter, the employer strategy in Europe of forming associations and insisting on multi-employer bargaining helped to move forward the transformation of European unions from the craft to the industrial form. In North America, the individualistic strategy of employers provided a favorable condition for the persistence of the craft form of organization. The dominant factor in that persistence was, however, the triumph of business unionism.

THE THEORY OF AMERICAN LABOR EXCEPTIONALISM

The exceptional choice of pure and simple unionism by American labor has long attracted the attention of students of labor. Why did the American labor movement not become socialist? (see, e.g., Sombart 1976; Galenson 1961). One of the most influential answers to that question was provided in the 1920s by Selig Perlman, a professor at the University of Wisconsin. Perlman was a student of John R. Commons who in the early decades of the twentieth century carried out the first in-depth research into the origins and development of American unions. Perlman was part of Commons' research team. Based on what he had learned working on Commons' project, as well as the knowledge that he brought with him from Europe about socialist ideology and developments, Perlman (1928) wrote *A Theory of the Labor Movement.* Not only did Perlman attempt to explain why the American labor movement had rejected socialism, he also provided a defense of the choice of pure and simple unionism. As a result, *A Theory of the Labor Movement* has long been considered an apologetic for the American labor movement.

Perlman began his analysis by fleshing out the theory implicit in what might be called unbound capitalism. The capitalist, according to Perlman, saw the world in terms of unlimited opportunities for individuals. Because so much opportunity existed, anyone could be successful on their own merits if only they put in sufficient effort. As a result, there was no need for trade unions whose function was to look after the collective interests of labor. Indeed, not only were unions unnecessary, they were also harmful because they interfered with the free working of the market and thus made the market less efficient. This theory suggested that the appropriate strategy for the worker was to save and invest in order to improve his/her lot individually.

Opposed to capitalist theory was socialist theory. As formulated by Karl Marx and his colleagues and successors, it held that capitalist theory was merely an ideological support for an unfair and unjust socioeconomic system. Everyone clearly could not get ahead as capitalist theory proposed. It was the few that prospered at the expense of the many. As a result, under capitalism typical working and living conditions were poor, income was very insecure since workers could be easily dismissed from their jobs, and businesses could be closed down. Income was also distributed very unevenly. While some individuals might improve their lot, the working class as a whole could not prosper under capitalism. Given this analysis, the proper role for labor was to pursue a new, more just society in which income and opportunity were distributed more equitably. The labor movement (and especially the political party) was the key instrument for the achievement of this new society.

Although it did not preach revolution, the Fabian Society in Britain also held that labor should organize with a view towards winning control of government democratically in order to remake society into one more equitable than that which existed under unbound capitalism. Sydney and Beatrice Webb (who Perlman referred to as efficiency intellectuals) argued that socialism would be a more efficient system than capitalism because it would insure that the talents of all members of society were utilized to their greatest extent (Webb and Webb 1902). Capitalism wasted too many human resources in unemployment and underemployment.

The program for labor suggested by socialist intellectuals called for the formation of unions and political parties which would seek politically (either by revolution or evolution) to remake capitalist society by distributing income and power more evenly. Instead of laissez-faire, the socialist program called for the state to play a major part in controlling the direction of the economy. Indeed, by early in the twentieth century state ownership and direction of the means of production had become the central element in the socialist program.

Perlman suggested that these were the two great bodies of ideas competing for the allegiance of the working person. Both, Perlman said, had been developed by intellectuals rather than by working people themselves. From his studies of American unionism, however, he claimed to have identified a third theory or ideology—one that had been developed organically by working people themselves. This was the theory of pure and simple, business, or, to use the term invented by Perlman himself, job-conscious unionism.

To understand Perlman it is necessary to review briefly the situation of the American labor movement in the 1920s. At that point it was predominantly a movement of craft unions that had come into existence in the mid-nineteenth century. In the 1880s, these organizations had formed a national federation which they named the American Federation of Labor. During the 1880s and 1890s, the AFL had fought a battle for labor supremacy with the reformist and more inclusive Knights of Labor. By the mid-1890s, the Knights were in decline. During the 1890s and first two decades of the twentieth century, another challenge to the hegemony of the AFL was offered by various, more radical labor organizations. The Industrial Workers of the World (IWW) after 1908 was basically anarcho-syndicalist in nature. It strongly opposed the capitalist system and refused to grant any legitimacy to capitalist authority in industry. The IWW attracted many adherents between about 1900 and 1920, but after a major recession in the early 1920s it faded away very rapidly.

Still another challenge was offered to the dominance of the AFL by the formation of an American Socialist Party which attracted the allegiance of several individual unions and gave promise of providing leadership to a European-like labor movement. By the mid-1920s, however, the Socialist Party had become insignificant politically and had lost the support of several unions. In short, at the time when Perlman was writing, the AFL had seen several challenges to its claim to be the major labor organization in the United States, having turned all others away.

As noted above, the policy of the AFL was to organize on the basis of craft and to bargain hard in order to win, according to the famous phrase symbolic of its outlook, "more, more, more" for its members. Unlike the movements on continental Europe, the AFL did not set as its prime goal the improvement of the condition of the working class as a whole. It was not opposed to the formation of unions by the unskilled, but its efforts were focused on securing benefits for its own members rather than for nonmembers—no matter how dire their straits.

This hard-hearted philosophy met with a great deal of criticism from European socialist unionists who considered American unions to be backward. Marx had proposed that early in their existence unions would always be economistic in their outlook. On their own, workers were unlikely to see past their immediate needs. As a result, they would attempt through unionism to improve their wages and hours of work but, untrained and uneducated, they would not be able to unravel the nature of the capitalist system in which they were enmeshed. They would not be able to understand that their efforts at raising wages and reducing hours were doomed to failure because of the macrodynamics of capitalism. That is why it was necessary for leaders (Perlman's intellectuals) to utilize unions as vehicles for training—as means to achieve greater consciousness of the class structure of capitalist society. From the perspective of this philosophy, American unionists were immature. They were still stuck in the economistic stage of development. They had yet to achieve understanding of the class dynamics of capitalist society.

Based on his studies of the American labor movement, Perlman rejected this analysis. Indeed, he turned it on its head and argued that it was the Europeans rather than the Americans who were immature. His basic argument was that the workers who formed the unions that made up the AFL had worked out their own home-grown philosophy. They had rejected the tenets both of capitalism and of socialism. They rejected capitalism because they realized that on the whole they were not all capable of becoming highly successful. The world from their perception was not one of abundance but rather one filled with insecurity. Instead of opportunity they mostly saw impending disaster. This led them to form trade unions which engaged in communism of opportunity. In short, the unions protected job territories and parcelled out the jobs available in an equitable fashion.

The AFL unionists also rejected the socialist analysis and agenda. Not only did "Tom, Dick and Harry" not see themselves capable of becoming millionaires by their individual efforts, but also they did not consider themselves capable collectively of running the complicated machinery of modern corporations and economies. They did not want to take over the operation of the economy as the socialist program called for. Instead their goals were more modest. They wanted no more than job and income security and an equitable wage. They were perfectly content to leave corporate management to corporate managers and the management of the economy to elected representatives and government bureaucrats.

This brand of unionism was more mature than the European brand because it was a true reflection of the wishes and needs of the workers themselves. It was not the result of an outside intellectual selling workers on some scheme dreamed up in an ivy tower. Intellectuals, according to Perlman, were not interested in real workers. They instead considered labor to be an abstract mass caught up in the abstract forces of history.

European unionists were immature, in Perlman's view, because they had been taken in by the arguments of the intellectuals. They had no confidence in adopting their own philosophy as the Americans had done. It was the Americans who were in the vanguard. Over time as labor movements matured, Perlman believed, they would all become more businesslike and less political. They would all begin to see that business unionism was the type of unionism most congruent with the real needs and wants of the working person.

BUT WHY THE UNITED STATES?

As noted above, Perlman's analysis stood Marx on his head. Rather than being backward, American workers were in the forefront of labor development. But the question then arose: why was it that American workers were mature enough to fend off the appeals of the educated and imposing intellectuals? Why was it only in America that workers were confident enough to adopt their own home-grown philosophy? Perlman's answer was that American unionism was exceptional because of factors peculiar to the American environment.

First of all, unlike the typical situation in Europe, universal male suffrage had been achieved early in the United States as was access to education. Moreover, the sorts of indignities suffered by European workers were never in place in America. American workers, for example, had not been required to produce workbooks signed by their previous employer in order to get a job. The American economy was also quite healthy during the nineteenth century. There was usually a shortage of labor. As a result (despite the scarcity consciousness of the typical worker), the experience of the worker was one of participating in a system that appeared to be successful. Furthermore, there was the frontier and free land in the event of depression and unemployment in the East.

In Europe, on the other hand, as population increased and the land was used more efficiently for profit, unemployment was high in the cities resulting in a more widespread negative perception of the capitalist system. Internal frontiers had long since been closed. Immigration from the poor conditions in Europe to the better opportunities that existed in North America was a common experience. In short, American workers did not have the sorts of political grievances that European workers had. As a result, they did not consider it necessary to change the political system radically. This objective experience was reinforced by the American cultural glorification of individualism and egalitarianism. As children, Americans were taught to believe that whatever their economic circumstance they were socially the equivalent of any other American—and superior to people in other countries. If social and political equality were a reality, then there was no reason to form organizations designed to achieve those ends.

In addition to the politico-economic environment in America, immigration also made it less likely that a philosophy based on class consciousness would be successful. Throughout the period when the American labor movement was taking shape, large segments of the American working class identified not so much with other workers as with other members of their ethnic community. When they came to America, Scandinavians, Italians, and Serbs tended to associate more with others like themselves than with workers generally. They were more likely to think of themselves as having common interests with others of their ethnic group rather than with workers from other ethnic communities (see especially Galenson 1961).

Perlman also argued that the early ascendence of the two-party system, with both parties staying close to the middle of the road, made it difficult for new social movements to be successful. Whenever new political issues arose, one party or the other would make them part of its platform. In Europe, on the other hand, political parties tended to represent class interests. Conservative parties represented the interests of the traditional landed class. Liberal parties represented the emerging business class. In that milieu, it was natural for socialist/labor parties to arise to represent the interests of the working class.

According to Perlman, job-conscious unionism fit the U.S. environment but it did not fit in Europe. Over time, however, as American conditions were approximated in Europe, the labor movement there would also become more mature.[6]

Perlman's theory provides a good deal of insight into the dynamics of American and European labor movements, but it is far from entirely satisfactory. The key proposition that workers form or join unions for short-term, job-oriented, pragmatic reasons rather than to change society fundamentally is no doubt correct. In a study done in the early 1970s in countries as diverse as

Brazil, India, Belgium, and the United States, William Form (1973) found that "while union officers were sympathetic to political unionism . . . it was unimportant to workers. . . . Whatever the political views of officers or workers, the vast majority of workers felt their unions should first pursue higher wages and better working conditions and then social solidarity" (237). He also pointed out, however, that these pragmatic needs might be met not only through collective bargaining, but also through government action; most workers were willing to defer to the judgement of their leaders regarding the appropriate strategy so long as the results were positive.

Perlman's theory seems to imply that American workers who did not unionize rejected both socialism and business unionism and embraced instead the abundance consciousness of the capitalist. For some that may be true, but for most it seems to be very unlikely. More convincing is the proposition that neither socialism nor industrial unionism were successful by the 1920s because of the massive repression of these institutions by both government and business (see Wilentz 1984). In addition, American courts were especially active in nullifying the meager legislative advances made by early labor organizations, thus leading labor to discount the efficacy of positive state intervention (see, e.g., Forbath 1991, Hattam 1993).

Another implication of Perlman's thesis is that European unionists were taken in by socialist intellectuals because of their lack of confidence in their own home-grown ideas. It is true that, especially early in the century, trade unionists were much more pragmatic in responding to their members' needs than political leaders in the socialist movement. It is for precisely that reason that in Sweden and Germany the unions split from the party umbrella to form their own organizations so that they could set their own agendas. On the other hand, in the long run most union leaders in Europe have not turned away from socialism. In fact, it has proven to be a very successful philosophy—one that is largely responsible for bringing to bear the political pressure and ideas that have produced the modern welfare state.

EMPLOYER POLICY AND THE LABOR-MANAGEMENT ACCORD OF THE 1940s

One might expect a priori that a labor movement more accepting of the basic tenets of capitalism would be more acceptable to business. But the American experience suggests the opposite. Because they were not a fundamental threat, employers generally did not feel that they had to reach a compromise with the AFL unions. Most insisted instead on dealing with unions on a case-by-case basis. If workers wanted to be represented by unions in specific plants that was one thing, but if they did not explicitly signify their desires to be so represented then that was an indication that they were content with the status quo and that the unions had no mandate to represent their interests.

In short, American employers refused to recognize the unions as the legitimate representatives of working class interests. Because of its elitist craft union strategy, the AFL could not put forth a credible claim that it was entitled to such general recognition. Employers also refused to recognize the claim of specific AFL unions to speak for the interests of, for example, all carpenters. The AFL was not strong enough politically to compel that end.

Because no national accommodation similar to those worked out in Germany and Sweden was achieved during the 1920s and 1930s, American employers felt no constraint in attempting to dissuade their employees from becoming union members. Indeed, the arsenal of weapons mentioned in chapter 1 designed to destroy unions (yellow-dog contracts, victimization, spies, blacklists, etc.) continued to be used with impunity in the United States long after they had come to be regarded as improper in Europe.

In the wake of German and Russian developments toward the end of World War I, as well as the growth of union membership and militancy in the United States, major American corporations reluctantly accepted that employees should be able to have a say in the making of firm-level decisions that critically affected their personal interests (Derber 1970; Conner 1983). Those employers insisted, however, that they should not be compelled by government fiat to establish any alien schemes developed elsewhere. Additionally, they should not be forced to deal with outsiders who had no commitment to the best interests of the firm. Instead, they argued, they would take the initiative to establish employee representation plans. This strategy clearly was influenced by European developments, and especially those in Germany (see, e.g., Douglas 1921; Conner 1983).

Because of the widespread adoption of this approach, employer-initiated representation plans proliferated throughout the 1920s and into the early 1930s. These schemes were condemned by the independent unions, but labor did not have the political or economic strength to forestall them. By the mid-1930s, there were nearly as many American workers in company unions as there were in independent unions.[7]

In 1932, Franklin D. Roosevelt was elected president and he immediately adopted the strategy of experimenting with various options in order to revitalize the depressed economy. One option that he was convinced to take was to support both the unions and the practice of collective bargaining. He was not a zealot for these, but he went along with members of his administration and of the Democratic Party who were. The bottom line was that it became the policy of the U.S. government to support the practice and procedure of collective bargaining. In the National Labor Relations Act (known generally as the Wagner

Act), passed in 1935, many of the tactics still used by employers to thwart unionization and collective representation of their employees were made illegal. A National Labor Relations Board (NLRB) was established which had the power to order employers to negotiate with unions chosen by a majority of relevant employees to act as their bargaining agent.[8] In this new policy environment, there was a rapid unionization of workers in the mass-production industries and a dramatic increase in the practice of collective bargaining.

By the mid-1940s, an informal understanding had been reached between the unions and, if not the employers as a whole, at least the largest corporations involved in manufacturing. It contained the following elements (see Adams 1989):

a. Union Recognition and Good Faith Dealing. Where unions had managed to win the allegiance of the majority of the employees, employers would no longer attempt to undercut them but would instead deal with them in good faith. This understanding applied only to unionized employers. Because of weak employer organization, non-union employers formulated their own policies separate from those of unionized employers. By and large, nonunionized organizations continued to maintain that if workers did not actively choose to unionize they obviously were satisfied with the status quo. Failure by workers to take active steps to unionize meant that they did not wish to be represented by unions. Nonunion employers continued to maintain the right to do everything within the law to encourage unorganized workers to maintain their status. Initially, however, the NLRB created under the Wagner Act forbade employers to say anything during union organizing campaigns for fear that employees would feel intimidated and threatened by public statements (Taylor and Witney 1987, 284). By the 1950s, that policy had fallen by the wayside—the victim of court challenges based on the notion of free speech and the passage of the Taft-Hartley Act in 1947.

b. Hard Bargaining and the Recognition of Management's Rights. Unions were expected to recognize that management had the right to make basic decisions about production, investment, and operations. Management would insist on this through the insertion of management's rights clauses in collective agreements reserving full discretion to make decisions about any issues not included in the agreement. This strategy was almost identical, in miniature, to the grand strategy followed by European employers in defense of their freedom to manage. In negotiations, it was understood that management would bargain hard in the interests of shareholders and unions were expected to bargain equally hard in the interests of workers.

From a labor perspective, this informal accord fell far short of the basic agreements which had come about in Europe. The unions were not recognized as the legitimate voice for the entire class of workers for which they intended to speak, but rather only for those who actively chose to become union members. Collective representation did not become a reality for the majority of workers, but only for the minority who took active efforts to have it installed. Most observers at the time expected that bargaining would eventually become standard, but they underestimated the resolve of nonunion employers to maintain the status quo. (see, e.g., Murphy 1987; Reynolds 1988).

DECENTRALIZED BARGAINING

One of the most notable exceptions of North American industrial relations is decentralized bargaining. In other industrialized democracies, the center of gravity of bargaining is at the multi-employer level. It is at that level because employers insisted on it. It was not difficult for employers to convince socialist unions that bargaining should be conducted on a multi-employer basis because socialist philosophy called for unions generally to raise the conditions of the working class, and this could best be done through broadbased bargaining. The idea was to protect the most sensitive areas of management's authority to organize and direct work by agreeing to codetermination of less sensitive issues such as the establishment of minimum wages and general wage increases.

United States' employer strategy was quite different. American employers decided to fight to maintain all of their rights by avoiding unions and collective bargaining altogether. Where they were unsuccessful, plant-level bargaining was the result. The Wagner Act did not create decentralized bargaining, but it did all but ensure that broadbased bargaining could not become an American reality by establishing plant-by-plant recognition procedures. Employees in an appropriate bargaining unit, such as blue-collar workers on the shop floor of a factory, could apply to have a union certified as their designated bargaining agent. But employees from two or more companies could not be certified together over employer objections; neither could employees from two classes (e.g., white-collar and blue-collar) within a single company normally be certified as a single unit.

THE THEORY OF AMERICAN LABOR EXCEPTIONALISM AGAIN—STURMTHAL'S SYNTHESIS

If Marx's analysis was the thesis and Perlman's the antithesis, in the 1960s, Adolf Sturmthal, a professor at the University of Illinois, provided a synthesis (Sturmthal 1966a, 1973). From the time when Perlman produced his *Theory of the Labor Movement* to the 1960s, there had been many developments in the philosophy and strategy of labor. First of all, the American labor movement moved to the left. In the 1930s, in the middle of the Great Depression, the unskilled and semiskilled workers in the mass-production industries organized in large numbers. Among the unions that came into being during that decade were those for steelworkers, autoworkers, packinghouse workers, and electrical workers. Within the AFL, some union leaders wanted to take the lead to organize the mass-production industries. Among the key unions involved were the mine workers, the clothing workers, the textile workers, and the oil workers (Taft 1964, 471). Other AFL unionists were, however, uneasy about the move. They continued to adhere to the initial analysis of the AFL which held that allowing unskilled workers into the federation would undercut the key basis of strength of the federated unions—the scarcity of their skill. The reformers, on the other hand, believed that the situation in the United States had changed and that the old philosophy was out of date.

The first response of the AFL was to place newly organized workers in federal locals under the direct authority of the federation from which they could be reassigned to the appropriate craft union (Taft 1964, 464). This format proved awkward and unsuccessful. It was reactive instead of proactive. Many AFL leaders felt that a more aggressive approach was required and that, given the conditions of the times, an industrial format might very well be appropriate for workers in the mass-production industries. Many felt that, instead of worrying about structural issues, organizing should be the first priority. When the AFL leadership procrastinated, several unions within the AFL at first set up a Committee for Industrial Organization (CIO) which devoted itself to organizing the workers in mass production. After bitter disputes with the old-line leadership, the committee later withdrew altogether from the AFL and established the Congress of Industrial Organization (Dulles and Dubofsky 1984). During this period, workers had a number of grievances due to the depression. When the government of the United States supported the practice of collective bargaining, the CIO unions grew rapidly. In a very short time, the AFL saw the handwriting on the wall. In order to avoid being overshadowed by the CIO, the AFL abruptly changed direction and began to compete vigorously with the new federation in order to organize the unorganized.

From the outset, the CIO was more political than the AFL. Several of its top leaders were declared socialists or communists. Others, such as Walter Reuther of the Autoworkers were, if not declared socialists, at least much closer emotionally and philosophically to their European counterparts than were the AFL leaders. The CIO itself was more interested in achieving general gains for workers through political action than the AFL ever had been. Towards that end, the CIO became very active in mobilizing support for the Democratic Party, although officially it remained nonpartisan. In short, the American labor movement was moving, if only very slowly, in the direction predicted by Marx. It was becoming more political, more apparently class conscious.

The same was true of the British and Canadian labor movements. In Britain, labor organization around 1880 could only be characterized as very pure and simple. The new model unions which had appeared about mid-century were well run, economically viable craft organizations that depended almost entirely on their own efforts (rather than those of a political party) to secure the interests of their members. According to Henry Pelling, the British labor historian, the American Federation of Labor was consciously modelled on the peak organization of these unions—the Trade Union Congress (1973, 118).

Towards the end of the century, however, unskilled and semiskilled workers began to organize, led by the gasworkers and the dockers. The new unions had low fees and depended, "not on benefits but on aggressive strike tactics to win concessions from their employers and so keep their members satisfied" (Pelling 1973, 102). These unions were more interested in political action than the older ones had been.

Although several trade unionists sat in Parliament in the 1880s, most of them did so as liberals even though the Liberal Party had no clear pro-labor platform. Many of the new unionists, on the other hand, gave their support to the formation and development of an independent labor party with close links to the trade unions. This approach slowly gained adherents until, early in the twentieth century, a crisis occurred for the labor movement. The House of Lords granted an employer damages against a union for losses incurred during a strike. This threatened the ability of the unions to be effective and provided the impetus that led to the formation of the Labour Party in 1906 (Pelling 1973, 126–27). At first, that party was no more than an instrument of the unions. Its philosophy was entirely pragmatic. During World War I, however, in a milieu of labor shortages, rising prices, and labor militancy, leftist philosophy became more attractive. In 1918, the party officially adopted the core socialist objective of state control of the means of production (Geary 1991, 33).

In Canada, the labor movement initially was very pragmatic. The first federation, the Trades and Labor Congress of Canada (TLC), had no identifiable philosophy. Its policy was to do whatever it could to promote the interests of its constituents. During the 1890s, however, several American-based unions acquired significant membership in Canada and by means of that link spread the gospel of business unionism. Until 1902, business unions, nationalist unions, socialist unions, Christian unions, and assemblies of the Knights of Labor all found a home in the TLC. In that year, however, the U.S.-based international unions precipitated a crisis. One of the tenets of the AFL was the proposition of one union for each jurisdiction. For example, there should only be one designated union for carpenters, one for plumbers, and so on. This policy was designed to avoid interunion rivalry and thus to conserve resources to better achieve improvements in conditions for the members. In 1902, the international unions in the TLC put forth a proposition that this principle should be honored by the Canadian federation. Since by that time the international unions dominated in most trades, the result would be that many purely Canadian organizations would be compelled to affiliate with American-based unions or leave the federation. The proposition passed and many Canadian unions did leave the TLC. In consequence, the Congress was dominated by the international unions that generally supported the ideology of the AFL. Many considered that the TLC became little more than a branch of the AFL (see, e.g., Horowitz 1968).

The apolitical character of business unionism was, however, never as strongly imbedded in Canada as it was in the United States. In 1906, impressed with the British example, the TLC gave its blessing to the establishment of labor parties at the provincial level, but that strategy was not initially very successful. Another attempt at party building was made during World War I when a national party was formed. That party, however, became very radical in the early 1920s and thus lost the support of the more conservative unionists. In the midst of the Great Depression of the 1930s, another working-class party came into existence—the Cooperative Commonwealth Federation. It was not formed by trade unionists, but rather by various groups of intellectual reformers. It was socialist in outlook, but certainly not revolutionary.

The excitement and spirit of the CIO organizing drive in the United States spilled over into Canada, and many Canadian workers in mass-production industries formed local unions and declared themselves to be part of the CIO movement (see, e.g., Abella 1974). As in the United States, the appearance of such unions caused a crisis in the still international-union-dominated TLC. The result was the withdrawal of the CIO associated unions which in 1940 set up the Canadian Congress of Labor (CCL). In 1943, the CCL formally designated the Cooperative Commonwealth Federation (CCF) to be labor's political arm in Canada. In the mid-1950s, shortly after the amalgamation of the U.S.-based CIO and AFL into the AFL-CIO, the two Canadian federations rejoined each other. Party affiliation was left to be worked out later. This issue was settled in the late 1950s when the parliamentary representation of the CCF was reduced to a very small number. The CCF agreed to meet with the leaders of the Canadian Labor Congress in order to reconstitute the party so that it would be acceptable to the reluctant pure and simple unionists in the new federation. In 1961, these discussions led to the formation of the New Democratic Party which received the full support of the CLC. As a result, today the dominant federation in Canada is social democratic in nature, although many of its constituent members are staunch supporters of the business union philosophy.

There had also been developments in Europe. Even in Perlman's time, radicalism in European labor movements was in decline. By the time Sturmthal took up his analysis of labor movement philosophy, the theme of the age was the end of ideology—a thesis put forth by Daniel Bell (1960) of Columbia University. European unions had become assimilated into the fabric of European society and, although they continued to support labor/socialist parties, most of their energies were spent negotiating collective agreements and servicing the employment needs of their members. In short, European unions, while certainly not giving up political objectives and strategies, had, nevertheless, become more job conscious in their behavior as Perlman had predicted they would (see, e.g., Kassalow 1969).

How was one to explain these developments? It was this question which intrigued Sturmthal. Clearly neither Marx nor Perlman was entirely correct. Labor movements do not inevitably become more political and they do not inevitably become more pure and simple. Indeed, by the 1960s, a kind of convergence had occurred in the methods used by the labor movements in Europe and North America. American unions (as well as British and Canadian unions) were making more use of political means to achieve advantages for their members, whereas European unions were relying more heavily on the economic technique of collective bargaining than they had in the past. What, then, were the factors which gave rise to these changes in strategy and implicitly in philosophy?

Looking back on the development of labor movements, Sturmthal argued that there were three major factors that gave rise to the philosophy and associated strategy chosen by labor movements: (1) the nature of the problems faced by workers in any given epoch, (2) the state of the labor market, and (3) the organizing principle chosen by the trade unions. If the key problems faced by workers were political in nature, the labor movement would choose a political strategy and supporting political ideology; otherwise, it would tend to choose an economic, pure and simple strategy. If the labor market was tight, the labor movement would be more likely to rely on collective bargaining to achieve gains for workers. It would do so because when labor is scarce the bargaining power of unions is strong, and their likelihood of success in bargaining is high. On the other hand, if the market is loose, if there is a lot of unemployment, collective bargaining is not likely to be very effective and thus a labor movement will be prone to expend more effort in attempting to win gains for workers through political means.

Finally, if a labor movement makes use of the craft principle of organization, it is more likely to adopt a nonpolitical strategy for two reasons. First, it is likely to have more bargaining power than it would if it chose to organize both skilled and unskilled workers, and second, it is likely to have less political clout because it will represent a smaller segment of society than a movement that organizes broadly.

These factors may be used to analyze the initial choice of strategy as well as the change in ideology and strategy in several countries. In the United States, workers in the late nineteenth century did not consider their key problems to be political since major political rights had already been instituted. Political unionism, in consequence, had low appeal. By choosing the craft principle of organization, the AFL ensured that its constituents would have substantial bargaining power, but insubstantial political power. Moreover, labor in the United States during the period when union federations were forming was, at least in comparison to Europe, quite scarce—thus, the AFL unions were able to be effective on their members behalf. During the Great Depression of the 1930s, unemployment shot up to high levels in the United States, and unskilled and semiskilled workers began to organize in large numbers. By becoming a mass movement, the CIO had more political influence than the AFL. The CIO could credibly claim to speak for the interests of a broader class of workers. Given these developments, there was a move left toward a more political and nascently more radical strategy.

In Britain, the labor movement moved left and formed a labor party as the direct consequence of the appearance of a major political problem at the turn of the twentieth century which could not be effectively addressed by institutions in place at that time. The move towards political action also coincided with the swelling of the ranks of trade unionists by the addition of many unskilled and semiskilled workers.

In Germany, the unions initially embraced a radical political strategy because workers were shut out of political and economic decision making. It was reasonable to believe that only by radically changing the system could progress be made. As the economy absorbed the rural workers in the twentieth century, and as labor won more and more political rights, the movement became more conservative. Because collective bargaining could be effective, the movement depended more and more on negotiations with employers as a prime means to achieve gains for its members.

In Canada, the labor movement became more political only after unskilled and semiskilled workers organized en masse in the 1930s. It was the broadly organized CCL, rather than the craftworker-based TLC, that first established a link with the socialist CCF.

Although very helpful in placing North American developments into a broader theoretical framework, Sturmthal's synthesis does leave some loose ends. As he proposes, almost everywhere craft or occupational unionists are less political than are industrial unions composed of skilled and unskilled workers. Even more recently organized occupational groups such as teachers and nurses tend to shun connections with socialist parties. The major exception is Denmark where a labor movement dominated by craft unionists is still very political in nature (Scheuer 1992).

The market, as a predictor of union philosophy and strategy, does not have the same degree of predictive accuracy. It is true that unions have more bargaining power where markets are tight and less where markets are weak. But markets are poor predictors of union strategy. Thus, labor markets were very tight in both of the world war periods, but in each case labor movements in the democratic countries became much more political. Unions also became more political in the tight labor market period of the 1970s when governments attempted to negotiate wage constraints with many of them. Of course, during these periods, serious political problems existed simultaneously with tight labor markets. Unravelling these forces is not a simple task. To those involved, they were experienced as a holistic environment rather than as discrete forces.

Another problem with Sturmthal's theory is that he proposes a congruence between the perceived problem and labor's choice of method. Labor movements that define their key problems as political are likely to adopt a political strategy to address those issues, and a labor movement that defines its key problem as economic is likely to embrace an economic strategy. Although the argument seems plausible, other combinations are possible and, indeed, may be observed. In France, for example, since the nineteenth century, unions have attempted to involve governments in wage disputes. Instead of exerting pressure on employers by striking for long periods, French unions often engage in demonstrations in order to convince the government to exert pressure on the employer to make concessions. In short, political means are being used to address the most basic of economic issues (Sellier 1978; Daley 1992).

It is also difficult to determine objectively whether the problems of a given period should be classified as economic or political. Indeed, economic issues have always had a major impact on politics, and governments rise and fall based on their perceived expertise to effectively address economic problems.

The oft cited relationship between access to free education and the franchise and labor conservatism in the United States is not entirely satisfying. French workers also achieved the right to vote and had broad access to free education early in the course of economic development (Meyer 1965). That did not stop them from formulating one of the most radical labor movements in Europe. No doubt, the conundrum is partially explained by noting that, despite the formality of an extensive franchise and widespread access to education, French governments have been very unresponsive to the concerns of labor. The conclusion would seem to be that the relationship between public policy and labor strategy is far from simple.

In short, while the theoretical perspectives of Marx, Perlman, and Sturmthal are all very helpful, an entirely satisfactory theory of the labor movement, into which American labor exceptionalism may be fitted, still remains to be formulated.

THE UNRAVELING OF THE ACCORD

During World War II, labor leaders were asked to participate on committees set up to administer various parts of the war effort. A War Labor Board encouraged employers to recognize and negotiate with unions over conditions of employment and had the power to impose settlements on those who were intransigent. Because unemployment was very low, the power of labor was high and union membership rose at a steep rate.

After the war, however, there was a backlash. Strikes broke out as workers demanded large wage increases to make up for wartime inflation and wage restraint. A conservative Republican majority was elected to Congress and the result was the introduction and passage of an act opposed to the interests of organized labor (Tomlins 1985). The Taft-Hartley Act was referred to by the unions as a slave labor bill. It granted legitimacy to the efforts of nonunion employers to actively oppose unionization as long as they did not engage in the activities that had been outlawed in the 1930s. It also allowed workers to decertify unions.

The specifics are probably not as important as the overall message emanating from Washington to employers. It was no longer clearly the policy of the government of the United States to encourage the practice and procedure of collective bargaining. Instead, the new policy was to allow unorganized employers to compete with unions for the allegiance of the worker—a competition strongly weighted in favor of employers because of the authority that they held over employees (Summers 1979; Gross 1985). Whereas prior to World War II there had been a widespread consensus that workers should be able to influence their conditions of work via some form of representative mechanism, the new policy legitimized the absence of any such mechanism in unorganized firms. It in essence certified that the normal condition in industry was industrial autocracy which should be replaced with a form of industrial democracy only when employers behaved so poorly as to stimulate their employee subjects to take action to institute a new industrial-political regime.

In this new milieu, some employers began to test the system around the margins. Lawyers found reasons to delay processing of complaints that employers were not refraining from the use of the tactics outlawed in the 1930s. By the 1960s, the incidence of cases in which employees were fired for engaging in union activity began to increase and that trajectory continued into the

1970s (Weiler 1990). Various court cases began to go against the unions (Atleson 1983). One case, for example, resulted in the restriction of issues that the union could negotiate to impasse (Knight and Sockell 1988, *NLRB v. Borg Warner* 1958). Another gave employers the permission to abrogate collective agreements when the company was in financial trouble (*NLRB v. Bildisco and Bildisco* 1984).

When a friendly government under Democratic president Jimmy Carter was elected in the 1970s, the labor movement pushed for labor law reform. A bill was introduced that would make it easier for the unions to organize and more difficult for employers to ignore the law. Employers organized effectively against this perceived political threat. Although the act passed the House of Representatives handily and acquired a substantial majority in the Senate, it did not attract a sufficient number of votes to override a filibuster by some U.S. senators.

In 1981, the conservative government of Republican Ronald Reagan broke an illegal strike by air traffic controllers and legally disbanded the union. That action was taken as a signal by many companies that they had been given carte blanche to disregard the terms of the postwar accord (Goldfield 1987).

By the mid-1980s, nonunion employers were breaking the law against victimization of unionists with impunity. Many were dealing fairly with unions in one plant, while at the same time actively attempting to keep the union out of other plants. Some employers in this category shut down unionized plants in order to open up nonunion plants in parts of the country where unions were weak (see Kochan, Katz, and McKersie 1986).

The result of these factors, as well as the impact of demographic shifts and industrial restructuring, was that union support began to collapse. By the early 1990s, less than 12 percent of private sector workers were still in unions and collective agreements probably did not cover more than 13–15 percent of private sector employees (Hirsh and Macpherson 1993).

CANADIAN DEVELOPMENTS

Events in Canada during the 1930s and 1940s were in many ways similar to those in the United States. After the passage of the Wagner Act, labor in Canada pushed for the passage of similar legislation. By that time, though, jurisdiction over labor affairs had devolved to the provinces. Several provinces passed legislation with provisions similar to the Wagner Act, although none of them provided for an administrative agency and thus, according to the major analysis of the period, they had little clear impact (Woods 1973). Nevertheless, union membership and militancy increased at a rate similar to that in the United States. This naturally occurring experiment throws in doubt the almost universal belief of American observers that union growth during the 1930s and 1940s was the direct result of the application of the Wagner Act. Canada and the United States are alike in that governments in both countries adopted a policy of supporting collective bargaining. They are dissimilar in that the procedures set up to accomplish that end in the United States were not initially adopted in Canada. Thus, the comparison suggests that it was the adoption of a positive policy by government towards unionism rather than the enforcement mechanisms embodied in the legislation that was the critical factor in propelling union growth (Adams 1993b).

During World War II, labor power based on a severe shortage of labor and the need for national unity increased substantially. The socialist CCF attracted a growing following and the CIO unions in Canada expanded at a rapid rate. Continued agitation by the labor movement for the passage of a federal Wagner-like Act (forbidding an employer to commit unfair labor practices and compelling employers to recognize and negotiate with unions where the unions had worker support) led to the federal government issuing Order in Council PC1003. This executive order put into practice all of the key elements of the U.S. National Labor Relations Act while retaining the long-term government policy of reserving the right to intervene in disputes and delay strikes in order that conciliation might be tried. This order was applicable to most of the labor force as a result of emergency measures adopted by the federal government as part of its war effort.

After World War II, the prerogative to legislate on labor issues reverted back to the provinces with the federal government retaining jurisdiction over the 10 percent of the labor force deemed to be working in interprovincial industries or industries critical to the nation as a whole (such as atomic energy). In the late 1940s, the federal government passed standing legislation embedding the Wagner Act principles and enforcement mechanisms, and by the early 1950s most of the provinces had done the same.

By the mid-1950s, it would have appeared to the objective observer that in Canada a labor-management accord with dimensions nearly identical to the ones described above for the United States had come into existence. In Canada, though, the terms of the implicit accord held up better than they did in the United States. From about the mid-1950s, the fortunes of the labor movements in the two countries began to diverge. In Canada, the movement grew stronger and in the United States it became weaker. By 1990, although only a minority of workers in both countries were covered by collective agreements, two times as many Canadian workers as American workers had their employment interests represented in negotiations with employers (Chaison and Rose 1990).

There are several reasons for the difference (Meltz 1985; Adams 1985, 1989; Chaison and Rose 1990; Kumar 1993). First of all, Canadian labor relations boards have been much more adamant in demanding that employers live up both to the letter and to the spirit of the law, and Canadian governments have stood firmly behind the accord. When some employers have attempted to take advantage of loopholes or ambiguities in the law, either new legislation has been introduced or labor boards have fashioned remedies very unpalatable to employers. In the 1970s, for example, an employer in Ontario refused to accede to a union's request that it deduct union dues from employee paychecks and transmit them to the union. The result was a bitter, headline getting, strike. In response, the conservative provincial government passed a law which stated that no employer could refuse to agree to such a union request in the future (Meltz 1985). In the early 1980s, a U.S. multinational company well known for its union avoiding tactics, refused to bargain in good faith with a government-certified union of its warehouse employees. After hearing all of the evidence, the Labor Board required that the employer apologize publicly to the union, pay the union for all of the expenses it had incurred as a result of the illicit behavior, and commence to negotiate with the union in good faith (Meltz 1985). Such actions as these sent a message to companies operating in Canada that illegal behavior would not be tolerated (see also Craig and Solomon 1993; Noël and Gardner 1990).

Second, changes in legislation and policy have generally (but not always) been designed to encourage the spread and effectiveness of collective bargaining. Canadian developments contrast sharply with the United States where court decisions have usually made it easier for employers to avoid or escape from bargaining. Among the innovations in that direction have been the introduction of first contract arbitration to overcome the propensity of employers to surface bargain in their first encounter with collective negotiations, and the outlawing of the use of strikebreakers in some jurisdictions (Sexton 1987; Craig and Solomon 1993). In the early 1970s, most provincial governments, following the recommendation of a federal commission, formally adopted the objective of encouraging collective bargaining (see Adams 1989). In short, whereas in the United States the government had moved from a clear position of encouraging collective bargaining to one often interpreted to be a policy of neutrality, Canadian governments moved from an absence of clear intent to one more specifically intended to encourage the practice of bargaining.

But why have Canadian governments and labor relations boards been more insistent than their counterparts in the United States that the accord be honored and strengthened? The key element is undoubtedly the existence of a viable social democratic party in Canada and its absence in the United States (Meltz 1985; Bruce 1989). After the war, the CCF established itself as a force both nationally and in many, if not all, of the provinces. By the 1960s, it had become the majority in only one province—Saskatchewan (where it introduced the first

North American universal health care system in the 1940s)—but it had also become a strong second or third party in several jurisdictions. In consequence, the other parties could not ignore its policies. The middle-of-the-road Liberal Party, in particular, had a tendency to adopt the policies whenever they attained increasing public support.

In 1959, however, the CCF was reduced to a rump group at the national level as the result of a Progressive Conservative Party sweep. Consequently, it held a series of conferences with leaders of various socialist groups as well as union leaders. From 1943, the CIO-associated CCL had given its support to the CCF, but that support had been withheld by the AFL-associated Trades and Labour Congress. The AFL and the CIO reaffiliated in the United States in 1955 and the next year the two Canadian federations did likewise, but support for the party was problematic. Discussions continued through the late 1950s and after the defeat of 1959, they intensified. The result was the formation of the New Democratic Party (NDP) in 1961. The NDP was more moderate than the CCF and was thus minimally acceptable to the craft unions which in the Gompers tradition, continued to distrust political action (Horowitz 1968).

Between 1961 and the 1990s, the NDP had many successes. It held the balance of power at the federal level a few times, and in the early 1990s was in office in three provinces: British Columbia, Saskatchewan, and Ontario. Throughout that period, it continued to maintain the allegiance of the dominant Canadian Labor Congress, although as a result of a dispute over several issues, of which political strategy was one, most of the international building trades unions out of the AFL tradition withdrew from the CLC in the early 1980s (see Rose 1983).[9]

It appears to be clear that within Canada, as the labor movement has moved down the ideological spectrum away from business unionism towards social-ism, it has increased in strength and effectiveness. Prior to the 1970s, Canadian unionists generally thought of themselves as junior partners in the North American labor movement. For the most part, they looked to the United States for inspiration and assistance. From the 1980s, however, the role has been reversed. The Canadian labor movement is today considered the more powerful and vig-orous of the two. It is now common for U.S. unionists to look north of the border for inspiration and guidance. In international perspective, however, from a labor point of view, Canadian industrial relations leave a lot to be desired. Although a larger percentage of Canadian workers have a means to effect the conditions under which they work, they still make up only a minority of the labor force and, although the slope has been less steep, union density and bar-gaining coverage in the private sector has been declining just as in the United States.

CONCLUSIONS—NORTH AMERICAN INDUSTRIAL RELATIONS IN COMPARATIVE PERSPECTIVE

One of the most widely noted and analyzed aspects of North American industrial relations was the apparent choice of the business union strategy by the mainstream of the labor movement. While the available theories provide us with considerable insight into the factors giving rise to labor's choice, none of them is altogether satisfactory. A thoroughly convincing theory of the labor movement remains to be formulated.

Whatever the explanation for the choice, it is clear that many of the characteristics of present-day industrial relations in Canada and the United States may be traced back to the dominance of the pure and simple union philosophy. In contrast to the European norm, in neither country did the labor movement pose a serious threat to the continued viability of liberal capitalism. Because labor was not a threat to employers as a class, for the most part they reverted to fundamental individualistic tendencies, common to employers everywhere, in dealing with the labor relations.[10] Instead of forming a national organization and attempting to reach a formal national accord as occurred in several European nations, employers decided to deal with trade unions on a case-by-case basis. There is, consequently, no national employer's confederation in either Canada or the United States, union-management negotiations are very decentralized, and a large percent of the labor force in both countries is without representation in employment decision making.

The decentralized character of the system was fortified by the passage of the National Labor Relations Act in the United States. By certifying unions on a plant-by-plant basis, it made any evolution towards multi-employer bargaining very difficult. Unionized and nonunionized employers had no common employment relations interest. Since they had good prospects of remaining free of union imposed constraints, there was no reason for nonunionized employers to associate with their unionized compatriots in order to reach a compromise with the unions. Indeed by compelling unorganized employees to take the initiative to establish a collective bargaining relationship, the Wagner Act could be interpreted as implying that individualist employment relations were the norm. Contrary to the European proposition that all employees have a right and should have the means to participate in the making of relevant collective decisions, an American theory developed which held that if workers were satisfied with conditions formulated unilaterally by their employers, they had no cause to unionize. Although the initial intent of the labor policy adopted during the New Deal era was to encourage universal collective bargaining, that intent quickly became reinterpreted to imply that workers should have a choice between individual and collective bargaining. Within the framework of this choice theory, employers and unions competed for the allegiance of the unorganized worker. Industrial autocracy, which was under severe attack during the first three decades of the twentieth century, was relegitimized.

In Canada, policymakers and administrators took more seriously the idea that employees should be able to establish a collective relationship free from coercion and, as such, continually reformed the law in order to ensure that end. They did so because of the pressure exerted by a labor movement that had become more of a political factor as a result of its developing an alliance with a social democratic party. The result was a collective bargaining coverage rate about twice that of the United States, but still one much lower than prevalent rates in Europe. As in the United States, the practice of industrial autocracy became fully legitimate once again.

Chapter 4

CONTEMPORARY COLLECTIVE BARGAINING

THE MODERN EMPLOYMENT RELATIONSHIP

The modern employment relationship is regulated by a complex web of rule. There are rules specifying the amount and nature of remuneration: wages, benefits, pensions, profit sharing, and so on. There are rules that define the nature of the job and the method whereby performance in carrying out job tasks will be evaluated. There are rules denoting appropriate and inappropriate behavior and rules regulating the discipline that may be imposed on those who engage in improper conduct. Within modern employment relations, employers and employees have rights and duties, and there are rules specifying what might be done if rights are not respected and sanctions that may be invoked if duty is not done (see Wheeler and Rojot 1992).

There are many methods for creating this web of rule. The government may establish the rules through the passage of laws and regulations. Under communism, this is the overwhelmingly dominant means for establishing conditions of employment. The rules may be established unilaterally by the employer. In the early nineteenth century, this was the dominant method in all of the countries that are now classified as liberal democracies. The rules may also be unilaterally established by labor organizations. Where they were strong, the early unions developed their own internal rules for minimum wage rates for the trade, for workload levels, and for apprenticeship training. Additionally, they demanded that employers abide by these rules if they wanted to employ any member of the union. More commonly today rules are established through bilateral (union-management negotiations) or multilateral (labor-management-government) processes.[1]

Throughout the contemporary industrialized world, the principle is accepted that employees should be able to influence the conditions under which they work. The dominant institution for putting that principle into action is the bilateral, union-management process of collective bargaining (Windmuller 1987b). In many countries, union-management bargaining is supplemented by the use of mechanisms such as workers participation on corporate boards of directors, by the establishment of statutory works councils, by the appointment of labor and business representatives to quasi governmental agencies, and by formal or informal tripartite consideration of socioeconomic policy. It is also supplemented to a degree by individual bargaining. However, most rules in the employment setting apply to everyone in a class (e.g., all production workers, all secretaries, all accountants) and cannot be individually varied. The wage system, pensions, operating hours, and health and safety policy are all critical to individual employees, but cannot be individually negotiated. They may be either imposed unilaterally or negotiated collectively.

North America, and the United States more particularly, is exceptional in its almost exclusive reliance on collective bargaining as the means to make the principle of participation operative. Also exceptional is the requirement that unions must be certified as bargaining agents in discreet bargaining units in order for employers to be expected to recognize and negotiate with them.[2] What we in North America refer to simply as collective bargaining is a very specific variant of bargaining with positive and negative aspects that are not necessarily generalizable. In this chapter, my goal is to place our practice in comparative perspective so that a judgement may be made of its relative merits and problems.

THEORETICAL JUSTIFICATION OF COLLECTIVE BARGAINING

In a democratic nation, the only legitimate justification for any institution is that it is beneficial (or at least not harmful) to the nation as a whole. There is also a widespread consensus that a defining attribute of democracy is that all citizens have a right to participate in the making of decisions that affect their essential interests (Commission of the European Communities 1975). To be legitimate, collective bargaining must stand up to these tests. Both in North America and elsewhere, one may find rationales that render collective bargaining consistent with these standards. The theory underpinning public support for collective bargaining in North America, however, is quite different from the one that is embraced in many of the other advanced liberal democratic countries.

Throughout the nineteenth and into the twentieth century, the labor movement and other forces for democracy marched side by side. In European countries, one of the key initial demands of the expanding labor organizations was for the universal adult franchise and for equal rights for all citizens (Kendall 1975; Hepple 1986b). The demand was for not only political democracy, but also industrial democracy (Malles 1973). Theorists argued that adults do not check their citizenship at the door of the factory or office.[3] They do not become subjects or wage slaves. Since the employment web of rule has such an enormous impact on their well being, they have a fundamental right to participate in the making of the rules under which they work. It is recognized that managers in modern corporations and bureaucracies also have responsibilities to share-holders, to the public, and to the local community as well as to the employees. Collective bargaining from this perspective is considered to be one means towards the achievement of industrial democracy.

Many of those in North America who are involved in industrial relations entirely accept this rationale (Derber 1970; Klare 1978). But there is another more prevalent theory that is accepted by most employers, government officials, and most likely trade union leaders as well. It is particularly prevalent in economic analysis. The theory holds that employees should have a right to bargain collectively if they choose to do so. They should have the right because individual employees have little bargaining power compared to the forces of the huge modern organization. Through unions and collective bargaining, this power may be offset. Implicitly, the employment relationship is regarded as an economic, market transaction rather than a social/political relationship. Even though the American Clayton Act of 1914 specifically declared that "the labor of a human being is not a commodity or an article of commerce," (Taft 1964, 243) in fact the bargaining power equalization theory, which is commonly cited as the justification for collective bargaining in the United States, seems to affirm the contrary. A corollary of this economic theory of employment relations is that if employees do not want to engage in collective bargaining they should not be compelled to do so. If they are satisfied with their wages, they should have no further interest in the myriad web of rule regulating the employment relationship. If there is no demand for union services then, like purveyors of an outmoded product, unions should wrap up their business and fade into history.[4] Whereas the political theory dictates a universal solution in which everyone is afforded a means to influence the rules under which they work, the economic theory suggests that it is reasonable for those who are receiving a satisfactory price for their labor to forego collective bargaining.[5]

The law regulating the establishment of collective bargaining in North America is based on this proposition of choice, and it has had profound effects on the culture of labor-management relations. No European country bases its regulations on this theory. Instead, most commonly, collective bargaining is accepted as the appropriate means for deciding wages, hours, and other basic conditions of employment. It is expected that all employers will agree voluntarily to enter into negotiations with freely chosen representatives of employees. Recognition, which is a key issue in North America, is of much less import elsewhere. There are indeed some employers who fight to remain beyond collective bargaining, but they are usually small and on the fringes of the system. In most other economically advanced liberal democracies, the large majority of employees have at least some of their conditions of employment established by collective bargaining. Recognition was settled early in the century as a result of the implicit or explicit basic agreements between trade union organizations and employer associations—often with the state as a third party. An implicit understanding supporting these agreements was that collective bargaining (as a form of industrial democracy) should be universally available just as the institutions of political democracy (e.g., the vote and political representation) were universally available. In short, not only did employee-citizens have a right to participate in decisions critical to their welfare, but also employers had a corresponding duty to recognize and negotiate with employee representatives.

No such accord could be reached in North America in the early years of the twentieth century. However, in the 1930s there was a great expansion of the labor movement in both Canada and the United States, and in both countries legislation was introduced to encourage the practice and procedure of collective bargaining. The implicit tripartite understanding that was reached appeared superficially to be similar to those previously achieved in Europe. Employees who wanted to engage in collective bargaining would have the free and unfettered choice to do so. Most industrial relations experts were fully confident that this stipulation would result in universal collective bargaining. After all, if offered the cost-free and unconstrained opportunity of being able to influence conditions of employment critical to their welfare, who would say no? In fact, the legal procedures that were instituted did not provide the clear choice that they were supposed to provide and, as a result, they did not have the affect they were initially intended to have.

After the cooperative milieu engendered by the war effort subsided, unorganized employers made it known that they had no intention of magnanimously accepting collective bargaining. Instead, they made it clear that they preferred the status quo and that they regarded collective bargaining as unnecessary except as a check on harsh and irresponsible companies. This attitude put employees in a position whereby to choose bargaining was to provoke the wrath of those who had the power to hire and fire. Under such conditions, the choice clearly was not a free one, but was instead constrained by fear of negative consequences. Despite the fettered nature of the process of unionization, many labor experts ingenuously portray the situation as one in which large numbers of North American employees have freely chosen not to become union members.

A favorite explanation for the implicit choice is the purported value of individualism. Thus, according to Bruce Kaufman, "American culture has a strong credo of individualism and a corresponding lack of class identity or consciousness." As a result, he proposes that "before the average American worker will seriously consider joining a union . . . he or she must feel unable to improve the situation at work through individual action" (1991, 471). In short, unionization is a reluctant step taken only as a last resort.

It is difficult to test the validity of such statements, but one way of doing so is to look at situations where employees actually have had a cost-free and unfettered choice. Two naturally occurring experiments of that type have happened in Canada. Prior to the 1960s, collective bargaining was not permitted for Canadian federal government employees. However, during that decade the federal government passed a law permitting employees to certify a union as their bargaining agent if they preferred to do so. It was made clear that the employer (the federal government) was entirely neutral with respect to the choice. It would be pleased to bargain with a union if the employees decided that they wanted to negotiate their conditions of work. No stigma of disloyalty would attach to any employees who took that step. On the other hand, if employees were satisfied with the status quo, the government would be pleased to continue unilaterally to establish terms and conditions of employment. Within a few years, essentially all federal government employees, white-collar and blue-collar, technical and administrative, both men and women, had opted for collective bargaining (Finkelman and Goldenberg 1983; Ponak and Thompson 1989). In the 1970s, essentially the same scenario was repeated for teachers in the province of Ontario. Indeed, I know of no case where employees have refused a bona fide employer offer to negotiate over the full range of conditions of employment without prejudice. If the Wagner Act's promise was kept, every employer would accept the duty to adopt such a policy. However, the reality is that such offers are practically never made.

CERTIFICATION

The framers of the U.S. National Labor Relations Act, which had as its fundamental purpose the encouragement of collective bargaining, had the following scenario in mind as the way that a bargaining relationship would come into existence. Employees in a factory or office would decide that they would like to discuss their conditions of employment with their employer. They would form or join a union and ask the union to open discussions with the employer. The result would be a mutually acceptable collective agreement. The framers of the act realized that this process might get more complicated. What if some employees wanted one union to represent them and others wanted a different one? What if some employees wanted union A but others were opposed to representation by that organization because of its policies and behavior but preferred union B? If the employer was not convinced that the first union was the choice of the employees, generally he/she could go to the Labor Board and ask it to conduct an investigation. If the board found that the majority of relevant employees wanted union A, then it would issue a certificate to that effect. Once the employer was presented with such a certificate, he/she would be legally required to enter into negotiations with the union with a view towards arriving at a collective agreement.

Voluntary recognition was initially the preferred means of establishing a collective bargaining relationship, but it occurred only infrequently. Employers quickly learned that it was a good idea always to refuse voluntarily to recognize a union no matter how certain they were that it was the choice of the employees. Consequently, the Labor Board had to get involved in nearly every case of recognition and issue orders insisting that a reluctant employer enter into negotiations.

In the early years of its operation, the Labor Board often issued a certificate when the union was able to present evidence that a majority of the relevant employees had become members or had signed cards authorizing the union to negotiate on their behalf (Gross 1981). Employer's argued that this method was prone to abuse. For example, some employees might be pressured to join a specific union against their wishes. A better method to determine employees' wishes was to hold a vote, even if the great majority of the employees had signed authorization cards.

This proposal seemed to be reasonable. What could be fairer than a vote? In practice, though, it provided employers with time to formulate a campaign designed to dissuade employees from authorizing a union to bargain on their behalf. Claims were made that certain unions were corrupt or undemocratic or prone to strike. These arguments often had a significant effect on employees. In the midst of representation election campaigns, employee support for the union almost always deteriorated once the employer began his/her campaign.[6]

In the early years of the NLRB, this type of campaign was forbidden. It reasoned that the choice of bargaining representative should be between the employee and the union. On that reasoning, employers were ordered to remain silent during organizing campaigns. But employers did not accept that dictum. They challenged it in the courts saying that it was an infringement of their right to free speech. When the Wagner Act was revised in 1947, the employer right to free speech was clearly recognized (Tomlins 1985). From then on the process of establishing collective bargaining was not a matter of free and unfettered employees accepting the opportunity to appoint an agent to represent their interests in the making of the rules of work; instead it became a contest between employers and unions for the hearts and minds of the workers involved, a contest in which employers had a significant advantage because of the authority which they exerted over the employees. An employee who went against the expressed wishes of the employer might very well find his/her prospects for advancement, if not continued employment, jeopardized even though this was supposed to be illegal. Indeed, by the 1960s and 1970s, the practice of illegal victimization of employees for becoming involved in union organizing campaigns had become commonplace (Weiler 1990). Not only might individual employees be victimized for making use of their right of association, but also the manager against whom an organizing campaign was initiated could have his/her career negatively affected as a result. American companies made union-free status a priority goal and managers who failed to maintain that status would suffer the consequences (Freeman and Kleiner 1990).

As a result of these developments, the process initially envisioned by the framers of the Wagner Act practically never happens today. The contemporary logic underlying the process of establishing a collective bargaining relationship is entirely different from what it was initially. First of all, nonunion employers almost always let their employees know that (contrary to the spirit of universal democratic participation and against the explicit intent of the law to encourage the practice of collective bargaining) they strongly prefer the status quo. As a result, employees who take the initiative to establish collective bargaining are almost certain to arouse the ire of their employer. They are likely to be identified as disloyal. In many cases, despite the injunction against threats and intimidation, they are likely to be dismissed for their involvement in the union (Weiler 1990). In consequence, the potential costs to any employee of becoming certified are great, and few take the initiative unless the conditions under which they are working are intolerable. Since only dissatisfied workers take the initiative to certify a union as their bargaining agent, the proposition has become established that employers get the union that they deserve. This phrase implies that if any given employer deals fairly with his/her workforce, the employees should have no reason to form or join a union. Instead of a universally desirable means of involving employees in the making of decisions which impact their interests at work, collective bargaining has come to be regarded as an antidote for incompetent or harsh management.

Since no manager wants to be considered incompetent, staying nonunion is a high priority personal goal. Moreover, since collective bargaining has, in popular thought, become transmuted from a universally desirable technique to allow employees to participate in employment decisions to a corrective antidote for bad management or a subsidy to a disadvantaged market haggler—morally there is no wrong seen in corporations actively pursuing a policy of remaining nonunion. Since corporate managers everywhere cherish control (rather than having to negotiate decisions with any other party), it has become the policy of most to avoid collective bargaining wherever possible. In short, a train of reasoning has been set in place that legitimizes the continuing existence of labor's exclusion from employment decision making and the active defense by employers of their right unilaterally to establish terms and conditions of employment.[7] In this rhetorical context, the establishment of a bargaining relationship is a very adversarial process.

Because employers actively oppose unionization, it is very difficult for collective bargaining to become established. Indeed, in recent years as unionized factories have restructured and downsized, and new service industries have appeared, collective bargaining has shrunk significantly. In the United States today, less than 15 percent of workers in the private sector have their employment interests represented through collective bargaining (Hirsh and Macpherson 1993). Ironically, the legal framework under which this situation has come about is the result of pressure exerted by the labor movement. Employers, by reinterpreting the theory underlying the legislation and by winning court and Labor Board judgements in their favor, have turned the law to their advantage.

From the industrial democracy perspective, the situation in the United States is indeed diabolical. A law intended to encourage collective bargaining is now being used to strangle it. The unions are, for the most part, acquiescing in their own asphyxiation. Many union activists agree with the phrase "the company gets the union it deserves" which suggests that if employees are satisfied with their conditions of work, they have no cause to institute collective bargaining. In addition, few unionists want to see a fundamental change in the law because within the shrinking perimeter where collective bargaining is still practiced, the law continues to be to their advantage. It requires that employers bargain in good faith. The law has permitted the establishment of practices under which the unions have considerable influence on terms and conditions of employment.

THE CANADIAN VARIANT

Although most American unionists do not support the abolition of the Wagner Act and its replacement by an entirely new approach, many would like to see it reformed. Canada provides the model they would like to see emulated. In the United States, employers as a matter of course contest certification elections and research shows that in the typical campaign, employers are quite successful in weakening support for the union. The Canadian version of the Wagner-Act model which, as in the United States, was first put in place as a result of strong agitation by the labor movement, does not (in most jurisdictions) require a vote. Instead, the union may be certified on the basis of cards—that is evidence that a majority of the relevant people have become union members or expressed their desire to have the union represent them in collective bargaining (see, e.g., Craig and Solomon 1993). Card signing campaigns are typically carried out in secret and majority support is achieved without the employer finding out that a campaign was underway.[8] In order to prevent the materialization of the fears voiced by American employers, commonly if there is any hint that the union has coerced any signature, the entire application is thrown out (Weiler 1980).

Canadian law is, from a labor perspective, preferable in other ways too. Procedures before the labor boards are more expedited (Bruce 1989). In the United States, lawyers are often able to delay proceedings while employers take action to make sure that they will win any election. Infringement of the law such as firing people for being involved in a unionization drive is dealt with more severely. Using their make whole authority, Canadian boards have imposed large financial penalties against employers who have engaged in such activities. Contrary to U.S. practice, Canadian boards will also certify unions even in the absence of a majority (see, e.g., Arthurs et al. 1988). A common tactic in the United States, even after certification, is for employers to engage in surface bargaining—going through the motions, but making no real attempt to achieve agreement. In several Canadian jurisdictions, this problem has been overcome by first contract arbitration. Labor boards have been given the power to have the first contract settled by an arbitrator in those situations where employers do not fulfill their responsibility to bargain in good faith (Sexton 1987).

These are only some of the ways in which Canadian legislation is more favorable to labor than U.S. law. The major reason for the difference is almost certainly the presence of a viable social democratic political party (Bruce 1989; Meltz 1989). In many instances, laws have been changed in labor's favor during periods when the NDP was insurgent (Bruce 1989; Meltz 1985). Even where it had little probability of achieving power, it still had an effect by dramatically publicizing and politicizing illicit employer behavior and thereby compelling more conservative governments to take action. In Ontario, for example, a Conservative Party government that was in power for over thirty years passed several apparently pro-labor bills despite a relatively low standing in the polls of the NDP. It was induced to take action because of the ability of the opposition to make political issues of the events giving rise to the change in law.[9]

The problem with the strategy of the U.S. labor movement on this issue is that, despite a much more favorable climate, the extent of bargaining in the Canadian private sector is still much lower than it is in the typical European country. Perhaps 25–30 percent of employees in the private sector are covered by collective agreements compared with a typical European situation of 70–80 percent coverage.[10] In short, adoption of the Canadian model in the United States is not likely to bring about universal participation consistent with the logic of democratic society.

Although there is no comparable system of union recognition in Europe, in France and Belgium there is a considerably different system. In order for unions to sign legally binding collective agreements, and to qualify for participation on various governmental and quasi governmental bodies, they must be certified (see, e.g., Windmuller 1987b). Certification is granted only to most representative unions. To be designated as most representative, a union or more often a federation of unions must have strength nationally or in a specific sector. But it need not have a majority. There are several union federations operating in France and most of them have most representative status (Goetschy and Jobert 1993). This system makes it difficult for newly formed unions to get established. Although there is no reason why a new union cannot negotiate on its members behalf, any agreements that it is able to secure are not legally binding. In Britain, it should be noted, no collective agreements are legally enforceable, but that has not stopped British unions and employers from establishing an extensive system of collective contracts that are usually honored.[11]

Some countries have a system in place which says that employers must negotiate with any union designated by two or more of its employees. Sweden adopted this approach in the 1930s specifically to encourage the recognition of white-collar worker unions (Adams 1975a). Although employers had extended general recognition to unions representing blue-collar workers in the December Compromise of 1906, they refused to recognize and bargain with their clerical and administrative workers. After the passage of the 1930 act, however, bargaining for white-collar workers was quickly established with the result that today more than 70 percent of those in the private sector are covered by collective agreements.

BARGAINING STRUCTURE

The employees to whom any collective agreement applies may be referred to as the bargaining unit. Such units are the basic elements of bargaining structure. A bargaining unit may be composed of a group of employees (e.g., production workers) working in a single plant. This is the most typical bargaining unit in North America. A bargaining unit may also be composed of a class of employees working in all the plants of a single employer. This type of unit is also common in North America. A third type of unit is one in which the collective agreement applies to all of the employees of a certain class who work for any employer who is a member of an employer's association. This is the most common European unit. Such agreements are typically negotiated between one or more unions and the employer's association. Sometimes such agreements are applicable across the whole country (commonly the case in smaller European countries) or only to a region of the country (a common pattern in Germany). In North America, such agreements are the exception, but they are found in industries such as construction, hospitals, shipping, and the railways.

A still different type of unit is one in which the collective agreement applies to all of the employees who are employed by all of the employers who belong to an association which is affiliated to an employer's federation. Such agreements are typically negotiated between national federations of employers and unions. This was the pattern in Sweden from the 1950s until the 1980s and in the other Scandinavian countries. Agreements of this sort on at least some issues have also been negotiated in, for example, Austria, Ireland, France, Belgium, the Netherlands, and Italy. In short, outside of North America these agreements are quite common.

Bargaining units are not mutually exclusive. They may, and commonly do, overlap. In Sweden, for example, for most of the period since World War II negotiations were first held between the national federation of blue-collar workers—LO—and the national confederation of employer associations—SAF. The result would be a frame agreement specifying the general level of wage movement for the next period (commonly a year but sometimes for longer), and some other very general conditions of employment. Additional negotiations would be carried out at industry level to flesh out the national agreement and still additional bargaining would go on at the company level in order to establish local conditions. The system was often referred to as centralized, but a much better term for it would be articulated.[12] Bargaining took place at all levels throughout the system (Forsebäck 1980; Kjellerg 1992).

In Europe, the center of gravity of bargaining since early in the century has been the industry level, whereas in Canada and the United States the dominant focus is the plant or enterprise. Why is North America different in this regard? It is because of the historical events discussed above. European employers granted recognition at the industry level and expressed a willingness to negotiate at that level in hopes of defending their control of employment and production decisions at the level of the enterprise. Unions agreed to this proposal (and were themselves sometimes the first party to put it forward) because of their object of establishing common rules for workers. Until after World War II, employer strategy was largely successful in minimizing labor influence on the day-to-day affairs of the enterprise. The works councils that had been established in Germany and Austria were largely advisory and had little impact on crucial managerial decisions inside the firm (Gulick 1948; Taft 1952). In other countries, union networks on the shop floor were generally opposed, and for the most part they were not well established (Crouch 1993). A major exception is Britain where shop steward movements during both world wars created a strong union shop floor presence. Until the last few decades, however, the shop stewards in Britain often operated independently of the national unions (see, e.g., Jackson 1991).

After World War II, works councils were reestablished in Germany and Austria and were adopted in several other countries. Over the past four decades, both the councils and union networks on the shop floor have been strengthened. In the 1970s, especially, changes in the law in several countries (Germany, Sweden, and the Netherlands) increased the power and authority of shop-floor labor representatives.

The North American employer strategy of contesting union representation on a plant-by-plant basis had an entirely different result. Where unions were strong enough to compel recognition, they were often also able to establish vigorous shop-floor networks. Initially simple, collective agreements over time became increasingly elaborate and placed a burgeoning network of constraints on managerial discretion at the shop floor. As this occurred, the determination of nonunion employers to avoid collective bargaining increased. As a result, American employers are often considered to be much more anti-union than European employers. Very likely, their behavior is more a function of the specific characteristics of the system in which they operate, rather than because of their "Americanness." Foreign companies operating in the American environment do not behave notably different from the American-owned companies. Indeed, many large Japanese corporations, which almost without exception recognize and bargain with a union in Japan, follow a policy of union avoidance in the United States. So, too, do German companies.

Decentralized bargaining has some real advantages for the workers involved. Because they are close to the bargaining process, they are more able than workers under broader-based bargaining to see the personal relevance of negotiations. They are able to have more control over it. This process also has advantages for employers. Agreements may be tailor-made to the needs of the particular company or plant whereas under broader-based bargaining, particular companies may be compelled to adhere to standards which they feel are inappropriate to their situation.

On the other hand, decentralized bargaining has some very problematic aspects. Under broadbased bargaining, the negotiators are more in the public spotlight and thus must consider the consequences of their actions on the public and the economy as a whole. In decentralized bargaining, however, the parties are interested only in their own circumstances. Although the cumulative effect of bargaining has significant consequences for the public welfare, no one takes responsibility for that effect. In inflationary times, decentralized bargaining tends to exacerbate wage-price spirals (Soskice 1990). The most preferable situation is probably one where general issues (such as general wage increases, pensions, and vacation plans) are negotiated at higher levels and specific issues (such as work scheduling, piece rates, and job structure) are negotiated at lower levels.

THE TREND TOWARDS DECENTRALIZED BARGAINING IN EUROPE

In recent years, the decentralization of bargaining in Europe has been a subject of increasing debate and discussion. This trend was first noticed in the 1970s and became more apparent during the 1980s (Windmuller 1987b; Ferner and Hyman 1992b). During the 1970s, an important precipitating factor seemed to be the increasing interest in the quality of worklife and the perceived need to involve workers in decision making at the point of production (Gaudier 1988). The primary objective of these initiatives was to make work more meaningful and satisfying and thereby to make it more attractive so that good workers could be recruited and retained. During that period, labor shortages and absenteeism were key problems. These initiatives required the involvement of unions and works councils, and thus labor-management interaction within the firm increased. The shortage of labor also increased the bargaining power of plant-level labor representatives. Wage bargaining at that level also increased.

In the 1980s, the socioeconomic milieu changed dramatically. As a consequence of the Great Recession of the early 1980s, unemployment increased to levels not seen since the 1930s and continued at high levels throughout the 1980s. At the same time, increased worldwide competition (Japan and the other newly industrializing economies had become serious global competitors) increased and required significant restructuring. Flexibility became a key organization goal. Employee representatives insisted on being involved in such restructuring efforts, and since such decisions were necessarily made by particular companies rather than by employer organizations, negotiations between worker representatives and particular companies expanded.

A good example of this is Germany. In the context of industry-wide bargaining, German unions in the early to mid-1980s began to make reduced hours a goal with the object of saving jobs (Turner 1991). In a dramatic breakthrough, the Metalworkers Union was able to win an agreement which committed employers to reducing scheduled weekly hours to 38.5 from 40. Employers, however, insisted that they must have some leeway in how to implement the reduction. In some cases, it might be best to reduce the workweek to 38.5 hours across the board. But in others, it might be better to have a more flexible system in which scheduled hours would stay at 40 hours a week, but average hours worked would be reduced to 38.5 hours via additional holidays, vacations, or some other configuration of time. The union felt compelled to agree with management's flexibilization proposal with one result being that bargaining over hours between the works councils and individual employers has expanded significantly (Jacobi, Keller, and Müller-Jentsch 1992).

New schemes of work organization have also been introduced widely throughout Europe and these initiatives have usually required some firm-level bargaining (Gaudier 1988). In France, the government in the early 1980s, observing that many workers were not covered by collective agreements (contrary to the accepted principle that all workers should be represented in the establishment of key conditions of employment) set out to alter that situation. It required that all employers had to enter into negotiations with representatives of their employees on a yearly basis in order to reach agreement over wages and hours.

Unlike North America, where the onus is entirely upon employees to take the initiative to negotiate, the French legislation placed that responsibility on the employers. This requirement greatly expanded the practice of local bargaining (Bridgford 1990).

Although these developments are often referred to as a growth in decentralized bargaining, they are more accurately described as the development of more articulated bargaining systems because bargaining at the employer association-union level and at the union federation-employer confederation level has not generally abated (Córdova 1990). In most countries, unions and employer organizations continue to negotiate at industry and national levels while expanding interaction at the company level. Two exceptions are Sweden and Britain.

In Sweden, national negotiations became increasingly difficult during the 1980s (Ahlén 1989). Employer representatives argued that the unions were insisting on agreements too detailed at the national level which produced too much uniform rigidity at a time when more flexibility was required. Consequently, the Employers Federation (SAF) became increasingly unwilling to negotiate at the top level. For a few years during the 1980s, it was cajoled by the unions and the government to enter into national agreements, but by the 1990s the system of national bargaining appeared to be at an end (Myrdal 1991).

In Britain, from World War I until the 1970s, the characteristic type of wage and hour bargaining was that between an employer organization and one or more unions at the national or regional level (Jackson 1991). During that period, there was, however, a good deal of variation and many single employer bargaining arrangements were in place. Moreover, in the 1960s, there was an expansion of bargaining at the local level which supplemented multi-employer bargaining. In the 1980s, industry-wide bargaining, however, began to break up (Brown 1993). It did so because, with the hostile government of Margaret Thatcher in power, the unions did not have enough power to compel the continuation of industry-wide bargaining. Employers in that decade increasingly came to prefer decentralized bargaining.

As noted above, industry-wide bargaining in Europe came about in large part because employers favored it. Unions also endorsed it because it allowed them to establish common rules for large groups of employees. It allowed them to take wages out of competition, an object which many employers also preferred. These preferences were clearly in place during World War I when industry bargaining was established in Britain. Why, by the 1980s, had they changed? There seems to be several reasons. First the industry agreements in Britain, like the national agreements in Sweden, were becoming too detailed and thus too rigid. Particular companies were being required to put practices in place which they considered to be inappropriate for their specific situation. Second, one reason why employers in Britain and elsewhere preferred industry agreements was to offset union influence at the company and plant level. By the 1970s, however, some British unions were, in a sense, having their cake and eating it too. It had become common practice for the unions to negotiate a multi-employer wage increase with an association and then to go to particular employers and make further demands. In short, many employers found themselves bargaining over the same issues at two levels. The third reason had to do with the changed milieu. Because the 1980s was a period of high unemployment, bargaining power was on the side of the employers—they could get pretty much what they wanted through domestic bargaining. The unions were generally so weak, it was not necessary to keep them at arms length. They simply did not have the power to impose local rigidities.

COLLECTIVE BARGAINING COVERAGE

Table 4.1 provides estimates of union density and bargaining coverage in Canada, the United States, and several European countries.[13]

It indicates, as mentioned several times above, that the percent of the labor force covered by collective agreements in Europe is much larger than it is in North America. This is due once again to the general agreements that were reached early in the twentieth century. It is also due in part to the existence of a legal instrument called extension of agreements. In countries with these stipulations, the government (usually at the joint request of the union or unions and the relevant employer organization) may extend the agreement to employers outside of the federation (Windmuller 1987b; Córdova 1990). The purpose of extension is to ensure that all relevant employees enjoy conditions of work generally in place in the industry involved and, very importantly, to protect employers in the association from low-wage competition by unassociated employers.

The existence of these requirements is one reason why European employers are very highly associated. In the typical country, a greater percentage of employers belong to their relevant association than do employees to their union. Only by joining are employers able to affect negotiations. Moreover, the unassociated employer is likely to be at a large disadvantage in negotiating with the union. Once the union has an agreement with the association, it can put all of its resources to work in negotiating with the independent employer. It might use the independent as a tool to win concessions that it was unable to win from the association. Faced with such a prospect, many employers have joined the association in order to get the advantage of the standard contract. Several American employers who set up in Europe after World War II went through precisely these steps.[14]

Table 4.1

Union Density and Bargaining Coverage Estimates, Early 1990s

	Density (percent)	Coverage (percent)
Austria	44-50	90+
Sweden	80-95	90+
Germany	39-45	90
Netherlands	24-30	75-80
United Kingdom	35-40	55[1]
Switzerland	28-35	65
France	8-12	70-80[2]
Canada	30-40	40-45
United States	15-17	18-22

Sources: Cordóva 1990; ILO 1985; Curme et al. 1990; Jackson 1991; Millward et al. 1992; Visser 1992; Brown 1993; Hirsch and Macpherson 1993.

Notes:
1. In the early 1980s, the British coverage rate was over 70 percent. It has fallen as a result of demographic changes and the policies of the Thatcher government.

2. The French rate was much lower in the 1970s. It has risen dramatically as a result of government legislation requiring employers to initiate wage bargaining on an annual basis.

Table 4.1 also indicates that in the typical country, union density is much lower than bargaining coverage. Many people who are covered by collective agreements are not union members. I will take up this subject in greater depth later on. For now, suffice it to say that the lower density rates are the result of what in North America would be referred to as a free-rider problem. In most European countries, the principle of freedom of association has been interpreted to mean that individuals have the right to join a union free from coercion, threat, or promise of benefit and that right has, unlike the North American situation, been made quite effective (von Prondzynski 1987). Dismissal of employees for membership or involvement in a union is not a significant problem on continental Europe. On the other hand, freedom of association has also been interpreted in Europe to mean that individuals must have the right not to belong if they so choose. The right of association is like freedom of religion; the right to join is meaningless without the right not to join. As a result, union membership as a condition of employment is illegal in most European countries.

In North America, an entirely different logic is in place. Since North American bargaining agents must fairly represent all of those in a bargaining unit, whether they are union members or not, it is considered reasonable that the union insist that, once the majority has opted for unionization, all of those in the unit should be required to contribute to the resource base which allows the union effectively to represent their interests. In some Canadian provinces, the clash of the two logics has given rise to a middle-of-the-road arrangement. In Ontario, for example, employers may refuse to compel all employees to become union members, but all of those covered by a collective agreement must, at the union's request, pay dues whether they are a union member or not. Although these agency shop agreements (known in Canada as the Rand formula) are sometimes negotiated in the United States, in six Canadian jurisdictions they have been put in place by law (Craig and Solomon 1993, 164–65). In those cases, the employer may not refuse the request of the union to have such a clause placed in the collective agreement. Canadian unions generally may, in addition, negotiate stronger clauses requiring that all covered employees be union members.

It seems clear that the European situation is much closer to the true meaning of freedom of association than is the North American approach (Beatty 1987). In North America, some workers are compelled to be union members against their wishes. They have no real freedom of association. This is one additional unfortunate aspect of the North America approach to labor policy. Mandatory membership (or at least dues payment) is a natural concomitant of unit certification. Without the latter, the need for the former would not be so pressing. In short, the Wagner-Act policy framework elicits behavior that is contrary to universally accepted labor standards.

SCOPE OF THE ISSUES

In most countries there is no legal restriction on the issues that may be the subject of collective bargaining. A union may initiate negotiations about everything from wages and hours to the nature of the product to be produced and the organization of the production process. In practice, though, collective bargaining in most countries is essentially concerned with wages, hours, benefits, employment security, and other conditions of work which directly effect employees (such as health and safety). Under industry-wide bargaining, the scope of the issues to be negotiated is typically narrower than under firm-level and plant-level bargaining because any agreement must be applicable to many different situations. Consequently, North American plant-level collective agreements are much longer and contain much more detail than do typical European agreements. Issues such as opening and closing times, lunch breaks, training, piece rates and other incentive pay schemes, vacation schedules, job transfer policies, plant shutdown, or reorganization decisions cannot easily be dealt with in multi-employer bargaining. In Germany and Austria, the works council is provided with a legal mandate to deal with such issues.

Even though European industry-wide bargaining deals with a narrower range of subjects than does decentralized bargaining in North America, it is incorrect to assert, as is sometimes done by North American writers, that European bargaining is over minimums. Annual wage bargaining, for example, typically determines not the minimum wage to be paid, but rather the general rate at which all wages and salaries of the relevant employees will increase.

Ironically, even though decentralized collective bargaining deals with a broader scope of issues than does broader-based bargaining in Europe, the scope of bargaining is more highly regulated in the United States than it is in any other countries. As the result of the Borg-Warner case in 1958, the U.S. Supreme Court divided issues into mandatory and permissible categories.[15] Mandatory issues must be negotiated at the request of one party; permissible issues need not be negotiated unless both parties agree to discuss them. In the specifics of the Borg-Warner case, the employer demanded that the union negotiate over certain issues that were considered by the union to be its internal affair. For example, the employer insisted that the union submit its last offer to the membership before calling a strike. The court agreed with the union that it should not have to negotiate over such issues. In subsequent cases, employers argued that by the same logic they should not have to negotiate over items that they considered to be internal management issues such as plant shutdowns and relocations, subcontracting, and work reorganization, and the courts agreed with them (Knight and Sockell 1988, 282). The mandatory versus permissive distinction has not been imported into Canada, however, and almost any issue that either party cares to put on the bargaining table is negotiable to impasse.

The limitation of the issues that may be negotiated is a stimulant to labor management conflict. It encourages management to exclude the union from discussions about issues critical to employee welfare and thus it exacerbates distrust and animosity. The European experience (and the Canadian experience as well) suggests that there is little to be gained by the exclusion of issues from the bargaining process.

BARGAINING PROCESS

In North America, the collective agreement is typically written, covers all negotiated issues, and lasts for a specific period of time. In Ontario, for example, by law there may be only one collective agreement, it must be written, and it must last for at least one year.

Towards the end of the contract period, the union (and increasingly during the 1980s, the company also) develops a long list of demands. Typically, the list contains many items that it does not legitimately expect to be included in the agreement. Some of these are new issues, and placing them on the agenda is an indication that the party is interested in the issue and that it may be pushed more vigorously in succeeding bargaining rounds. Some issues are on the agenda because some individual or subgroup in the bargaining unit asked that they be included. These issues commonly "fall off the table" in the course of bargaining.

The parties exchange their list of items, a common agenda is set, and bargaining commences. The bargaining process may take some time. In Canada, it has been estimated that it takes from fifteen to twenty-five meetings in a typical bargaining round for the parties to reach agreement (Labour Canada, various years).

In Europe, there is more variation on these issues. Bargaining in Northern Europe (Germany, the Low Countries, and Scandinavia) always ends, as it does in North America, in a written agreement which lasts for a specific period of time. But in Southern Europe and Britain, this is not always the case. Much bargaining in Britain (and France and Italy as well) is informal and results in no more than an oral understanding sometimes embodied in notes taken by one of the attendees at a bargaining session (Jackson 1991). In such cases, the agreement lasts only so long as both parties agree that it will remain in place. When either party wants to alter current understandings it notifies the other. In Britain during the inflationary 1970s, this custom meant that wage negotiations were occurring in some industries every three to six months. In France, the open-endedness of the bargaining that took place prior the reform of the 1980s meant that there would be intense negotiations during some periods and relatively little activity during others (see, e.g., Bunel and Saglio 1984). After a period of intense bargaining from the late 1960s to the mid-1970s it slowed down in many industries almost to a halt.

Formal and informal bargaining are not mutually exclusive. Even though there are many oral agreements in Britain, there are also many written collective agreements in effect (Jackson 1991, 140). That is also true of North America, of course. Many issues come up on a day-to-day basis and they cannot wait for resolution until the contract expires. In North America, however, the typical collective agreement contains a management's rights clause. This clause commonly specifies that any issue not included in the collective agreement may be unilaterally decided by management. During the time that the collective agreement is in effect, management may do whatever it pleases with respect to issues not in the collective agreement.

The typical situation in Europe is quite different. Despite the attempt by employers early in the century to maintain control over internal issues by requiring agreements or understandings like the Swedish December Compromise of 1906, over the years labor's influence over internal issues has increased. Standards generally in effect today require that as new issues not included in the collective agreement arise, the parties will discuss them and attempt to come to an agreement. Indeed in Northern Europe, although unions may not go on strike during the term of the collective agreement over issues included in the agreement, they may raise and strike over issues not included in the agreement. European unions are not compelled or expected by tradition to sign only one collective agreement. In fact, in most countries there are simultaneously several agreements in effect. Wages are typically negotiated separately from other issues on an annual or biannual basis. Agreements over other issues such as training, technological change, and pensions may be renegotiated periodically, or they may stay in place until one party or the other initiates new negotiations.

The theory behind the single agreement in North America seems to be that employers should not frequently be placed in a strike-threat position because that would be disruptive and inefficient. European practice does not support the theory. Indeed, most strikes are over major issues such as wages and job security. Only rarely do strikes occur between wage rounds. On the other hand, continuous consultation takes considerable pressure off of wage bargaining. In the North American case, the parties must discuss and resolve disputes over as many as 150–200 issues in a bargaining round. Europeans, in any round, focus on only a few, and thus the probability of breakdown is lower.

Note that single-issue bargaining is quite different from multi-issue bargaining. When 150 issues must be resolved in a three or four month period it is almost certain that many of them will fall off the table. On the other hand, if negotiations are over a single issue it is very likely that the parties will find some way to resolve their differences. The North American system practically ensures that many issues, instead of being jointly regulated, will remain in the domain of management's reserved rights.[16]

Another significant difference between European and North American bargaining has to do with initial offers and demands. North American custom requires that the unions ask for much more than they expect to get and that management initially offer much less that it is prepared to settle for. This ritual allows both parties scope for bargaining. They have issues to trade off. Typical

European bargaining is much different. When, for example, unions make a wage increase demand, they expect that the final settlement will be very close to the initial proposal. A far-fetched proposal would be ridiculed both by employers and by the press. Indeed, it is generally expected (especially in Northern Europe) that any demand be backed up by serious economic analysis of the likely consequences of the adoption of the proposal. Bargaining in these circumstances often takes on the character of a debate between employer and union representatives over the quality of their economic forecasts and the assumptions on which they are based. It also allows for a good deal of public scrutiny of the process. Many observers have suggested that these characteristics produce results that are economically more sensible and in the overall public interest (e.g., Pekkarinen et al. 1992).

CONTRACT RATIFICATION AND BARGAINING AUTHORITY

In North America, if tentative agreement is reached in any bargaining round that agreement is almost always submitted to the membership of the union for ratification. If the members accept the tentative deal, bargaining comes to a halt, if not bargaining must resume under very difficult conditions. North American employers have complained about this practice for many decades. They argue that since the management bargaining team is expected to be able authoritatively to commit the company to any agreement, the union leadership should have the same power. In Europe, commonly union leaders do have such power (Windmuller 1987b). It removes some control from the hands of the membership, but it is felt that it puts pressure on union leaders to negotiate responsible agreements. One major problem with such systems is that in periods of rapid economic change, the leadership may not be able properly to estimate the members interests. The result may be, as there was in the late 1960s and early 1970s, a rash of wildcat strikes (Barkin 1975). Ratification is practiced by some British unions and is used in some cases in Belgium, Finland, Germany, Switzerland, Norway, and Denmark (see Córdova 1990; Windmuller 1987b; Kjellberg 1992).

LEGALITY OF COLLECTIVE AGREEMENTS

Written collective agreements are legally binding in the United States and almost everywhere else except Britain. In the United Kingdom, collective contracts are only gentleperson's agreements (Córdova 1990, 22). This is one aspect of the so-called voluntaristic policy that was followed by British governments throughout much of the twentieth century. The policy has been that the issues, structure, and process of bargaining should be left up to the parties and that the state should refrain from involvement. That policy has changed significantly in recent decades, however. The Thatcher government, during the 1980s, passed several laws regulating bargaining—for the most part to the disadvantage of the unions (Towers 1989).

Typically in Europe, collectively bargained terms become part of the individual contract of each covered employee (Córdova 1990). That individual contract, though, is much broader in scope than the collective agreement. Theoretically, it contains the entire panoply of rights and duties that regulate the relationship between the employer and the individual employee. If, for example, the employee was hired on the understanding that he/she would be eligible for promotion within six months, then that understanding, whether written or not, is considered to be part of the individual contract of employment. Indeed all explicit or implicit understandings between the individual employee and the employer are deemed to be included in the individual contract, including the terms of any and all collective agreements that establish minimum conditions. Collective agreements almost always contain minimums that cannot be legally negotiated away, but, in many situations and with respect to many issues, individuals may be able to negotiate terms better than those in the collective agreement. This is different from the typical situation in North America where negotiated terms are usually the actual terms.[17] In most countries, individuals may go to court to make effective terms of the contract that employers do not honor. Labor courts in countries such as Germany and France are kept quite busy settling such individual disputes.

Under the Wagner Act model, a different situation exists in Canada and the United States. The Wagner model delegates to the union exclusive bargaining rights. This means that individuals give up their right to enter into individual understandings outside of the collective agreement unless, of course, the collective agreement explicitly provides them with that capacity. The result is that the individual contract of employment, for all practical purposes, ceases to exist in North America where collective agreements prevail. In some cases, this can be to the detriment of the employees. For example, an unorganized employee in Canada may, if dismissed, sue the employer for wrongful dismissal with hopes of winning a settlement of several months pay. Unionized employees lose the right to sue for wrongful dismissal and have only the rights embedded in the union-negotiated collective agreement.

A common misperception of casual North American inquiry into European practice is that European labor courts are, more or less, equivalent to North American grievance procedures. Although there are similarities, there is one difference of such consequence that it renders comparison all but irrelevant. In North America, the grievance procedure is used largely to settle disputes arising in the context of an on-going employment relationship. Employees with problems take them to their shop stewards with the intention that the steward will work out a satisfactory solution with management. In Europe, most disputes that are settled by labor courts are those which occur at the point of separation. Most individuals who file claims with labor courts are no longer employed by the company against which the claim is made. For the most part, claimants are complaining that employers failed to provide them with appropriate compensation (pay in lieu of notice, severance, and vacation pay due) at the point of separation. In North America, similar claims are filed by unorganized employees either with the regular courts or commonly with departments of labor. Grievances in the North American sense of the word are generally settled informally in Europe, although on occasion full-time union officials will intervene on behalf of their members.

CONCILIATION AND MEDIATION

Not infrequently, the parties to the collective bargaining process reach an impasse. They are no longer able to make progress in negotiations. To get beyond these blockages to the achievement of agreement, the countries of the liberal democratic world have invented a wide assortment of techniques.

In the United States, under Wagner-Act model bargaining, if the parties reach an impasse and the collective agreement has expired, the union may initiate a strike or the employer may engage in a lockout. There is no requirement (except in the railroad and airline industries of the United States or when the president declares a national emergency) for the parties to engage in conciliation or mediation although they are required to notify the National Mediation Service that an impasse has occurred. The service may then offer voluntary assistance to the parties (Katz and Kochan 1992). In Canada, however, the parties are not permitted to take unilateral industrial action unless they have first gone through a series of government specified procedures. In Ontario, for example, either party must notify the Ministry of Labour that an impasse has occurred. At that point the ministry appoints a conciliator who meets with the parties to see if anything can be done to help them resume negotiating. If, in the judgement of the conciliator, additional efforts would be futile or a hindrance to further progress, he/she must file a report with the minister recommending either the establishment of a conciliation board or that the parties be permitted to strike and/or lockout. No strike or lockout is permitted during conciliation or during the proceedings of a conciliation board should one be established. Although fairly common until the 1960s, in recent decades conciliation boards have been used only rarely (Woods 1973; Saxe 1992).

In this respect the general situation is more like that in the United States than the procedure in Canada. The most common philosophy under liberal democracy is for the state to adhere to the principle of bargaining autonomy. This principle holds that the parties should be left to their own devices to come up with a mutually acceptable agreement and that the state should become involved in the process only to protect the overall public interest. During certain periods, especially times of high inflation, this principle is honored more in the breech than in fact. Only a few countries (Belgium, Australia) mandate conciliation or mediation although many governments make those services available. The situation in Canada is due, according to the most well-known student of the issue, to the fixation of the state with minimizing industrial conflict (Woods 1973).

INTEREST ARBITRATION

One apparently simple way to avoid overt conflict is to forbid its use while providing another means for dispute resolution. The most common alternative to the strike threat is arbitration. Issues that cannot be settled by negotiation are submitted to a neutral third person who decides those issues.

This procedure is rarely used in the private sector in North America and most other liberal democratic countries. During some periods, however, it has been used. In Britain, for example, interest arbitration was in effect throughout World War II and continued in effect until 1959 (Clegg 1972, 170). It was used primarily by public sector and quasi public sector employees. Voluntary arbitration, which required agreement by both sides to a dispute, continued to be available after 1959, but was rarely used. In recent years, however, a form or binding arbitration known in Britain as pendulum arbitration and in North America as final offer selection has been gaining momentum. Voluntary procedures have been established in several companies, most notably those under Japanese ownership (Blain et al. 1987, 196).

Some form of interest arbitration exists in several U.S. jurisdictions for at least some employees (Olson 1988; Aaron, Najita, and Stern 1988), and it is widely used in the public sector in Canada. In fact, about 50 percent of all public sector employees in Canada negotiate under a system in which strikes are forbidden and impasses are settled by reference to binding arbitration (Ponak and Thompson 1989). In the United States, a much smaller percent of the public sector is covered by binding interest arbitration procedures. Outside of North America, interest arbitration is not used widely in the public sector (see Ozaki 1987a, 1987b, 1990).

Until after World War II, it was generally considered that civil servants had a special obligation to the public that precluded the right to strike. By that time, most civil servants had formed trade unions or associations and they engaged in lobbying and other tactics to influence their conditions of work, but they were not permitted to engage in strike threat bargaining. During the 1960s, however, a wave of public sector reform swept over the liberal democratic world and when it settled public sector employees in many countries, including most western European countries, had acquired the right to strike. In many countries, however, civil servants still are forbidden to strike and have no right to invoke binding arbitration. In a survey carried out in the early 1980s, Córdova found only twenty-seven countries worldwide with an explicit or tacitly recognized right to strike for civil servants (Córdova 1985).

In both Germany and Japan, civil servants are well organized and procedures exist for them to put their case for changes in conditions of employment, but government makes the final decision. This has resulted in very stormy relations in Japan (much less so in Germany) where public sector unions tend to be more militant and radical than those in the private sector. For a few years after World War II, public sector employees in Japan did have the right to strike but when they threatened to use it widely to disrupt government, it was rescinded (Yamaguchi 1983, 306). This system, sometimes referred to as "meet and confer," is widely in evidence in the United States (Aaron, Najita, and Stern 1988). In essence, it is a unilateral system of employment decision making, although in practice employee associations in many situations have a considerable amount of influence over the decisions. Informal understandings exist that serious efforts will be made to achieve informal consensus. This seems to be the basic situation in Germany where associations representing civil servants have been very successful in defending and improving the conditions of work for their members despite the formal absence of the right to strike (Keller 1981).

The two most notable countries where interest arbitration has been used as a universal dispute resolution device are Australia and New Zealand. In both of those countries during the 1890s, there were major national disputes that became significant foci for political debate. In order to ensure that such disputes would not happen again, first New Zealand and then Australia forbade strikes and gave unions access to arbitration instead. By the early 1980s, more than 80 percent of those in the Australian and New Zealand labor forces were covered by interest arbitration awards.[18] The Australasian experience provides useful evidence relative to a continuing North American debate about the utility of interest arbitration.

It suggests, in support of a popular North American theory, that arbitration has a chilling effect on bargaining (see, e.g., Katz and Kochan 1992). Instead of bargaining to a successful conclusion on their own, the parties quickly grew reliant on the intervention and services of the government appointed neutrals to assist them in achieving agreement. It also suggests that arbitration is addictive. Once a party becomes skilled at utilizing the system, it continues to utilize the system. Indeed, it has been argued by some Australasian scholars that the legal system had the effect of molding union activity. Indeed in some cases unions were brought into existence in order to make use of the provisions of the law (Hince 1993). A third bit of evidence from Australasia is that the existence of arbitration does not necessarily put an end to strikes. Indeed, in many years in recent decades, Australia had more strikes per capita than any other developed country. These strikes were characteristically short and thus not much time was lost, but there were a lot of them. A final lesson from Australasia is that arbitration systems have a levelling effect on incomes. The dispersion of incomes from employment is somewhat smaller in Australia than it is in other countries, and there is a more pervasive sense of social equality (see, e.g., Gardner and Palmer 1992).

STRIKE VOTES

In North America, essentially every union has a requirement that a strike vote has to be taken before a strike may take place. That is also the norm in Europe and in Japan. In fact, it is very common for unions to have a high threshold for a strike to commence. In Germany, for example, commonly two-thirds to three-fourths of the members must approve strike action. This is probably one of the reasons for the very low incidence of strikes in Germany.

Exceptions to this standard have sometimes produced dramatic situations. The coal miners strike in Britain in the mid-1980s was initiated by a decision taken by Arthur Scargill, the president of the union. He simply directed union members to lay down their tools and leave work, and he ordered the establishment of picket lines in front of many mine sites (Towers 1989). As in North America, the British tradition is that it is improper to cross a picket line and miners generally honored that tradition. Despite considerable pressure to hold a vote, Scargill refused, arguing that it was a leadership issue. In part, because of the controversy over Scargill's action, the conservative British government later passed a new act requiring unions to hold strike votes.

Another exception to the standard has to do with what North Americans would call wildcat strikes—that is, unplanned strikes which occur on the spur of the moment. These strikes are rarely preceded by a formal vote; more characteristically, the decision to walk out is taken by a committee of local union leaders or the walkout simply occurs spontaneously.

LEGALITY OF STRIKES

During the nineteenth and into the twentieth century, in some cases strikes were illegal. Slowly, the right to strike was granted. Today it is considered to be a fundamental principle of liberal democratic nations. In such countries the right to strike is recognized everywhere in the private sector, but not without qualification. Strikes and other industrial action (slowdowns, work to rule) are regulated in various ways. For example, in Germany a strike is defined as a work stoppage undertaken in pursuit of a collective agreement with respect to terms and conditions of work (Weiss, Simitis, and Rydzy 1984). By defining it in that manner, political strikes are not classified as strikes and are illegal. This is a common practice in many countries. In Canada, for example, any concerted action to reduce production, such as a slowdown or a work to rule, is defined in most jurisdictions as a strike. It is also usual for governments to require a peace obligation during the period when the agreement is in effect—although commonly the obligation, as noted above, applies only to disputes over issues included in the collective agreement. Usually, if disputes occur over new issues not enshrined in a contract, those issues are negotiable, and if no agreement can be reached strikes may occur over them.

Since the right to strike is a constitutional right in both France and Italy, "no strike" clauses do not exist in statute and cannot be enforced if included in collective agreements.

In the United States, the National Labor Relations Act gives even unorganized employees a strong right to strike. It states that all employees covered by the act have a right to engage in concerted activities (including the right to stop work) for the purpose of mutual aid or protection. Although the courts and the Labor Board have narrowed this right by their interpretation of what it means (e.g., a single employee cannot engage in concerted action), it is still a strong right (Summers 1990a, 1992). In practice, though, it is of little significance. There are few nonunion employees who make use of the right. Even though they have the protection of law to do so, it is likely that those who took advantage of the right would be subject to some form of retribution by their employer. The procedures for ensuring adherence to the letter of the law are inadequate and under administrations that are not enthusiastic about applying the law, protection for the worker has been very weak. As a result, the strong right does not have a great deal of practical effect.

In Canada, the situation is quite different. In most jurisdictions unorganized workers do not have the right to strike. If they want to acquire that right they must form a union and take steps to bring themselves under the terms of the appropriate labor relations act (Craig and Solomon 1993). This policy would seem to be very contrary to the international standard that the right to strike should be universal except for clearly defined exceptions—such as forbidding the withdrawal of services that could have serious effects on innocent third parties or the prohibiting of industrial action during periods of national emergency such as wartime.

For the most part, workers who might cause a public emergency by withdrawing their services are employed in the public sector and it is common to have strike restrictions on such employees as police, fire, the military, and the health sector. As noted above, many countries have a blanket prohibition on withdrawal of services by civil servants. Even in France where the right to strike is embedded in the constitution, there are restrictions on the right of certain public sector employees to strike (Ozaki 1987b).

As in North America, the state as sovereign may step in and legislate the end of any specific dispute. That step has been taken, not infrequently, in Scandinavia, for example. Although ad hoc legislation to end strikes is very rare in the United States, it is common in Canada, and during the 1970s and 1980s it grew in use. That development led two Canadian observers to argue that the rights of Canadian workers—those in the public sector, at least—were being trampled by the state (Panitch and Swartz 1984).

CONTINUATION OF EMPLOYMENT

In the United States, when workers go out on strike it is legal for their employers to hire permanent replacement workers in their stead (Taylor and Witney 1987, 467–70). In short, if workers go on strike in the United States, the result may be the same as quitting their jobs. Only if their union is strong enough to negotiate their return to work will they get their job back from a srikebreaker.[19] This approach is very rare internationally. Indeed, the common situation within the liberal democratic world is for strikers to continue to be considered employees at least for some period of time. Although many countries permit companies to operate during strikes with temporary replacements, once the strike is over the strikers must be given their jobs back. Unlike the United States, Canada follows the international standard on this issue. In the mid-1980s, one province that did not adopt this approach, Alberta, had a major conflict over the issue. When the dust settled it revised its law to fit the Canadian and international standard (Noël and Gardner 1990).

LOCKOUTS

The lockout is the traditional employer counterpart to the strike. If an impasse occurs in negotiations, the employer, or more commonly several employers in an association, tell their employees not to come to work until the dispute is settled. Most commonly, the lockout is used as a counter to a union strategy of striking one or a few plants of a multi-plant employer, or one or a few employers in an employer association. The lockout is used with considerable vigor throughout Northern Europe. In Sweden, the Swedish Employers Federation maintains a large strike insurance fund and has the right to order any member organization to lockout its employees (Skogh 1984). A few European countries (France, Italy, Portugal) have statutes prohibiting employers from locking out employees.

The lockout is legal in North America. However, because of the prevalence of plant-level bargaining, employers have little need to use it and it occurs only infrequently. Occasionally it is used, however, as an offensive weapon to compel union concessions or to shortcut the union strategy of calling a strike during a favorable time of year.

GRIEVANCE PROCEDURES

Disputes occur not only over the terms of new agreements, but also over the interpretation of collective agreements and other understandings which in total compose the contract of employment. To settle interpretation or rights disputes, labor and management in North America have invented the institution of the grievance procedure. Commonly a grievance will begin with an individual employee who believes that some aspect of the collective agreement is not being applied correctly to him/her. The individual will complain to the local union officer—the shop steward who, if the case has merit, will file a formal written grievance. Most probably the issue will first be discussed with the individual's supervisor. If no mutually acceptable solution can be found, the grievance may go to the departmental level and, failing agreement, to the company level. The final step in the procedure in North America is, almost always, binding arbitration by an arbitrator jointly chosen, and jointly paid, by the employer and the union. In this manner, hundreds of thousands of problems are settled every year (Lewin and Peterson 1988).

Although arbitration is, in theory, officially a private institution, a custom has arisen for arbitrators to consult the reasoning of others who have settled similar cases. Because there is a market for them, arbitration cases are published.[20] This custom has led to the establishment of a body of workplace jurisprudence which, although it has little standing in law, has had an enormous effect on the operation of the workplace. For example, a typical North American collective agreement gives management the right to discipline or discharge employees for just cause, but it is left up to arbitrators to decide what the phrase just cause means. Over the years, arbitrators have made it clear that it is permissible for employers to dismiss employees for such behaviors as stealing, drinking or using drugs on the job, excessive absenteeism, and several other offenses (Adams and Adell 1992; Wheeler and Nolan 1992). If an employee, through the union, challenges a dismissal, arbitrators across North America generally will insist that the penalty reflect the seriousness of the offense, that the employer conducted an equitable investigation and permitted the employee to state his/her case, took the past record and length of service of the employee into account, made sure that the rules were known and applied consistently, and put a system of progressive discipline into effect (Begin and Beal 1985, 406–7).[21]

Grievance procedures in Europe are typically much less formal than are those in North America (Wheeler and Rojot 1992). If an employee has a problem, commonly the procedure is for him/her to take the issue up first with the supervisor. If the result is not satisfactory, several options are then available. In Britain, the employee will go to the shop steward who will then try to work out a solution. Should none be reached, the workers might go out on strike in support of the individual's claim.

In France, there is a statute requiring a special elected official, the *delegue du personnel,* whose job it is to work out grievances. Depending on the issue the *delegue* might call in various government officials and might assist the individual to go to the *prudhommes*—the bipartite (labor and management) French employment courts. In Germany and Austria, the individual might very well go to one of the works counselors or to the union office in the town. Either a works councillor or a union officer might then try to settle the dispute amicably.

In most European countries, the final step in such informal systems is a labor court—a government institution designed commonly to settle disputes over a range of issues emerging not only from collective agreements, but also from individual agreements and statutes (Aaron 1990). Individual agreements are very important in Europe, contrary to the situation in the United States and to an extent in Canada. According to common law, whenever anyone accepts employment that person enters into an agreement with the employer which establishes a body of rights and responsibilities for both parties. In fact, all of the understandings entered into by the employer and the employee with respect to each other are considered to be part of the individual contract. Most commonly, collective agreement terms are considered to become part of the individual contract and individuals usually may process their own complaints to court.

Although European labor courts are part of the overall legal system, commonly judges are appointed only after consultation with labor and employer organizations, and they are expected to understand and respect industrial relations customs. In a few countries (Italy, the Netherlands) instead of a labor court, grievances in the last resort are settled by the regular courts. Even in those countries, however, there are special sections overseen by judges sensitive to the concerns of labor and management.

The substantive rules produced by European labor courts and North American arbitration are not that much different. Remarkably, perhaps, the standards of conduct expected of employers and employees in both Europe (under labor courts) and North America (under arbitration) are very similar (see Wheeler and Rojot 1992; Adell and Adams 1993) despite obvious outward differences. The major difference between Europe and North America is the way that the unorganized are treated. As noted above, in the typical European country the great majority of employees are covered by collective agreements and almost all employees have access to labor courts. In the United States, on the other hand, 80–85 percent of employees are not covered by collective agreements, do not have access to grievance procedures ending in binding arbitration, and do not have the benefit of arbitral jurisprudence. As a result, the rights enjoyed by employees under collective bargaining do not extend to the unorganized. The basic principle in the United States is that the unorganized employee may be dismissed at any time for any reason, or for no reason whatsoever. A similar principle holds in Canada except that the employer must provide the employee with reasonable notice. The bottom line is that American workers are liable to much more arbitrary treatment than are workers in most of the liberal democratic world. This is one more result of the exceptional pattern of American labor relations developments related in the first few chapters (see also Bok 1971). With no class-conscious labor movement to look after their interests, the unorganized in America have acquired fewer rights and privileges than have workers in most other countries. The quality of their industrial citizenship is second-class.

In one respect, North American grievance procedures are much more favorable to workers than are European systems for resolving employment grievances. According to common practice in North America, workers who are unjustly dismissed are reinstated. In Europe, reinstatement is not common (Sherman 1981). It is available in several countries but, instead of reinstatement, judges commonly have the option of awarding the unjustly dismissed employee financial compensation, and the award of compensation is the usual practice. That is why, as noted above, most claims brought by individual employees to labor courts are claims filed by workers no longer employed by the firm against which the relief is sought. The result is that if an employer is determined to dismiss an employee, he/she may do so contingent upon paying a penalty. As a result, the European employee is perhaps less secure from arbitrary treatment than is the American unionized worker. This is a subject on which future research needs to be done. Do European and North American organized employees enjoy the same or different degrees of freedom from arbitrary treatment? Theoretically, it appears that the North American worker is better protected, but empirical work is needed to test the theory.

THE RIGHT OF FIRST INTERPRETATION

In North America, if there is a dispute over the terms of a collective agreement the employer has the right of first interpretation. What this means in practice is that if an employer decides that an employee should be fired, that employee is dismissed immediately and removed from the payroll. The arbitrator has the discretion of reinstating the employee with or without back pay depending upon how egregiously mistaken the employer was in carrying out the dismissal in the first place. This principle, which is a sacrosanct aspect of North American practice, is not so universal elsewhere. In Sweden, legislation introduced in the mid-1970s explicitly gave the local union the right of first interpretation in dismissal cases. If the employer wanted to fire someone and the local union did not agree, the individual would continue working and drawing a salary pending the decision of the labor court. In order to prevent the union from making use of this right to disrupt production in pursuit of other objectives (e.g., wage increases) the law called for heavy penalties for unions that made use of its first interpretation rights frivolously. In Germany, also, employees cannot be dismissed individually unless the works council agrees to the dismissal. If the works council disagrees and no mutually acceptable solution can be worked out the issue is settled by reference to a process similar to North American arbitration (Weiss et al. 1984). Although it is generally accepted in North America that management must have the right of first interpretation in order to prevent chaos, contrary practice in Germany and Sweden has not created intolerable problems. In both countries, the system has worked reasonably well. In short, European experience casts considerable doubt upon North American theory.

COLLECTIVE BARGAINING AND
THE NEW INDUSTRIAL RELATIONS

The traditional policy of North American unions has been to bargain hard to win their members the best conditions of employment. Traditionally, the unions have not been interested in becoming involved in the management of the enterprise. Management, on the other hand, generally defined its role as being that of an agent for shareholder interests. As a result, management would seek to acquire labor at the best possible price. Given these perspectives, bargaining was clearly adversarial. Unions always demanded and managers always gave in reluctantly, if at all. Wage bargaining in Europe was similar, although, because it was conducted at higher levels than in North America, the parties were generally more concerned to justify their positions as being in the overall economic interests of the industry and nation.

In recent years, adversarial assumptions have begun to be challenged in North America. According to the tenets of the "New Industrial Relations," companies are most productive if they are able to induce the thorough involvement of employees in their work rather than simply eliciting unenthusiastic acquiescence to orders given (see, e.g., Kochan and Barocci 1985; Barbash 1988; Godard 1994). Japanese experience suggests that this is best done if employees are organized in groups and given broad job responsibilities. It also suggests that union-management cooperation over a broad range of issues helps to engender the trust necessary to produce employees highly committed to continuous improvements in quality and productivity. As a result, over the past decade many North American companies have been seeking union cooperation in the establishment of new forms of production and human resource organization. That initiative has produced a heated debate in the labor movement. Many labor leaders are completely set against cooperation because they fear that employers will abuse the process by inducing workers to accept more responsibility and to exert more effort without any clear long-term benefit (Parker and Slaughter 1988; Wells 1987; Godard 1994). Others have been convinced, usually after initial reluctance, to give the process a chance (see, e.g., Banks and Metzgar 1989). To date, although there have been notable experiments, the spread of labor-management cooperation at the level of the enterprise has been limited and uneven (Godard 1994). It is being held back by adversarial traditions and by institutions that elicit distrust rather than a propensity to cooperate (see, e.g., Kochan et al. 1986). As Kochan and Wever (1991, 377) note "no [American] union has so far placed support for alternative forms of participation and representation in the center of its agenda for the future."

In Europe, the situation is quite different. From the early 1970s, Scandinavian unions were leaders in cooperating with management in order to reorganize work to make it simultaneously more satisfying and rewarding to the workers and more productive (Berggren 1992). In Germany, after some initial reticence, unions have gotten firmly behind work reorganization schemes (Jacobi et al. 1992).

In North America, adversarial suspicion traditionally has made unions reject the idea of workers' participation on boards of directors, although that reluctance has softened in the 1980s.[22] In Europe, on the other hand, German and Austrian unions have long insisted on board participation and, in the 1970s, as a result of labor demands, worker representation on boards of directors was extended to several other European countries. Because of the broader recognition of labor's critical and constructive role in society, European unions are less reluctant to become involved in participatory schemes. They have less reason to fear that such schemes are plots to wrangle concessions that could not be won through adversarial bargaining.

CONCLUSIONS

The objective of this chapter has been to place contemporary North American collective bargaining in comparative perspective. On many dimensions, North American practice is different from the norm elsewhere. Union recognition, the structure of bargaining, the process of bargaining, and dispute resolution techniques such as formal grievance procedures ending in binding arbitration are all unusual in comparative perspective. In some cases, the North American approach is superior to those more common elsewhere. For example, effective reinstatement of unfairly dismissed employees to their jobs is clearly superior to reimbursing employees for the injury sustained. Decentralized bargaining is also advantageous to the extent that it may be tailor-made to the situation of the parties involved, and may be more easily influenced by those regulated by the resultant agreement. On the other hand, the North American industrial relations system has features that are undesirable in comparative perspective.

The concept of union certification has resulted in the establishment of two systems of employment relations. In one, employment decision making is a unilateral employer process. The governance system is authoritarian. The employees have been excluded from the decision-making process altogether. Formally, those employees have the opportunity to opt for collective bargaining, but it is a hobbled and costly choice to be undertaken only in the most dire circumstances. As a result, most North American employees have no representation in the making of rules which critically impact their working lives.

Decentralized bargaining is also problematic in that under such a system no one has any responsibility for the cumulative effect of negotiations. The results of such negotiations are based largely on power rather than principle, and it is very difficult to coordinate fragmentary bargaining with socioeconomic policy.

Power also plays an important part in bargaining in Europe, of course. However, high-level bargaining is inevitably influenced by general policy considerations. Although imperfect, there is in many European countries a general consensus that bargaining should produce outcomes that are consistent with the policy goals of price stability and international competitiveness. There is also broad agreement that wage increases in the aggregate should not exceed what is possible as the result of the advance of productivity.

Because of distrustful attitudes stimulated and perpetuated by the legal framework regulating bargaining in North America, it has been difficult for the parties to embrace the new cooperative systems of production and human resource organization which generally seem to be more efficient and effective than the older Taylorist form of work organization. These systems seem to require labor-management cooperation, but the institutions of bargaining in North America do little to elicit cooperation.

Chapter 5

THE ORGANIZED AND THE UNORGANIZED

THE TWO NORTH AMERICAN
INDUSTRIAL RELATIONS SYSTEMS

As noted in chapter 4, what we in North America refer to simply as collective bargaining is a very specific variant of bargaining. Like so many other characteristics of North American industrial relations, our practice of collective bargaining is exceptional. Even more exceptional, however, is the overall structure of industrial relations in Canada and the United States. In most countries, there is a single dominant industrial relations system whose characteristics apply to the great majority of working people. In North America, however, we have two systems—one for the organized and one for the unorganized—and the rights and duties of the parties, terms and conditions of employment, and structures and processes of decision making are quite different in the two. Some of the key differences are discussed below.

Unionized employees have an agent to represent their employment interests to the employer while for the most part unorganized employees do not. They may bargain individually, but only a very small number of such workers have the bargaining power to negotiate effectively, and even those employees are unable to influence policies which of practical necessity must apply to all members of relevant groups. For example, individual employees cannot negotiate the wage and salary structure, the health and safety policy, the impact of technological change on the structure of work, decisions to open or close plants, or company strategy to implement equal employment opportunity programs. These policies may be established either through collective mechanisms such as collective bargaining, works council-management discussions, through deliberations on corporate boards of directors on which employees have representation, or they may be established unilaterally by management. For the most part in North America, where there is no collective bargaining there is unilateral management policymaking. One exception has to do with the implementation of health and safety policy. In several Canadian provinces, the law requires that health and safety committees be established in both union and nonunion companies, and those bodies have the statutory right to participate in the making of key decisions with respect to the formulation and implementation of company health and safety policy (see Adams 1986).

Unionized employees are generally paid better and have better benefits than comparable unorganized employees. For example, in the United States there is, unlike most countries, no statutory right to paid holidays and annual vacation with pay. Almost all unionized employees have such advantages embedded into their collective agreements. Unorganized employees in large corporations also usually have these advantages, but still there are many thousands of workers in the United States who do not receive any paid time off during the year. Most European countries provide at least four weeks annual vacation with pay to all employees after one year of work. Collective agreements, which apply to most working people, often add from two to four more weeks (see, e.g., Brewster et al. 1992). In Canada, all of the provinces require at least two weeks paid vacation a year, but workers under collective agreements are almost always entitled to more generous benefits.

Although both Canada and the United States have social security schemes that provide all workers with a pension, regardless of union status, unionized workers are much more likely than comparable unorganized workers to have access to private pension plans that provide much better benefits than the public scheme. They are also more likely to have better health and life insurance plans, severance pay, bonuses, and access to leave for various reasons (Lewin 1978; Freeman and Medoff 1984). Overall it is estimated that in a typical year in the United States, the wage and benefit premium of unionized workers is about 10–15 percent (Wachtel 1992, 142). A similar effect would seem to hold in Canada (Gunderson 1989).

Unionized employees also have superior employment rights to the unorganized. In Canada and the United States, the great majority of collective agreements contain just cause clauses. These provisions state that the employer may dismiss an employee individually only for just cause. The term just cause is not defined, but rather it has come to have a specific meaning as the result of accumulated decisions taken by arbitrators who are charged with adjudicating disputes over the interpretation of the collective agreement. Over time, these decisions have created a sort of common law of the workplace that ensures that workers under collective bargaining will be treated fairly and equitably.

Workplace common law under collective bargaining in both Canada and the United States permits employers to dismiss employees, but only if the employee committed a very serious offense such as stealing from the company or lying on an employment application, or for the accumulation of several minor infractions such a repeatedly missing work for no legitimate reason. Under collective bargaining, the employer may establish rules, but they must be reasonable, consistently applied and enforced, and be widely disseminated. If accused of an offense such as stealing, the employer must conduct an equitable investigation and allow the employee to be heard. The employee's past record and length of service with the company should also be taken into account. In general, arbitrators under collective bargaining will not permit the dismissal of a long-service employee with a good record for a first offense, unless it is a very grievous premeditated misdeed (Wheeler and Nolan 1992; Adams and Adell 1992). These rights are very strong in North America because of the ability of the arbitrator to reinstate an unjustly fired employee to his/her job, and because of the vigilance of union shop steward networks in ensuring that the provisions are respected.

Rights very similar to these also apply generally to employees in most advanced liberal democratic countries, but they are not as strong because of the weaker shop-floor presence of the union and because there is no tradition of effective reinstatement (Wheeler and Rojot 1992). Although use of reinstatement or reemployment is expanding somewhat in Europe, unjustly dismissed employees generally settle for a financial package (Hepple 1990). This is one way in which organized North American workers are considerably better off than are their European counterparts. On the other hand the unorganized worker in North America is much worse off than is the European equivalent. In the United States, an unorganized employee is hired at will. That means that he/she may be fired at any time for nearly any reason, or for no reason. The employer does not have to take long and good service into account. There is no requirement that a charge be investigated and proven. The rules can be arbitrary and there is no need for the employer to listen to the employee's explanation of events.

In the past decade and a half, or so, that harsh doctrine has been ameliorated to some extent by court decisions that have assessed penalties against employers for dismissing employees contrary, for example, to guarantees embedded in unilaterally established company personnel manuals (Adams, Adell, and Wheeler 1990). It is also illegal to fire an employee because of his race or creed and for a few other legally specified reasons. Nevertheless, the basic standard remains in place. No matter how good and how long the service given to the company, the unorganized worker in the United States may be dismissed instantly at the whim of the employer. In Canada, the system is different. Unorganized employees may be dismissed for any or no reason, but only with reasonable notice which provides something of a deterrent to arbitrary behavior. A few Canadian jurisdictions in addition have instituted the just cause provision for all employees, both unionized and nonunionized. Research suggests, however, that these provisions are more effective under collective bargaining than they are in the organized sphere (Adams, Adell, and Wheeler 1990; Eden 1993–94).

In both Canada and the United States, all employees have certain statutory rights. There are, for example, minimum wage laws in both countries. These laws are administered by labor departments which often have inadequate budgets to ensure that the law is obeyed. As a result, for the most part these departments depend on complaints by employees before they act. The result is that a very large percent of those employees for whom the minimum wage laws are directly applicable do not get what they are entitled to (Adams 1987; Ashenfelter and Smith 1979). Studies in both the United States and Canada have found that most employees are paid above the minimum wage and thus the law does not affect them. In addition, there are thousands of workers who get paid exactly the minimum wage and, incredibly, thousands of others who get paid (illegally) less than the minimum (Adams 1987; Ashenfelter and Smith 1979).

Why do they not complain and ask the government authorities to compel the employer to obey the law? Most likely because they fear that they will be dismissed for making a complaint. In both Canada and the United States, it is illegal to dismiss an employee for making a complaint about minimum conditions of employment, but procedures for making sure that employees who complain are protected are woefully inadequate. Minimum condition problems almost always occur within the unorganized industrial relations system with the result that the employees involved do not have the protection of the union and of the just cause provisions of collective agreements. As a result, if the employer makes their life very difficult there is not much that the government can do to protect the employee. In the unionized sphere, wages and hours are usually better, but even where minimum conditions apply the presence of the union goes a long way towards ensuring that the stipulations will be respected.

ORGANIZING THE UNORGANIZED

The brief review above makes it very clear that the conditions under which the unionized labor in North America are much better, in general, than are the conditions of the nonunionized. Why then are so many workers unorganized? A partial answer to that question is suggested by the discussion on certification procedures in chapter 5. Getting certified against the objections of the employer is a difficult and potentially job threatening process. A fuller answer to the question emerges from a review of theory and research on union density.

A long line of research has linked the growth and decline of unions to the business cycle (see Webb and Webb 1894; Commons et al. 1918; Davis 1941; Ashenfelter and Pencavel 1969; Bain and Elsheik 1976; Freeman 1990a). Membership grows in good times and falls in bad times. Membership expands in times of economic growth and prosperity for several reasons. According to most theorists, these are times in which prices are rising thereby undermining the purchasing power of wages. Workers have an incentive to join unions in order to pressure employers to restore the balance. Another effect of inflation, generally neglected by union growth theorists, is that it greatly upsets relativities between groups in the labor market and produces a high level of insecurity and anxiety. Providing a means to reduce such threats is one of the primary functions of trade unions and collective bargaining.

Second, boom times are generally times when unemployment is low—providing workers with considerable bargaining power to achieve their aims. In bad economic times, opposite forces go into effect. Prices stabilize, sometimes wages go down (in real terms at least), and many workers lose their jobs. It might seem that under these conditions workers would have just as much incentive to organize as in inflationary times, and certainly they do, but generally unionization has little to offer as a means of addressing these problems. Since unemployment is high, and thus bargaining power low, unions are unlikely to be able to be very effective against the economic insecurity brought on by recession.

In general terms, the effect of these forces may be seen in the overall course of union membership development during the twentieth century. Membership increased greatly in World War I, but declined precipitously with the onset of the major recession of the early 1920s (see table 5.1). It increased again during World War II in the Allied countries, but flattened out in the postwar period only to expand significantly again during the Vietnam era. When the Great Recession of the 1980s hit, it fell again.

Although the business cycle presents a general guide to membership ups and downs, recent research has indicated that the cycle explanation works in some times better than others, and in some countries better than others (see Visser 1990; Freeman 1990; Price 1991; Chaison and Rose 1991). If it had the same effect everywhere, the overall level of union membership should be fairly similar because the economies of the liberal democratic world have been closely tied together since the advent of the industrial revolution. But that is not the case. Union density varies very widely (see table 5.2) and the reasons for that variance must be sought by looking at factors other than the cumulative effects of past economic booms and busts.[1]

In the early 1970s, I wrote an article arguing that the low rate of union membership density in North America could be explained largely by reference to the peculiar nature of collective bargaining in Canada and the United States (Adams 1974), and in turn to the historical developments giving rise to that institutional configuration. A few years later, one of Britain's most outstanding industrial relations academics—Hugh Clegg—systematically compared six countries on various dimensions (Clegg 1976). He came to basically the same conclusion as I had a few years earlier. Union density variation was essentially

Table 5.1

Union Density in Eighteen Countries, 1900-1990

	Median	Range	N
1900	6	3-13	10
1910	8	5-18	15
1920	32	11-53	16
1930	28.5	8-44	16
1940	29	7-67	15
1950	40.5	28-67	18
1960	38	19-70	18
1970	41	22-66	18
1980	46.5	18-78	18
1989	36.5	10-81	18

Source: Visser 1992a.

a function of variation in certain characteristics of industrial relations systems. Since Clegg's version of the theory is more well known, I will make use of his terminology.

Clegg claimed that international variations in union membership density could be explained by reference to three critical aspects of industrial relations systems: the extent of collective bargaining, the depth of bargaining, and union security. By the extent of collective bargaining he meant the number of working people whose conditions of work are decided by bargaining. The more people covered by collective agreements, the greater the extent of bargaining. In turn, bargaining coverage is essentially a function of recognition. The larger the number of working people for whom employers recognize unions as bargaining agents, the greater the extent of bargaining. By depth of bargaining, Clegg meant the extent to which the union organizational apparatus extended down to the shop floor. If union officers and activists came into daily contact with those they represented, and if they continually negotiated with management about employment problems as they arose on an every day basis, then bargaining could be said to have considerable depth. If, on the other hand, unions had little presence in the enterprise, then bargaining depth could be referred to as shallow.

Clegg used the term union security in a very specialized and nonintuitive manner. In North America, union security is a term used entirely to refer to various versions of mandatory union membership or the deduction of union dues from the paychecks of workers and the transmission of that money to the union. Clegg's union security would include those specific procedures, but he intended the term to encompass much more. Indeed, union security was seen to be not merely a function of specific techniques but rather of the overall attitude and behavior of employers. If the employer fully accepted the union, then the union could be said to be very secure.

Clegg proposed that union membership would be very high where collective bargaining was extensive and deep, and where employers fully accepted the legitimacy and role of the unions as bargaining agents for their employees. The power of this observation may be seen by reference to the situation in a few different countries—beginning with Germany.

Clegg proposed that, whatever their historical mission, one of the most important functions of contemporary unions is collective bargaining over conditions of work. For a union to carry out that function, however, it must be recognized. It must have a bargaining partner with whom to negotiate. In Germany, recognition is, by and large, not a problem. Most employers belong to employer associations that recognize the right and responsibility of the unions to bargain on behalf of the employees. Recognition is an issue that was settled on the national stage long ago, although it went into hiatus during the Nazi era. There are also some small employers who try to stay beyond the net of collective contracts, but union avoidance is relatively rare.

Table 5.2

Union Membership Estimates as a Percent of Civilian Wage and Salary

Employees in Twelve Countries, 1955-1990

	1955	1960	1965	1970	1975	1980	1985	1990
United Kingdom	46	45	45	50	53	56	51	46(1988)
United States	33	31	28	30[1]	29(22)[2]	25(22)	(17)	(16)
Canada	31	30	28	31	34	35	36	36
Australia[3]	64	61	46	43	48	47	47	43
Japan	36	33	36	35	35	31	29	25
Denmark	59	63	63	64	72	86	92	88
France	21	20	20	22	23	19	17	11(1989)
Germany	44	40	38	37	39	40	40	39(1989)
Italy	57	34	33	43	56	62	61	65(1988)
Netherlands	41	42	40	38	42	41	34	28
Sweden	62	62	68	75	83	88	95	95(1989)
Switzerland	32	33	32	31	35	35	32	31
Median	42.5	37	37	37.5	40.5	40.5	38	37.5

Source: Chang and Sorrentino 1991.

Notes:
1. From this year, the series included members in employee associations. In the 1970s, without association membership, the union density was 27 percent.

2. In parentheses are estimates from a new series based on data from the Current Population Survey. Before then, data is based on surveys of unions and employee associations.

3. Data are from union reports. Household surveys consistently showed lower density. For 1976, 42 percent; for 1982, 40 percent; for 1986, 37 percent; and for 1990, 34 percent.

German unions do not have the benefit of mandatory membership provisions because it is illegal to compel anyone to become a union member or refrain from becoming a member. This standard is seen to be the natural concomitant of the right of every worker to join a union, free from intimidation or threat. The unions fought hard for the second principle and, by and large, they have succeeded in making it effective. Few German employers make active attempts to dissuade the employees from becoming union members. Such behavior is not only illegal it is seen as being highly improper—tantamount to interfering with the right of a citizen to vote as he/she prefers. As a result, even though German unions do not have the right to compel individuals to become members, they do have a good deal of security. Employers recognize their role in society and attempt to cooperate with the unions, rather than attempt to avoid or destroy them.

Thus, on two of Clegg's dimensions the German unions do well; but the unions do not do so well on the third. Generally, the unions in Germany have only a weak presence on the shop floor. In most industries, shop steward networks are not well organized and, even where they exist, employers are very reluctant to have anything to do with them and their role is usually marginal. The main reason for this situation is because of the negotiations which took place after World War I that led to the institution of works councils. In Germany, works councils carry out many of the tasks that trade unions do elsewhere. Most works counselors are trade unionists and some engage in organizing the unorganized, but they have a separate source of authority and a specified set of responsibilities laid down by law (Visser 1993; Markovits 1986).

One consequence of this system is that large numbers of German workers do not come into close, daily contact with the union institution. If they have a complaint, they know that they can go to the union office and that a union officer will intervene on their behalf—that peace of mind is of considerable value to many (see, e.g., van de Vall 1970). On the other hand, it is not difficult for the typical German worker to reason that, if he/she is getting all of the benefits of collective bargaining and other union efforts without being a member (and paying dues), then there is no hurry to change things around. In short, the German unions have a serious problem of what in North America are called free riders—people who benefit from union efforts, but do not contribute to the resource base of the union. In those industries where they have managed to build up a shop-floor network, such as metalworking, membership density is higher.

The German situation is approximated, more or less, in Australia and the Netherlands. Although in Australia, unions have been able to win union preference clauses in some agreements thereby giving them a greater degree of security than the German unions (Brooks 1992).

At first glance, the Swedish situation does not appear to be much different from the one in Germany. Bargaining coverage in Sweden is very extensive—employers fully accept the role of unions in society and make few efforts to dissuade workers from becoming union members. Although compulsory unionism is not illegal, it is strongly opposed by the Swedish Employers Federation. That organization has a policy which forbids any member to sign a mandatory membership clause. Moreover, many Swedish trade unionists agree that it is improper to compel a reluctant employee to be a member. As a result, mandatory membership is rare.

Despite these similarities, Swedish workers are nearly twice as well organized as German workers. There are at least two major reasons for this difference. First, despite the strong words of the December Compromise of 1906 granting the employer the right to hire, fire, and direct work, the Swedish unions did not accept the intention of the employers to keep them out of the shop. As a result, they worked hard over the years to build up strong shop-floor networks and they were in many cases successful. Thus, workers in Swedish firms are much more likely than workers in German firms to come into contact daily with local union officers who are carrying out important functions and who are likely to exert considerable moral pressure on them to join up.

In addition, the Swedes have cajoled employers into cooperating with them on organizing drives. In the early 1970s, when I was doing research in Sweden, one of the least well-organized unions was Handelsanstelldaforbundet, the Retail Workers Union. It is very difficult to unionize retail employees because so many of them work in small shops and have close personal relationships with the employer or manager who may not issue threats, but might find it difficult not to indicate that he/she would prefer to be free from the necessity of dealing with the unions. Coming from a North American background, I was amazed to find that the Retail Workers Union had convinced many employers to cooperate with their organizing drives by, for example, providing the union with lists of employees and by allowing the union to talk to new employees.

Commonly when new employees start work, they are given a union membership application to fill out along with the other paper work required to be completed in the first few days. Many probably believe that joining the union is as much one of the expectations as doing a diligent job and showing up for work regularly and on time. In fact, Swedes join unions and pay dues more regularly than they show up for work.[2] In the context of Clegg's theory, it is fair to say that the Swedish unions have even more security than do the German unions. Why do employers cooperate to such an extent with union organizing? A major reason, no doubt, is because the Social Democratic Party has been in power for most of the period since 1932 (even though they were out of power in the early 1990s) and employers did not want to antagonize the political wing of the labor movement by refusing to cooperate with its economic branch. Moreover, since they had to deal with the union at any rate, there was not a significant incentive to refuse union requests for cooperation with organizing. The Swedish situation is much different from that in North America where union certification depends on employee support, and the avoidance of certification means the maintenance of managerial control.

The Swedes have yet another advantage over the Germans—one that does not fit well into the Clegg theoretical framework. The Swedish unions administer the unemployment insurance fund. Instead of establishing a government-run system, the Swedes (along with a few other European countries) decided instead to provide subsidies to unions so that they would expand their already existing unemployment insurance schemes (Gordon 1988). Because of the subsidization and government regulations, it is not necessary to be a union member to get access to unemployment, but it is necessary to go into a union office to sign up. By and large, those Swedes who go into a union office for unemployment insurance also join the union. As a result, during the 1980s when unemployment was high in most countries, thereby undermining union strength, the fear of unemployment in Sweden (especially by white-collar and professional workers) led to very significant increases not only in absolute membership, but also in membership density. For similar reasons, union membership in the 1980s also increased in Denmark, Norway, and Belgium (see Freeman 1990a; Visser 1990; Price 1991).

In the 1960s, there was a thesis fashionable in the United States known as the saturation hypothesis. The proposition was that all of the organizable workers in the United States had already been organized and therefore it was unlikely that the unions would grow in the future.[3] As it turned out, unions have not grown, but not because of any saturation effect. The Swedish experience suggests that given the proper circumstances, almost everyone is unionizable.[4] One of the strongest unions in Sweden is the Union of White Collar Workers in Private Industry (SIF). In many countries, these workers are not well organized and are considered to be unlikely candidates for membership. The Swedish case clearly shows that trade unionism and collective bargaining are not just institutions appropriate for some employees, but not for others, as a line of North American thought has suggested (reviewed in Chaison and Rose 1991; Wheeler and McClendon 1991). Almost all employed people in Sweden—men and women, blue-collar and white-collar workers, private sector and public sector, those performing the most menial jobs as well as highly educated professionals and managers—have found those institutions to be of value. The Swedish case is approximated in Denmark, another very high density country.

The French case is an unusual one. Until the 1980s, it resembled in many ways the German situation. The bargaining that took place happened largely at the multi-employer level—mandatory membership was illegal and the unions were weak inside most companies. French governments of the past addressed this gap by instituting both works councils with only advisory powers on most issues and the position of *delegue du personnel,* a legally instituted grievance committeeperson. Like the works counselors in Germany, the *delegues* are mostly unionists, but their power and authority comes not from the unions but from the law. In 1968, there was a massive general strike in France and, in the negotiations which eventually brought the crisis to a close, unions were given the legal right to establish local union branches in the plant and to make use of bulletin boards, for example, to keep in touch with the workers (Goetschy and Rosenblatt 1992). Employers, however, continued to do all that they could to minimize the influence of the unions on the shop floor so that their position was only marginally improved.

Although it has similarities to the German and Swedish cases, the French situation is quite different because of the character of the unions. The mainstream of French unions have been very far to the left, both ideologically and strategically, for most of the twentieth century. For members, they wanted individuals who had embraced the ideology and wanted to work for the goals of the organization. They did not consider that their principle function was the periodic negotiation of wage and benefit improvements. They did engage in negotiations but, more importantly, they engaged in daily agitation. They believed that their central task was not to build up large strike funds in order to wring another few francs out of management. Instead, their job was to point out injustices and to demand change. Trade union leaders in France are frequent interviewees of television and newspaper journalists. They have demonstrated more skill at organizing demonstrations and manipulating the media than at negotiating new agreements. In short (although this may now be changing), the unions in France are not very well organized because they have not tried nearly as hard as the Swedes (who are obsessed with bringing every employed person into the fold) to organize the unorganized.

While this explanation was very satisfactory to me in 1980, events have occurred since then that I find difficult to understand. In 1981, François Mitterand, long-time leader of the Socialist Party, became president of France and began a program of significant reform. Among other things, the Auroux laws (named after the minister who developed them) required employers to institute wage bargaining with the unions one time every year and to bargain with them over the wage structure at least once every five years. In North America or Britain, this type of a law would, without question, be a great boon to the unions. It would certainly lead to a significant increase in union membership. In France, however, union membership fell during the 1980s at the same time when bargaining expanded significantly. For several decades, union density hovered around 20–25 percent of the labor force, but during the 1980s it fell by almost half.

Several reasons have been offered for this development (see, e.g., Bridgford 1990, Aldir 1989, Segrestin 1990, and Goetschy and Rozenblatt 1992). First, the Auroux laws gave workers the right to express their feelings and concerns about the enterprise at meetings to be organized by the employer. Many employers took advantage of this proposition to encourage employees to formulate informal organizations with which they were more willing to negotiate than the ideological unions. It is argued that the appeal of strong ideologies has faded in France during the 1980s and, as a result, unions have been less attractive. Given the availability of a forum for communicating with the employer that was not tainted by the brush of ideology, many workers took the option and dropped their union membership despite the fact that the unions were now negotiating on their behalf. The wage negotiations which took place annually during the 1980s and early 1990s were concluded mostly on terms proposed by employers (Delamotte 1988). Because of high unemployment, and therefore low bargaining power, the unions were not able to achieve a great deal.

Nevertheless, the French case of the 1980s and 1990s is puzzling because, in the past, when governments in liberal democratic countries have taken clear policy stands encouraging unions and collective bargaining, those institutions have almost always expanded. Recently, I reviewed twenty-three cases in eight countries over two centuries where governments engaged in clear attempts to encourage or discourage unions and collective bargaining. The French case of the 1980s was the only one in which union membership fell during a period of active government encouragement (Adams 1993a).

With these cases in mind, we turn to Canada and the United States. As indicated in table 5.2 union membership density in the United States is very low in international comparison, while the Canadian rate is about average but much lower than the rates in several Northern European countries. The North American situation is the result of an institutional configuration much different from those in Europe. Bargaining coverage in North America is nearly the same as union density, whereas in Europe coverage quite often exceeds density by a considerable amount. Because no general recognition agreement came to pass early in the twentieth century, bargaining continued to be decentralized and that bargaining structure was solidified with the introduction of the Wagner-Act policy model in the 1930s in the United States and the 1940s in Canada. As discussed in previous chapters, the Wagner-Act model instituted a kind of game in which, for the most part, unions negotiated only for workers in certified bargaining units. Where unions were not certified, employers had the right totally to refuse to deal with them and, almost without exception, they have taken up the offer. The big problem that North American unions have in their efforts to expand membership is to achieve recognition. Where they are not recognized, they have essentially no capacity to be of value to workers as agents in dealing with the employer.[5]

Whereas the extent of bargaining is very restricted, bargaining depth in North America is, in international comparison, excellent. Where they have managed to win recognition, the unions have also generally managed to set up strong shop steward networks and formal, very active grievance procedures leading to binding arbitration. In many instances, these procedures provide the unions with leverage to influence informally many of the day-to-day activities of their members. Formally, collective agreements have expanded to regulate the shop-floor employment relation in considerable detail.

Because of strong shop steward networks, unions are continually in touch with their members. In many companies, union stewards see those they represent almost on a daily basis. The union is an ever-present reality, not a distant, faceless, bureaucratic institution. Because of these characteristics, it is not as easy for the North American worker in a certified bargaining unit to allow his/her membership to go unpaid out of neglect. But North American unions do not depend solely on shop-floor contact. Unlike Europe, most collective agreements contain mandatory union membership clauses or at least agency shop (Rand formula in Canadian terminology) clauses which require that all bargaining unit members must pay union dues even if they choose not to become a union member. Under such conditions, some bargaining unit members prefer not to become union members for ideological reasons (fanatical individualists or people who belong to religious sects who have rules against membership in other organizations), but most simply join. As a result, union membership and bargaining coverage is very close (see Curme et al. 1990). North American unions have a good deal of union security where they are recognized, but none where they lack recognition.

North American unions almost always attempt to negotiate mandatory membership or mandatory dues payment clauses in collective agreements, but in some states of the United States such clauses cannot be made legally binding.[6] If employees fail to pay, there is nothing, legally, that the union can do about it. In these right to work states, union membership is somewhat lower than it is in states without such prohibitions, but in companies where unions are recognized, union membership is very high (see table 5.3). Even without coercive clauses, unions are able to sign up and maintain membership in such situations because of their depth of bargaining.

Although the rate of union density in Canada and Germany is roughly the same, the rates are the result of quite different forces in effect. Because of those forces, the membership recruitment problem faced by the unions is entirely different. In Canada (and the United States), the critical problem is the acquisition of recognition; in Germany, on the other hand, there is no recognition problem. Instead the challenge to the unions is to get access to the unorganized and

Table 5.3

Union Density and Bargaining Coverage in American Right to Work States, 1988

	Density (percent)	Coverage (percent)
Alabama	14.2	16.1
Arizona	6.9	8.6
Arkansas	9.5	11.6
Florida	7.8	10.6
Georgia	10.4	12.3
Iowa	14.4	18.2
Kansas	12.1	14.1
Louisiana	9.5	11.1
Mississippi	7.5	9.0
Nebraska	11.6	16.8
Nevada	18.0	20.8
North Carolina	6.3	7.6
South Carolina	5.1	6.6
South Dakota	8.7	10.8
Tennessee	12.3	14.7
Texas	6.9	8.9
Utah	11.9	15.1
Virginia	9.2	11.4
Wyoming	13.1	16.2

Sources: Curme et al. 1990.

to convince them that there is value in being a union member. In Germany, the added personal value of union membership is somewhat marginal and subjective. One gets more peace of mind in knowing that should a personal problem occur in relations with the employer, the union would be available to intervene and assist in working out a mutually satisfactory solution. One also gets the peace of mind of knowing that one is paying a fair share for services rendered. One may also get satisfaction in supporting an institution considered by many to be critical to the health of liberal democratic society. And, of course, in some situations, one may join to get a nagging steward off his/her back. In Canada, on the other hand, the added value of union membership is very substantial. In general, union members are better paid than nonunion members for doing the same job, but that is only a small aspect of the union-nonunion differential. More importantly, in the estimation of many, is the fact that unionized workers have considerably more protection against arbitrary, unjust behavior on the part of the employer (van de Vall 1970). For example, union members may be dismissed only for just cause. This means that if one does one's job with a reasonable amount of diligence and the job continues to exist, then one cannot be dismissed. In the unorganized sphere, however, the employee may be dismissed at the whim of the employer if proper notice is given. If there is an improper dismissal in the union situation, the employee will be reinstated to the job; if there is an improper dismissal of an unorganized employee, a financial settlement is the most that the person can hope for in most jurisdictions.[7] In the United States, the relative status of the unorganized employee is even worse. The contract regulating the individual employment relationship is said to exist at the will of the two parties. What this means in practice is that the employer may dismiss any employee for no reason, and with no notice whatsoever, no matter how many years of faithful service the person has rendered. The practical effect is that employees so dismissed are entitled neither to notice nor to compensation for the mental and financial violence done to them (Adams, Adell, and Wheeler 1990).

There is a considerable difference in union density between the United States and Canada. The main reason for this difference is the extent of recognition. In Canada, recognition has been extended to a much greater percentage of public sector employees (Rose 1984). In the private sector, Canadian labor relations boards, as discussed in previous chapters, have been much more adamant in insisting that employers recognize the right of employees to opt for collective bargaining without fear of retribution. This difference in turn is almost certainly the result of the greater political strength of the Canadian labor movement, and particularly of the links between the trade unions and the New Democratic Party (see, e.g., Meltz 1985; Bruce 1989; Adams 1989; Chaison and Rose 1990).[8]

Table 5.4

Union Density and Collective Bargaining Coverage

United States and Canada, 1990

	United States		Canada	
	Unionized	Coverage	Unionized	Coverage
	(percent)		(percent)	
Agriculture	1.9	2.1	5.9	6.7
Mining	18.0	20.2	37.5	40.9
Construction	21.0	22.2	32.7	35.2
Manufacturing	20.6	22.2	39.3	43.5
Transportation	31.6	34.1	47.9	51.5
Commun. & Pub. Util.	34.6	38.3	60.1	66.2
Wholesale Trade	6.5	7.3	12.4	14.2
Retail Trade	6.2	6.9	12.4	15.6
Finance, Ins., and Real Estate	2.5	3.4	9.0	13.1
Services	5.7	7.1	34.3	38.8
Government	36.5	43.3	61.3	72.3
TOTAL	16.1	18.3	33.1	37.6

Source: Kumar 1993.

The situation in Japan is, in many ways, similar to that in North America. Where the union is recognized generally, everyone in the company including white-collar, lower-level managerial (but not top managers), and professional employees becomes a member even though formal mandatory membership is unusual. But since bargaining is company by company, in those companies where no union is recognized union membership is likely to be nonexistent. Since the main authority and financial strength of the union movement is at the level of the enterprise, union organizing is limited. The union of Toyota employees has no reason to want to spend money organizing the employees of some other company. Some union federations have made attempts to organize the unorganized, but those organizations have only meager resources.

Unlike North America, Japanese employers are supposed to recognize and bargain with even minority unions. But, in fact, many nonunion employers attempt to remain nonunion by, for example, setting up consultation committees (which in North America would be referred to a company unions) and letting it be known, in subtle ways, that management prefers the nonunion status. As in North America, victimization of employees for involvement in the union is illegal, but such tactics as transferring internal union organizers and even promoting them into managerial jobs in order to dampen their ardor for unionization has been known to happen (see Freeman and Rebick 1989). Japan is an oddity in that union density is more extensive than collective bargaining coverage. This is primarily the result of civil servants being highly organized, but being forbidden to engage in collective bargaining.

The British case has similarities to both North America and to continental Europe. There is a considerable amount of multi-employer bargaining between unions, and employer associations and in those situations unions are recognized as the agent for all relevant employees (e.g., production workers). As a result, as in Europe, unions may be strongly organized in one plant and weakly organized in another. On the other hand, increasing numbers of employers in Britain choose to stay out of associations, and (as in North America) it is not unusual for an employer to adopt a policy of attempting to manage free from the constraints of collective bargaining. Although some small employers make strong efforts to convince employees to stay out of unions, the principle of the right of association in Britain is more firmly embedded than it is in North America, and victimization for union membership is much less usual.

Like North America, British unions do try to organize the unorganized, but union dues in Britain are low and the unions have chronic financial problems (Edwards et al. 1992). As a result, compared to Sweden, or even Canada and the United States, organizing efforts are restricted.

CONCLUSION

This review suggests that a large percent of the variation in union density may be explained by reference to a single factor: the attitude and behavior of employers. Where employers recognize unions to be the legitimate bargaining agents of their employees, or make it clearly known that they have no objections to their employees nominating a union to bargain on their behalf, and where they allow unions free access to employees and agree to negotiate over the full range of issues of importance to employees, then the great majority of workers become union members. There are some who will choose not to be members for personal reasons, but when given the unfettered choice to have representation or to have their conditions of employment established unilaterally, most choose representation.

Consider this mental experiment: A large corporation acquires a new managerial team. The new president announces to the employees that he/she would be pleased to meet with the freely chosen representative of the employees in order to discuss the full panoply of rights and duties with a view towards reaching a consensus with respect to them. In how many situations would the employees say no? Very few, it seems to me.

Employer behavior is, in turn, primarily a function of government policy. Employers always and everywhere prefer to maintain full control over every critical aspect of the production process, including the hiring, dismissal, and organization of employees. Unions and collective bargaining make life more difficult for managers. There is another party that has to be consulted and dealt with; another uncertainty on the way to action.

For the most part, employers only deal with unions because the unions themselves have compelled them to do so by making creditable threats to disrupt production or because pressure has been exerted by government policy. Of the two, government policy is much more important. Without some degree of political support, unions have rarely been able to pose a serious, widespread threat to managerial authority and control. The Swedes are well organized because of more than a half century of Social Democratic government, and the clear message from that government that cooperation with the unions was expected. Canadians are better organized than Americans because of the pressure exerted by the union-supported New Democratic Party on various governments over the years. Although not in power a great deal, nevertheless, the threat of an NDP breakthrough compelled various liberal and conservative governments to pay close attention to the concerns and complaints of labor (Meltz 1985; Bruce 1989). The weakness of the labor-Democratic Party link in the United States and the long tenure of the Republicans in power has had the opposite effect.

Recent international, comparative research shows a very close link between union density and long-term political makeup of the government. The longer a left government had been in power between 1919 and 1980, the higher the union density in 1980 (Wallerstein 1989; Visser 1992a). In the short run, the election of a moderate or left government can aid union growth and right-wing, conservative governments generally act as a damper on growth (see Ng 1987; Bean and Holden 1989).

What this, in turn, means is that union density is, in the last analysis, essentially a function of government policy. If union density is low, it is because governments are pursuing policies which have that effect; if union density is high, it is because governments have seen to it that employers recognize and deal with the unions, and that the unions are able to offer potential members a range of valued benefits. Union density in the United States is low not because of the pervasiveness of American values of rugged independence, as some writers would have us believe, but rather because American governments have pursued policies that have made it very difficult for unions to provide valued service to potential members.

If government influence is the key to employer behavior, how do governments exert that influence? There are many mechanisms. First, governments may, as the British government did from the early 1930s until the advent of the Thatcher regime in 1979, make it clear to their own employees that collective bargaining is the preferred method for establishing terms and conditions of employment. They may also, as the British government did in that period, deal only with government contractors who clearly respected the right of their employees to be represented by trade unions (see Adams 1993a). Governments may also pass laws intended to elicit appropriate behavior. One of the objectives of the Australian and New Zealand legislation of the 1890s was to remove union recognition as a source of labor-management contention (Plowman 1989). The Thatcher government's labor laws were explicitly designed to weaken unions and permit employers to regain a higher level of control over employment conditions and organization (Edwards et al. 1992).

Of course, the unions also play a significant role in determining their own future. Unions vary considerably in the amount of resources they devote to organizing the unorganized. The Swedes are very avid organizers, but the French, Japanese, and British are not. Unions also vary in the amount of pressure that they are able to exert on employers and governments. American unions have very little political clout compared to the unions in North Europe, and the result is a much less favorable milieu for organizing.

The interactions between labor, management, and governments produce an institutional configuration which we call an industrial relations system. Although there are similarities between them, each has its own detailed dynamics.

Where unions are involved in the administration of unemployment funds, membership goes up during periods of high unemployment; where they have no such connection, membership is more likely to go down.[9] Where all wages and prices are indexed (as they were in Australia for much of the century), inflation is much less likely to provide a significant incentive for union growth or formation than it is where workers have to struggle to maintain relativities (Price 1991).

But industrial relations systems configurations are not permanent. There does not appear to be an ideal state toward which industrial relations systems are moving. Instead, as Price (1991) has recently argued, systems change as the result of the emergence of crises. Key changes occurred in industrial relations systems in several countries in the 1918–1920 period and in Eastern Europe in the years following World War II. Germany, Japan, and Italy all operated under fascist regimes in the 1930s and during World War II, but when those countries lost the war their political and industrial relations systems were thoroughly altered. A major change in course occurred in the U.S. system in the 1930s. These changes are most likely unpredictable. What we can say in the context of this chapter is that the dynamics of union growth and decline will change along with them. No single formula is likely to be found valid in communist, fascist, and capitalist countries. Although certain general principles are certainly identifiable, such as the impact of employers and governments on union growth, the dynamics for each system have to be separately traced and defined.

Chapter 6

INDUSTRIAL RELATIONS AND SOCIOECONOMIC PERFORMANCE

In the previous chapters, I have tried to indicate several ways in which the North American systems of industrial relations are different from those of other economically advanced liberal democratic countries. I have also tried to provide explanations for the differences. Now it is appropriate to ask: do the differences make a difference? Are we better or worse off because of the differences? The data clearly show that in many ways we are considerably worse off than we need to be.

In the years after World War II, all of the countries of the liberal democratic world adopted similar socioeconomic objectives. They all set out simultaneously to achieve full employment, steady economic growth, and price stability. Because of the great hardships encountered during the depression of the 1930s, they promised to develop welfare systems that would shelter all citizens from those hazards in future. If they had not already done so, they also promised to provide labor with means to participate in the making of decisions critical to the welfare of workers, in part to avoid a repetition of the turmoil experienced in several periods in the past, especially the 1930s and 1940s, and in part to fulfill the promise of full citizenship in both political and economic spheres. Furthermore, they promised the public that all of the above goals would be accomplished in a milieu of social peace and stability. The institutions of industrial relations in any country may be helpful in pursuit of those aims or they may hinder progress toward those goals. In general, our institutions have been much less helpful than institutions in other countries in allowing us to fulfill the implicit consensus that emerged in the wake of World War II. To begin with, we have been much more prone to conflict than have many nations.

INDUSTRIAL CONFLICT—THE CONTEMPORARY PATTERN

As one might expect, the adversarial systems that we have created are in fact very conflict prone. Table 6.1 reports the number of days lost, standardized for the size of the labor force, in thirteen liberal democratic countries. Although there is a good deal of minor international variation in the way that statistics are

118

compiled (very short strikes and political strikes are often excluded, for example), nevertheless, broad comparisons provide a generally accurate picture
of major differences.

The data in table 6.1 report strikes in a selected group of industries that in
the United States are relatively well organized. One of the problems with making strike comparisons between the United States and other countries is that

Table 6.1

Days Lost Per Thousand Employees in Selected Industries*, 1970-1979 and 1981-1990

	1970-1979	1981-1990
Austria	<15 [1]	<5 [1]
Norway	90	170
Sweden	40	90
Netherlands	80	40
Japan	220 [2]	20 [3]
Germany	90	50
United States	1210	290
Canada	1840	880
New Zealand	n/a	1070
Australia	1300	770
United Kingdom	1090	740
Italy	1650 [2]	290 [3]
France	300 [2]	150 [3]

Source: Bird 1991; Bamber and Whitehouse 1992; Ferner and Hyman 1992.

Notes:
*   Mining and quarrying, Manufacturing, Construction, Transport and communication. Annual
averages.

1. Estimates from Ferner and Hyman for conflict across entire economy.

2. Bamber and Whitehouse figures for years 1974-1978.

3. Bamber and Whitehouse figures for years 1980-1989.

such a large number of American workers are not unionized, and unorganized workers in the United States almost never strike (although they certainly have done so in the past and may do so again in the future). Thus, comparisons of whole economies do not properly indicate the disputatious nature of union-management relations in the United States.

The data in the table indicate that in the 1970s the United States and Canada were among the most conflict prone of developed nations. The level of conflict dropped in the 1980s, more so in the United States where the milieu was much more antilabor than in Canada. Nevertheless, the level of conflict in the United States, even during the 1980s, was considerably higher than in several countries in which labor and management had achieved a high level of social partnership.[1] Particularly notable in that regard were the Scandinavian countries, as well as Austria, Germany, the Netherlands, and Japan. Where adversarialism persisted, such as in the United Kingdom, Italy, France, and New Zealand, conflict continued at high levels. In Australia, although conflict was high, it decreased markedly after the achievement of a labor-management-government accord in the early 1980s (Lewis and Spiers 1990).

To see more clearly the nature of industrial conflict in North America it is useful to disaggregate the strike data into its constituent parts. Strikes have four dimensions: size (the number of participants taking part in each strike), frequency (number of strikes occurring in any given period), length (the amount of time consumed by each strike), and volume (days lost due to industrial conflict).

The data reported in table 6.2 indicate the pattern of industrial conflict during the period 1970–1992. These data are broadly representative of the pattern that has been in place since the end of World War II and, although strike volume has decreased during the 1980s and early 1990s, there is no reason to believe that the overall pattern has changed (see Paldam and Pederson 1984; Lacroix 1986; Malles 1977).

Why do Canada and the United States lose so much time due to strikes? That question may be answered in several ways. One explanation emerges from the structure of strikes. Those with only a passing acquaintance of the configuration of conflict sometimes say that the North American industrial relations systems are very strike prone. But that is not exactly the case. It is certainly true that strikes occur with a greater frequency in Canada than in many other countries, but U.S. strike frequency for the entire economy is below average. Workers in several countries (Australia, New Zealand, France, Italy) went on strike more often than either Canadians or Americans during this period. The high strike volume in Canada and the United States is due in part to a moderately high strike rate in the Canadian case, but even more so to the average length of strikes in both countries. In France, strikes occur four times as often as in the

Table 6.2

Volume, Frequency, Size, and Duration of Industrial Conflict,

Annual Averages, 1970-1992

	Days lost per thousand employees (volume)	No. of strikes per hundred thousand workers (frequency)	Days lost per worker on strike (duration)	Workers involved per strike (size)
Italy	678	13	2	2891
Canada	571	7	14	541
Australia	367	31	2	527
United States	205	3	14	475
United Kingdom	263	5	8	707
New Zealand	280	24	3	348
France	98	13	2	371
West Germany	32	n/a	5	n/a
Sweden	104	2	6	673
Netherlands	23	0.5	5	952
Austria	5	0.2	1	2348
Japan	39	3	3	558

Sources: International Labour Office, Yearbook of Labour Statistics, various issues.

Notes:
Italy reported hours lost which were converted to days by dividing by seven. From 1983 to 1992 the United States reported only days lost from strikes of 1000 or more workers; those numbers were inflated by 1.6, the average difference between all strikes and strikes of 1000 or more workers between 1976-1981 for which both series are available. An equivalent procedure was used to estimate the number of workers on strike. France reports average number of strikers per month which were converted to years by multiplying by 12.

United States, but total time lost in France is only about half that of the United States. Strikes in France are frequent, but of very short duration.

Why, in international comparison, do North American strikes last so long? That question can be answered best by discussing some specific comparisons. In the United States and Canada bargaining is very decentralized. The most common form of bargaining is that which occurs between one union and one employer over the conditions of employment of a specific group of employees in one worksite. In Germany (and other continental European countries) where bargaining is more centralized, the typical bargaining round involves negotiations between a union and an employer's association over the conditions of all of the relevant employees who work for the companies affiliated in the association. In the United States, there are many more bargaining rounds than there are in Germany because of the decentralization, and thus there are many more situations in which something might go wrong. Moreover, there is more political pressure to avoid multi-employer strikes that might very well have significant effects on the neutral public than there is to avoid smaller strikes that impact only the parties involved.

Another difference has to do with the scope of bargaining. In the typical bargaining round in North America, there are a great many items under discussion—in large bargaining units, for example, there can be as many as 150–200 items on the bargaining table. Not all of these issues are of equal concern to the bargaining parties, but, nevertheless, they all must be discussed and assessed and a complicated process of well timed trade-offs must occur for a bargaining round to reach a successful conclusion without a breakdown. In Germany, on the other hand, far fewer items are under discussion in any one bargaining round. Commonly, the focus of bargaining is on a single issue such as wages, hours, or the impact of the introduction of new technology and work processes.

Not only are there more items on the bargaining table in the United States, but also the results of bargaining are more critical to the welfare of the employee because far fewer conditions of work are regulated by legislation. In Germany, all employees are entitled to health insurance, good pensions, and maternity benefits, and substantial statutory holidays, whereas there is no national health insurance system in the United States—social security pensions replace only a small part of income and employees must negotiate for any or all time off from work (for Europe, see, e.g., Jacobi et al. 1992; Brewster et al. 1992). Canada is more generous on these dimensions than the United States, but less so than Germany. For example, in most Canadian provinces, employees are entitled by law to at least two weeks off with pay after working one year.

Still another reason for the difference has to do with the impact of strike funds. Both American and German unions maintain substantial strike funds. However, the result of a multi-employer strike is to draw down strikes funds very quickly. On the other hand, a large union can afford to finance a strike by some of its members if most continue to work and draw wages.

Another way to explain the higher volume in the United States compared with, for example, Germany is by reference to the qualitative nature of the la-bor-management relationship. There are significant differences in the tenor of labor relations in Germany as compared to the United States and Canada. Ger-man labor has been assimilated into the basic fabric of societal decision mak-ing. The unions are always consulted on important national decisions that affect the interests of their members. They appoint members to various agencies criti-cal to the functioning of the economy. For all intents and purposes, they co-manage labor market policy and training policy. Given these very substantial rights, the unions have accepted considerable responsibility for the efficient performance of the economy. All labor market parties are strongly committed to reaching mutually acceptable solutions to key labor related issues (Turner 1991; Thelen 1991). In short, the term social partner is not just a euphemism. As a result, strikes are undertaken only with great reluctance.

The situation in the United States is far different. Until very recently, in-dustrial employers followed a policy of stringent labor exclusion from decision making. The general policy of American business was to restrict bargaining to the smallest number of issues. The scope of bargaining in the United States has continually expanded, but only as a result of major labor-management conflict. Each new item that found its way into a collective agreement was typically the result of a major battle at the bargaining table. In the political sphere, under a string of conservative presidents, labor was excluded from influence over na-tional policy. The result was a good deal of animosity and distrust which often manifested itself in overt conflict. In this respect, Canada is only marginally better than the United States. As in the United States, Canadian employers have insisted on management's rights clauses in collective agreements which are used as a means to exclude labor representatives from participating in any deci-sion making over issues not in the collective agreement.[2]

Japan is an interesting case which falls in between North America and Germany, and illustrates the importance of what might be called labor integra-tion. Structurally, bargaining in Japan is similar to bargaining in Canada and the United States. It is decentralized down to the level of the individual company, although not down to different plants. On the other hand, like Germany, in the typical bargaining round negotiations are over a small range of issues. Wage bargaining occurs annually in the spring across Japan. In addition, the amount of consultation between labor and management at the level of the enterprise is more like the German case. Union leaders are commonly taken into the confi-dence of corporate leaders rather than being excluded. Although some would argue that German labor has more influence over key industrial decisions, nevertheless, continuous consultation over all facets of productive enterprise is a characteristic aspect of both German and Japanese industrial relations (Kuwahara 1990; Shimada 1992; Jacobi et al. 1992).

There are, in addition, other significant differences between Japanese and North American unionism. As noted above, unions in Japan are organized on an enterprise basis. All regular employees in a corporation normally belong to the enterprise union. For example, all Toyota employees, including white-collar and clerical workers up to middle management, belong to a single Toyota employees association. In the Japanese system, too, once a core employee takes a job with a company like Toyota, he/she is expected to stay with the company for his/her whole career. As a result, employees identify with the fortunes of the company to an even greater extent than they do elsewhere. This union structure and attitude no doubt helps to moderate the incidence of industrial conflict. Since it would be difficult to find equivalent work elsewhere, and because essentially all employees except those at the higher echelons are in a single employee union, it is not difficult for Japanese employees to accept the notion that their best interests and the best interests of the company are closely aligned.

In addition, Japanese firms have very narrow wage bands between the top level and the rank and file, and most have in place a system for the equitable sharing of enterprise income through bonuses. Nevertheless, strike frequency and volume are not so minimal in Japan as some people seem to think. During the 1970–1992 period, strikes occurred more often in that country than they did in Austria, Sweden, or the Netherlands and probably Germany. Given the similarities with those other low conflict countries, the Japanese case supports the proposition that decentralized bargaining is more strike prone than multi-employer bargaining.

By and large, in North America the strike is a tool of the trade unions. Although as many as one strike in three is illegal, almost all strikes are organized and led by union leaders. Nonunion members rarely go on strike. In essence, laws designed to contain strikes within the province of union-management relations have been successful. That is not the case everywhere.

In France, for example, the pattern of conflict is much different from North America. Strikes are frequent, short and often spontaneous. In North America we would call many of them wildcat strikes, but such strikes are not illegal in France because there is a constitutional right to strike. In the French case, strikes may occur at any time and, unlike North America, they are not typically the last step in a tightly choreographed bargaining ritual. Neither are there well-developed schemes for settling disputes over the interpretation of previously agreed to terms (Clegg 1976). As a result, many French strikes are the result of disagreements between worker representatives and management at the shop-floor level that could not be satisfactorily and peacefully resolved; others take on more the character of a public demonstration. Often they are designed not to win concessions directly from management, but rather to cajole the government to intervene in the dispute (Sellier 1978).

One reason strikes do not last longer in France is because unions do not have extensive strike funds and cannot afford to underwrite the costs of long strikes. But even more fundamentally, most unions have not seen fit to build up the sort of strong administrative organizations necessary to successfully engage in strike-threat bargaining. They have defined themselves more as protest organizations whose job it is to raise questions and have them appear on the public agenda. Maximizing the economic rewards of specific workers in specific plants is seen as much less important than raising the overall condition of the working class.[3]

The French pattern of frequent, short strikes is also evident in Australia, although there is no constitutional right to strike and walkouts in that country have been illegal throughout much of the twentieth century. Less clearly, the pattern also exists in Britain. As discussed in the last chapter, grievance procedures are highly developed and regularly used in North American industrial relations. Because these procedures have been successfully institutionalized, many disputes over the interpretation of the collective agreement that might have ended in strikes are now resolved without resort to conflict. Grievance procedures are also institutionalized and accepted in Scandinavia, but they are rudimentary or very informal in Britain, France, and Australia. When those negotiations break down, strikes are not uncommon over what, in North America, would be called rights issues.

In Britain, instead of a single general pattern of union-management relations there is great diversity. One finds multi-employer bargaining and single employer bargaining; informal bargaining and bargaining which, like North America, ends in a written agreement. One also finds grievance procedures like those in North America in some situations, but more often one finds informal dispute resolution. Britain has, perhaps, more internal variation than any other country and the strike figures are a reflection of that variation.

In North America, the tradition of business unionism has led unions to build up significant strike funds. Moreover, as a result of the tight ordering of collective bargaining brought about by the introduction of the Wagner-Act model, strikes are largely predictable. Being predictable both employees and companies may prepare for them. Companies stockpile and employees arrange casual employment and make special arrangements with creditors in expectation of a strike. As a result strikes last a long time. None of these characteristics hold in France or Australia or, for the most part, in Britain where unions do not have significant strike funds. Northern European unions, those in Germany and Scandinavia, do have large strike funds but when multi-employer strikes occur those funds are drained very quickly. Consequently, many of the strikes that do occur are short and illegal.

The Italian pattern is again quite different from either the North American model, the Northern European model, or the short, small strike pattern evident in France and Australia. In Italy, political strikes are very common and are counted. These strikes are designed either to influence government policy or to influence the government as employer. The typical strike is very short, but it includes a great many people. That is why Italy loses so many days of work each year (Ferner and Hyman 1992a).

Although there are many similarities between Canada and the United States, there are also some important differences. The data on time lost due to strikes suggests that Canada in recent decades has been more than twice as conflict prone as the United States. The difference between the two countries is not so great as it appears, however. When data for the private sector are compared and adjusted for the level of union membership, the difference largely disappears. Industrial conflict between the two countries diverged sharply in the 1970s and it was just at that time that large differences in union membership density began to be felt (see table 6.3).

Table 6.3

Days Lost Due To Strikes in Mining, Manufacturing, Construction and Transport

Per Thousand Employees, 1962-1981

	1962-1966	1967-1971	1972-1976	1977-1981
Canada				
Annual Averages	766	1687	2203	1569
Union Membership Density (percent)	29.7 (1965)	33.6 (1970)	36.9 (1975)	37.6 (1980)
United States				
Annual Averages	790	1649	1054	900
Union Membership Density (percent)	28.4 (1965)	27.3 (1970)	25.5 (1975)	21.9 (1980)

Sources: Jackson 1987, table 2.6; Craig 1986, table 4.1; Katz and Kochan 1992, exhibit 6.1.

By the mid-1970s, a considerably larger percentage of private sector employees in Canada were in trade unions as compared to the United States. The Canada-U.S. comparison by itself might lead one to the conclusion that strike rates are closely correlated with union density. But that is definitely not a good generalization. It is quite clear that organized workers are more likely to engage in strikes than unorganized workers because there is leadership available to organize and direct the effort (see, e.g., Snyder 1975). But that does not mean that strikes rates are closely correlated with union density across nations. In fact, a study by Haas and Stack (1983) of seventy-one countries found that when other factors were controlled, such as the level of economic development, there was no relationship between union density and industrial conflict as a few previous sociological studies (Britt and Gallie 1972, 1974; Shorter and Tilly 1971; Snyder 1975, 1977) had suggested.

The experience of the industrialized, market economy countries seems to be that there is a positive relationship between conflict and the rate of union organization at low organization levels, but a negative correlation at high union density levels. Once unions organize a sizable portion of the labor force, they acquire a greater interest in overall economic performance and a greater awareness of their potential impact on that performance. As a result, the strike weapon is used more judiciously. They also acquire more influence over national and enterprise decisions with the result that the use of the strike is less necessary. At low levels of density, not only is there a general positive relationship with industrial conflict, but it also appears that conflict is more likely to occur in unpredictable damaging strike waves. In short, high union density contributes both to low levels of conflict and better overall economic performance.

THE LONG-RUN PATTERN

Karl Marx argued that over time as workers became more conscious of the exploitative nature of the capitalist system, industrial conflict would build to a crescendo resulting in a revolution in which capitalism would be destroyed. During the 1960s, four prominent labor economists—Clark Kerr, John Dunlop, Frederick Harbison, and Charles Myers—acquired a large grant to study the reaction of labor to the advent of industrialization. One of their most publicized findings was that, contrary to Marx, strikes do not increase in frequency or intensity over time. Instead, they peak relatively early in the process of industrialization and decline from that point with, of course, periodic fluctuations. Their thesis was supported by a more detailed investigation which focused squarely on industrial conflict. Ross and Hartman (1960), in a phrase which became famous, argued that the strike was withering away. Worldwide, they said, strikes were receding as industrial relations became institutionalized, and the parties came to accept one another and grew more skilled at negotiating.

The withering away thesis disappeared not long after it was published. By the late 1960s and early 1970s, the level of industrial conflict was up everywhere and books were being written on the resurgence of class conflict (Barkin 1975; Crouch and Pizzorno 1978). This reemergence of conflict gave rise to a substantial amount of research on strikes in the 1970s and 1980s. What the researchers found was that neither Marx nor Kerr were entirely correct. In some countries, notably those of Northern Europe, strikes had indeed over the long run fallen to very low levels in comparison to what they had been in the first part of the twentieth century (Hibbs 1978; Paldam and Pedersen 1982, 1984). In other countries—the Anglo-Saxon group of Britain, Australasia, and North America—conflict had increased in the post-World War II period to levels exceeding those prior to World War II. Why the variance? Although there is still debate over this long-run development, the most widely held theory is that industrial conflict has decreased in countries where labor has become assimilated into the fabric of socioeconomic decision making. In all of the Northern European countries, labor is fully accepted as a social partner, whereas in the Anglo-Saxon countries labor's influence and acceptance has been less complete. Moreover, in the Northern European countries, the success of the labor movements has led to the development of very generous welfare states, whereas in the Anglo-Saxon countries the welfare state is comparatively underdeveloped. On the basis of his analysis of the experience of eleven liberal democratic countries, Hibbs (1978, 1976) argued that conflict in those countries where labor had become assimilated had shifted from the economic to the political sphere. Instead of bargaining and strikes there were national consultations and parliamentary debates. This is probably the main reason why industrial conflict is very low in several countries which have very high rates of union density. They are precisely the countries where labor has been assimilated and has considerable political power.

In the long run, another pattern is also evident. Strikes vary with intensity as a function of socioeconomic developments. During both world wars, when there was high inflation, low unemployment, and considerable uncertainty, industrial conflict rose to peak levels. It receded in the interwar years and during the 1950s and early 1960s. It was this recession that Ross and Hartman mistook for a long-term decline. Conflict rose in the late 1960s and 1970s again driven by essentially the same forces as were in effect during the war periods—inflation, which upset many relativities and caused considerable uncertainty, and low unemployment, which provided workers with the bargaining power they required in order aggressively to attempt to shelter themselves from the uncertainties of the economic environment. With the onslaught of the Great Recession of the early 1980s, conflict again receded and stayed at low levels throughout the decade. Even though there was considerable economic growth during that decade, unemployment was high in most countries and inflation was low. The relationship between unemployment, inflation, and strikes has been fairly stable throughout the twentieth century, and there is every reason to believe that it is still in effect.

GENERALIZATIONS

Can any general conclusions be drawn from this international comparison? Is there anything of practical value that we, in North America, can learn from the international experience? The answer to both questions is definitely yes.

In general, strikes are less likely to occur where labor is fully accepted as a social partner and brought into the forums where key economic decisions at both the enterprise and national level are made. The conflict and animosity between labor and management that continues to exist in North America is the legacy of the failure of the parties to reach a full accord on their respective places in the system. With some notable exceptions, business still begrudges organized labor any legitimate place in the system of economic decision making other than as a threat to the egregious employer and a penalty to those employers who have sinned in the past. That is less true in Canada than in the United States, but still the two countries taken together are more like each other on this score than like the nations of North Europe who have achieved serious integration.[4]

A second generalization is that decentralized, multi-issue bargaining is more likely to result in frequent strikes than is multi-employer, issue-by-issue bargaining. As long as decentralized bargaining remains a key characteristic of North American systems, we can expect to have higher levels of conflict than countries with more articulated bargaining.

A third generalization is that the amount of conflict (if other things are equal) has, if anything, a negative relationship with the density of unionization. Indeed, the very highly unionized countries of Scandinavia have some of the most enviable records of industrial peace. Previously, I mentioned that in the typical Japanese corporation the propensity of employees to strike was low because almost all enterprise employees were members of a single enterprise union and, because they did not have good prospects for finding similar jobs elsewhere, were prone to see their interests in common with the firm. In Sweden, Austria, and other Northern European countries a similar logic holds at the national level. When essentially all employees become union members, union leaders begin to see that it is important for them to be concerned with the overall performance of the economy rather than solely with sectoral interests. In the United States and Canada, because such a small part of the labor force is organized and because union leaders are primarily responsible to their own members rather than to workers as a whole, they are naturally less concerned with the effects of their decisions on overall economic performance.

A fourth generalization is that the relationship between levels and incidents of conflict is far from simple. Government policies outlawing strikes do not, as the Australasian experience indicates, necessarily put an end to overt conflict. On the other hand, some governments have been able to formulate policies that do contain conflict. In Northern Europe, low conflict has been achieved by the assimilation of labor into national and corporate decisions making; in North America, labor policy has quelled strikes of the unorganized (at least in the short run) at the cost of much conflict in the union-management sphere. The relationship between government policy and industrial conflict is still not very well understood.

DO CONFLICT LEVELS MATTER?

One final question needs to be addressed. Is the level of conflict in North America really problematic? Some economists argue that because the amount of working time lost due to industrial conflict is a very small percent of potential time worked and, because much of it is made up before and after strikes, it is not really a problem of consequence. Many are fond of noting that much more time is lost each year due to accidents and illness than is lost due to strikes. The figures are indisputable but the benign conclusion does not flow as easily as it seems at first glance. The low conflict which exists in Germany, Sweden, Japan, Austria, and other countries is indicative of a healthy functioning labor-management relationship which every year produces gains in the efficiency and quality of the overall economic relationship. The numbers that the benign analysts quote are perhaps the least important. It is much more difficult to calculate the positive gains from labor-management cooperation, but it is those gains that are really significant.[5] As we shall see below, there is a strong correlation between economic performance and industrial conflict. Low conflict countries do substantially better than those characterized by animosity and overt belligerence.

PARTICIPATION

Despite our assertions in North America of being democratic countries, we deny to the majority of employees any say in the determination of critical conditions under which they work. Our major labor policy framework has failed to deliver on the promise of universal participation. Well over half of the labor forces in both Canada and the United States function every day within a system of enterprise governance characterized by command and obey authoritarianism.

As noted by prominent political scientists, the persistence of that system is entirely contrary to principles which we consider fundamental to our way of life (Dahl 1984; Lindblom 1977). Command and obey authoritarianism in the economic sphere is a throwback to the elitist undemocratic political systems which dominated the world prior to the nineteenth and twentieth centuries.

Instead of industrial citizens, those who work under such regimes are better described as subjects, or even wage slaves. As under classical slavery, their labor is owned by the employer who may do with it as he/she pleases within the bounds established by society. Although it is fashionable in North America to consider employer initiated participation schemes to be an alternative to independent employee representation, the two phenomena are not equivalent (see, e.g., Mahoney and Watson 1993; and the discussion in Godard 1994, chap. 5). Enlightened employers may unilaterally grant rights to employees, but as long as those privileges may be arbitrarily withdrawn, they cannot be thought of as being on the same political plane with constitutional rights of citizenship. Employers in such situations behave paternalistically, not democratically. Unlike the classical slave, the wage slave may leave any individual employer. On the other hand, in modern society it is impractical for most adults to avoid the wage system altogether. In all modern economies, the income of 80 percent or more of all households is acquired through wage earning.

We have already seen that most other countries do much better than North America in providing for labor participation in the making of employment decision. By some combination of collective bargaining, works councils, and workers' participation on boards of directors, they ensure that most working people have a means to influence the making of rules that are critical to their welfare. In those countries, employees have acquired significant industrial citizenship rights.

JUSTICE AND DIGNITY

One of the main objectives of labor movements everywhere has been the achievement of justice and dignity for the working person. For those they have organized, the Canadian and American labor movements have fashioned institutions that provide a high level of these desirable qualities. As discussed in more detail in the chapter on the organized and the unorganized, the organized worker in North America has a good deal of assurance that he/she will not be arbitrarily discriminated against or treated in a demeaning manner. The unorganized, however, have few protections against such treatments other than the goodwill of their employers, and general social standards that have their most significant impact in large organizations. As Summers (1984, 1438) has remarked, they are at "best objects of employer benevolence."

Outside of North America, general standards of just treatment are equivalent to those in effect in unionized firms in North America (Summers 1984; Wheeler and Rojot 1992). However, because reinstatement for unjust dismissal is rare outside of Canada and the United States, just treatment is less well assured. To date, there has been little research on the actual behavior prevailing in organizations outside of North America. Nevertheless, it is clear that very significant gains have been achieved everywhere over standards common at the beginning of the twentieth century.

SECURITY

As noted in a previous chapter, the individual employment security of those covered by collective agreements in North America is very good. Unionized workers can only be dismissed from their jobs for just cause and the protection against arbitrary employer behavior is strong. For unorganized employees, however, especially in the United States, individual employment security is dismal. Effective protection against arbitrary and unfair dismissal is all but nonexistent.

Collective employment security in North America is also inferior to that provided in many other countries. Even though every liberal democratic country adopted full employment as a goal after World War II, that goal has never been met in either Canada or the United States (see table 6.4). Although economists argue about the definition of unemployment, most would consider a rate under 3 percent as meeting that definition. Because of people entering and leaving the labor force and moving between jobs, there will always be some unemployment.

Most European countries had unemployment rates at or below 3 percent prior to the first oil crisis of the 1970s. The rates edged up after the oil crises and skyrocketed after the Great Recession of the early 1980s. Unemployment in Canada and the United States has continually been above 3 percent since World War II and continually above the average for all OECD countries outside of North America (see table 6.4).[6]

In comparison to Europe, in fact, the U.S. rate is artificially low. Most European countries have, by North American standards, very generous unemployment insurance schemes. A larger percentage of people without jobs are covered by the systems—the unemployed receive a larger percentage of their last paycheck in unemployment benefits, and benefits are paid for a longer period of time. Indeed, several countries have indefinite unemployment benefit periods (Layard, Nickell, and Jackman 1991). Because, by European standards, U.S. benefits are so meager many Americans quickly accept jobs for which they are overqualified in order to acquire some income (Rowthorn 1992). The

Table 6.4

Unemployment as a Percent of the Total Labor Force

	60-67	68-73	74-79	80-90	60-90
United States	5.0	4.6	6.7	7.0	6.0
Canada	4.9	5.1	6.4	8.9	6.6
United Kingdom	1.7	3.2	5.2	10.9	5.9
Australia	1.3	1.4	4.0	6.9	3.6
France	1.0	n/a	3.1	6.9	3.1
Italy	3.9	4.0	4.2	6.6	5.0
New Zealand	n/a	0.3	n/a	n/a	n/a
Sweden	1.3	2.1	1.6	2.3	1.9
Germany	0.9	0.8	2.9	6.0	3.1
Japan	1.2	1.3	2.0	2.4	1.8
Austria	1.4	1.0	1.3	3.0	1.9
Netherlands	0.8	1.7	4.8	n/a	n/a
Norway	1.1	n/a	1.4	2.8	n/a
Total OECD less United States	1.7	2.1	3.3	6.2	3.7

Sources: OECD Economic Outlook, Historical Statistics 1960-1990; OECD Observer (February/March) 1993.

result is a large underemployment rate in the United States. If European style benefit plans were available in the United States, the unemployment rate would certainly be much worse than the current reported rate.[7]

There is an enormous technical literature on the causes of unemployment that it would not be appropriate to review here. A few data stand out sharply in international comparison. Throughout the twentieth century, there has been a worldwide capitalist economy. All capitalist nations were impacted by the effects of the recessions of the early 1920s, the 1930s, the early 1980s, and the early 1990s. They all experienced overheated economies as a result of the two world wars and the Vietnam era. But within that general pattern, there has been variation which suggests that despite global forces nations still have some choices. The fact that Sweden and Japan (as well as Switzerland and Austria) were able to maintain full employment through the crisis years of the 1980s suggests that meeting the objective is mostly a matter of political will. If that is so, the failure to achieve full employment in North America must be seen as a social choice.[8]

High unemployment means that many people must live with considerable insecurity. That insecurity is enhanced by our practices at the company level. Standard practice in North American manufacturing during most of the post-World War II period has been to hire people in good times and lay them off in bad. In many other countries, industrial relations institutions have fashioned very high employment security at least for core full-time employees. Several European countries have forbidden large employers to layoff workers without first notifying the government and justifying that action. In addition to legal constraints, social sanctions also mitigate against casual layoffs.

The primary union instrument for achieving employment security in North America is the application of the seniority principle. Most collective agreements provide that layoffs will occur on the basis of reverse seniority. This provides long-service employees with some protection from the ups and downs of the business cycle. On the other hand, seniority is a much less effective barrier against the impact of the major downsizing efforts that have occurred since the Great Recession of the early 1980s. Although the seniority principle is also generally applied by managers of unorganized companies, it is done so at the discretion of management. Employees have no assurance that a fair and unbiased principle will be generally applied should layoffs and dismissals occur.

Employment security is one way to secure the general material quality of life; another is to fashion a social security system that ensures the flow of income if individuals are cut off from employment. All of the liberal democracies have fashioned welfare states in the last half-century, but some have done so more thoroughly than others. Table 6.5 provides some idea of the extent to which this has been accomplished. As noted above, unemployment benefits in North America are very poor in international comparison. So too, are many other aspects of social security. The United States, with Canada not too far behind, is one of the least well-developed welfare states. As a result, both employment and financial insecurity are higher than they are elsewhere (see also Esping-Anderson 1990).

Table 6.5

Expenditures on Social Security as a Percentage of Gross Domestic Product, 1970-1986

	1970	1975	1980	1986
Australia	8.0	10.3	11.4	9.1
Sweden	18.6	25.0	31.9	31.3
Netherlands	18.9	25.5	28.3	28.6
Denmark	14.8	20.2	26.9	26.3
France	15.1	23.9	26.3	28.6
Belgium	18.1	24.0	26.2	26.4
West Germany	17.1	23.7	24.0	23.4
Austria	18.5	20.2	22.5	25.4
Italy	14.1	19.2	18.8	n/a
United Kingdom	13.7	17.1	18.1	20.4
Canada	14.4	13.8	13.6	16.2
United States	9.3	12.8	12.3	12.5
Japan	5.6	8.9	11.2	12.2

Source: The Cost of Social Security, Thirteenth International Inquiry, 1984-1986, Comparative Tables (Geneva, International Labour Office, 1989).

Note: Social security is defined to include medical care, sickness benefit, unemployment benefit, old-age benefit, employment-injury benefit, family benefit, maternity benefit, invalidity benefit, and survivor's benefit.

PRODUCTIVITY AND GROWTH

In the past, we have done very well in becoming two of the richest nations on earth but our relative position (especially that of the United States) has slipped considerably over the past three decades (see table 6.6).[9] Outside of North America, the industrialized market economy countries have increased production per capita by an average of better than 3 percent a year, while the United States has advanced at only 2 percent a year. Canada has been closer to, but still beneath, the foreign norm.

Table 6.6

Real Gross Domestic Product Per Capita

Year-to-Year Percentage Changes

	60-68	68-73	73-79	79-90	60-90
United States	3.1	2.0	1.4	1.6	2.0
Canada	3.6	4.1	2.9	1.8	2.9
United Kingdom	2.4	3.0	1.5	1.9	2.1
Australia	3.0	3.5	1.5	1.6	2.3
France	4.2	4.5	2.3	1.7	2.6
Italy	5.0	3.9	3.2	2.2	3.4
New Zealand	1.4	3.4	-0.2	0.8	1.2
Sweden	3.6	3.1	1.5	1.6	2.4
Germany	3.1	4.1	2.5	1.7	2.6
Japan	9.1	7.1	2.5	3.5	5.3
Austria	3.6	5.4	3.0	2.1	3.2
Netherlands	3.5	3.7	1.9	1.2	2.4
Norway	3.6	3.3	4.4	2.2	3.2
Total OECD less United States	4.4	4.6	2.1	2.1	3.1

Sources: OECD Economic Outlook, Historical Statistics, 1960-1990 (Paris, 1992); OECD Observer (February/March) 1993.

One of the key contributors to this underperformance internationally has been the slower growth of manufacturing productivity in North America (see table 6.7).

Although there are multiple causes for the relatively poor productivity performance of Canada and the United States during the past three decades, it is becoming increasingly clear that the institutions of industrial relations play a

Table 6.7

Manufacturing Productivity

Average Annual Change in Output Per Hour, 1960-1990

Norway	3.3
Sweden	4.0
Netherlands	5.4
Germany	4.0
Japan	6.9
France	4.9
Italy	5.3
United Kingdom	3.7
Canada	2.9
United States	2.9
Median	4.0

Source: Neef and Kask 1991.

critical role in the achievement of high and increasing productivity. We seem to have achieved our current level in spite of, rather than because of, our system of industrial relations adversarialism. Countries which have been able to integrate labor into socioeconomic decision making and develop cooperative labor management relations are now generally able to outperform us.

PRICE STABILITY

We have done moderately well in pursuit of price stability, but only at the cost of high unemployment (see tables 6.4 and 6.8). Other countries have done much better at achieving a more optimal trade off.

Table 6.8

Consumer Prices

Annual Percent Change

	1960-1980	1973-1980	1985-1991
Germany	3.8	4.3	2.1
Belgium	5.5	7.8	2.6
Denmark	7.8	10.6	4.2
Netherlands	6.2	7.0	1.7
Sweden	6.4	10.2	8.4
United States	5.1	8.6	4.7
Canada	5.3	9.1	5.3
Japan	7.7	8.7	1.9
United Kingdom	8.6	15.6	7.3
Median	6.2	8.7	4.2

Sources: Monthly Labor Review December, 1981; OECD in Figures (June/July) 1992.

COOPERATION AND SOCIOECONOMIC PERFORMANCE

One way to classify industrial relations systems is by the extent to which they may be characterized as adversarial or cooperative. In a recent comparative study of the steel industry, Trevor Bain (1992) utilized this approach. He found that both cooperative and adversarial countries were responsive to the needs of the world market. However, in cooperative countries human needs were handled with more care and compassion, and had results that were more beneficial to both the people involved and to the nations concerned. Table 6.9 organizes countries into cooperative and adversarial categories. To be classified as cooperative, a country had to contain structures in which labor was recognized as the appropriate voice for working people, and it had to be highly integrated into political and industrial decision making. In the adversarial countries, labor was either weakly integrated or entirely excluded from participation in the making of socioeconomic decisions critical to the welfare of working people during most if not all of the relevant period.[10] Within table 6.9, a socioeconomic performance index is created which shows the success of the countries in achieving the combination of low unemployment, high economic growth, and low inflation. It also shows the relationship between socioeconomic performance and industrial conflict. As one would expect, the cooperative countries have a much lower incidence of overt industrial conflict than do the adversarial countries. The unequivocal conclusion is that cooperative countries perform much better than adversarial countries. Our adversarial legacy has begun to be a major hindrance in the pursuit of high socioeconomic performance.

CONCLUSIONS

The American choice of business unionism has resulted in labor having relatively little political power. In consequence, U.S. governments have had more license to permit high levels of unemployment. They have also been under less pressure to ensure high social standards across the economy. As a result, job and income insecurity are very high when compared internationally. Until the last few decades, the situation in Canada was the same. However, as the labor movement has become more political in nature, social protection has expanded significantly—but it still has a long way to go to approach standards common in Europe.

The apolitical strategy of focusing squarely on the interests of members rather than workers generally also resulted in a very large part of the North American labor force being left without any form of representation in the making of the regulations determining their daily conduct. In short, pure and simple unionism has resulted in a poorer quality of democracy than has European social unionism.

Table 6.9

Socioeconomic Performance in Cooperative and Adversarial Countries, 1970-1992

	A. Growth[1] (percent)	B. Inflation[2] (percent)	C. Unemployment[3] (percent)	Socioeconomic performance index[4]	Days lost to strikes[5]
Cooperative Countries					
Austria	3.0	4.8	2.6	15.6	5.2
Norway	3.1	7.7	2.7	12.7	65.6
Sweden	1.6	8.1	2.3	11.2	104.1
Netherlands	1.9	4.7	8.1	9.1	22.8
Germany	2.6	3.8	4.6	14.2	32.4
Japan	3.8	5.4	2.1	16.3	39.4
Mean	2.7	5.8	3.7	13.2	44.9
Adversarial Countries					
United States	1.8	6.0	6.6	9.2	205.0
Canada	2.5	6.6	8.2	7.7	571.0
New Zealand	1.0	10.6	3.4	7.0	280.3
Australia	2.0	8.4	5.9	7.7	366.9
United Kingdom	1.8	9.6	6.3	5.9	262.5
Italy	2.9	11.0	8.4	3.5	677.5
France	2.4	7.4	6.8	8.2	97.8
Mean	2.1	8.5	6.5	7.0	351.6

Sources: OECD Economic Outlook, Historical Statistics; OECD Labour Force Statistics; ILO, Yearbook of Labour Statistics.

Notes:
1. Real GDP per capita, average year-to-year percent change.
2. Consumer Price Indices, average annual percentage changes.
3. Average rate of unemployment as a percentage of total labor force.
4. The sum B subtracted from 10 and C subtracted from 10 and A.
5. Working days lost per thousand workers.

Business unionism led to the Wagner Act which perpetuated adversarial industrial relations by establishing a contest between unions and employers for the hearts and minds of employees, and by legitimizing labor exclusion from participation in the making of many strategic decisions. In turn, adversarialism produced a great deal of conflict and little attempt to reach labor-management-government consensus. Conflict and the absence of consensus in the past few decades has resulted in economic performance inferior to the countries that have been able to overcome confrontation in order to establish labor-management-government cooperation in pursuit of socioeconomic excellence.

In the next chapter, I will trace the development of industrial relations in Germany, Japan, and Sweden—three countries highly successful by the socioeconomic criteria identified above. All three are also models of labor-management-government cooperation. However, each of the three had to overcome an adversarial legacy in order to achieve labor-management-government cooperation. One of the three—Sweden—seems to be falling back into an adversarial pattern.

Chapter 7

FROM CONFRONTATION TO COOPERATION: A TALE OF THREE COUNTRIES

Although considerable reference has been made to Germany, Japan, and Sweden in the chapters above, it is useful to bring together the scattered observations into a whole pattern. In this chapter, the most critical aspects of these model systems with respect to the socioeconomic goals noted in the last chapter will be discussed in order to show how the whole pattern in each country fits together.

GERMANY

Germany has been much studied by foreign economists and industrial relations experts because of its enormous success in the post-World War II era (see Adams and Rummel 1977; Fuerstenberg 1993; Helm 1986; Streeck 1984a, 1984b; Thelen 1987, 1991; Berghahn and Karsten 1987; Turner 1991; Jacobi et al. 1992). Despite losing the war, having its economy largely destroyed, and having its territorial integrity compromised, West Germany had established itself as the economic engine of Europe by the 1980s. Germany had attained that high level of economic performance and competitiveness in the context of a substantial societal consensus, very low levels of industrial conflict, and one of the best records in the West for controlling inflation. It also built an extensive social welfare system that ensured cradle to grave security. From the 1950s until the early 1980s, there was near full employment. However, the deep recession/depression of the early 1980s resulted in a major rise in unemployment that persisted throughout the decade. There are a number of key elements in the development of the German system that have come to define the relationships between business, labor, and governments at the national, sectoral, and enterprise/workplace levels.

The Legien-Stinnes Accord

This agreement was signed at the national level just after World War I between the leaders of the major trade union federation and the major employer federation (Slomp 1990; Grebing 1969; Berghahn and Karsten 1987). The employers agreed, under some pressure from government, to recognize the unions as the legitimate representatives of workers, and agreed no longer to attempt to dissuade individual employees from becoming union members. They also agreed to negotiate wages and other conditions of employment with the unions on a multi-employer, industrial basis.

Note that multi-employer bargaining was sought by both labor and management. The unions wanted that format because it allowed them to be of service to the widest range of workers. The employers wanted it because it meant that negotiations would be over basic terms and conditions of employment, and general increases that they expected would allow them to maintain considerable discretion at the enterprise and plant levels.

Codetermination

From early in their history, a key object of German unions was the achievement of industrial democracy as a natural and essential counterpart of political democracy. German employers were, however, adamantly opposed to dealing with unions on a daily basis in the shop. They argued that they needed discretion to make quick decisions free from constraint in order to operate the production process in an efficient and effective manner. They also argued that the unions had a political agenda that, if manifested in the shop, would result in disruption to the production process. The independent unions, argued the employers, had no commitment to the success of the enterprise.

These opposed positions resulted in a compromise. Employers recognized that employees should have a right to representation at the level of the enterprise, and unions recognized that the right to representation should be universal—that is, it should be available to all employees not just to union members. Legislation putting these principles into effect was passed. It required the establishment of works councils elected by all employees in a company, whether union members/supporters or not. These councils were to have legally specified rights and duties. Unions could nominate candidates in works council elections, but one did not have to be a union member to stand for election. The legislation also required that workers have a minority representation on corporate supervisory boards.

Neither the unions nor the employers were entirely happy with this compromise, but it contained positive and negative aspects from both perspectives. Labor leaders feared that the councils might become competitors for the allegiance of employees and thus insisted that the unions retain the exclusive right to negotiate wages, hours, and other basic conditions of work. As noted above, the unions also insisted on the right to nominate candidates for council election, and in fact most of those elected were active trade unionists. Many nonunionists who were elected joined a union subsequently because of the training and consultative services available from the unions.

From the management perspective, being compelled to deal with employee representatives on a day-to-day basis was hard to accept. It was better, however, to deal with local leaders elected by their peers rather than with outsiders. This preference for dealing with insiders rather than outsiders is very widespread among managements in industrialized countries. Indeed, while this debate was occurring in Germany, a dialogue framed in almost exactly the same terms was taking place in the United States. Woodrow Wilson's attempt at reaching a labor-management accord after World War I broke down when the employers refused to recognize the right of independent unions to represent workers' interests (Taft 1964; Dulles and Dubofsky 1984). Many were willing to concede at that time that workers should be able to choose representatives to represent their interests to their employers, but they argued that the appropriate way for that to come about was for employers voluntarily to establish employee representation plans (Derber 1970). The result was the company union movement of the 1920s and 1930s.

In the early 1920s, a deep worldwide recession put an end to the period of labor militancy. The pendulum of power swung back in the direction of business. During the 1920s in Germany, employers seized the initiative and were able to reinstitute their authority and their ability to make unconstrained decisions. Since very little changed inside the firm as a result of the Weimar legislation, many labor spokespersons considered it to be a failure. Although they were supposed to create a form of industrial democracy, the new institutions were not strong enough to prevent many large companies from supporting the rise to power of the Nazi Party (Sturmthal 1944).

During the Nazi era, the entire system was dismantled. However, codetermination was reestablished after the war. Initially, in the coal and steel industry, employees were granted parity representation on supervisory boards. Chairpersons were to be neutral outsiders who would have the power to break voting ties. The labor side of the directing board, in addition, would be able to designate one of the top corporate executives—the one with responsibility for human resources management. Many of these top management positions were filled by trade union activists who previously had experience as works counselors. The labor movement wanted this parity codetermination system extended to the whole of German industry, but management was opposed and indeed attempted, unsuccessfully, to have the system dismantled once normalcy was reestablished (Adams and Rummel 1977; Thelen 1991). Outside of coal and steel, as a result, the government reestablished minority labor representation on directing boards. Employees were to elect one-third of the board members and the top executive corps was to be appointed by the board as a whole.

Labor was not satisfied with the situation and, in the mid-1970s, it succeeded in having the law changed to require near parity in large corporations.

Both employees and stockholders would elect half the supervisory board members, but there would be no neutral chairperson. Instead, the shareholder side would select the chair who, in the event of a tie, would be able to cast a second tie-breaking vote.

Works councils were also reestablished after World War II with powers similar to those of the Weimar Republic. Because the unions were not granted more authority over the councils than they had during the Weimar era, they opposed the Works Constitution Act of 1952. They still were concerned that the councils would become competitors as employee representation agents. However, as a result of diligent organizing efforts, the unions were able to dominate the works councils elections and, by the mid-1960s, the overwhelming majority of councillors were union activists (see Thelen 1991; Markovits 1986).

The Works Constitution Act simply states that "works councils shall be elected in all establishments ('Betriebe') that normally have five or more permanent employees with voting rights, including three who are eligible" (Federal Minister of Labour and Social Affairs 1980, 103). Administratively, however, it is left up to the unions or to the individual employees to set up the councils. As a result, the preponderance of large- and middle-sized firms have councils, but commonly in very small firms the necessary steps have not been taken.

In 1972, the powers of the councils were extended considerably. They now have codecision rights over a wide range of firm level issues such as working hours, wage payment procedures, piece rates, individual employment contracts, occupational health and safety, the implementation of vocational training, job classification, and dismissals both individual and mass. On these issues, no decision may be taken unless the works council agrees (Federal Minister of Labour and Social Affairs 1980). Deadlocks are generally settled by reference to binding arbitration, although impasses requiring arbitration occur only very infrequently. The councils are also entitled to economic information about the plans and prospects of the firm, and they must be consulted before technological or work organization changes may be put in place. But, they do not have codetermination rights with respect to such issues.[1] In addition, they oversee the implementation of collective agreements and statutory requirements and negotiate plant agreements necessary to put them in place. The councils are not permitted to organize strikes. Most active works councillors are also trade unionists. The unions have very extensive research and education facilities to provide councillors with the skills they need in order responsibly and effectively to carry out their statutory duties.

Although this system was initially opposed by both labor and management, there is currently a very strong labor-management consensus that it has worked remarkably well (Wever 1992; Freeman and Rogers 1993). It has allowed change to be introduced without major disruption. Employee representatives (both board members and councillors) have to be informed about tentative plans well in advance of their implementation. The consequences of the change are discussed and means to deal with them are built into implementation plans. Since consensus is sought before implementation, resistance subsequent to the change is kept to a minimum. Moreover, the quality of the decisions taken are considered by many to be better than they otherwise would have been because of the broad base of input. There is general agreement that the requirement to consult and to reach consensus rather than submit disputes to third parties (who might very well hand down inappropriate decisions) has substantially modified managerial style. Traditionally, German culture elicited an authoritarian approach to employment relations. The institutions of codetermination have resulted in a much more collaborative managerial approach. Employee representatives, on the other hand, have been able to become acquainted first hand with the difficult and complex decisions continually facing management. This greater understanding has helped to ensure more cooperation and commitment to decisions taken.

In short, employees have improved their situation because their interests are taken into account when critical enterprise decisions are under discussion, and because there is a genuine effort to reach consensus with respect to those decisions. Employers have also gained because the quality of the decisions has been enhanced and resistance to change has been significantly reduced.

Employers feared that decision making would be slowed down to the point of inefficiency but, in general, that has not happened. For the most part, employee representatives have been willing to defer to managers in areas beyond their expertise. Problems have occurred primarily where managers have failed to produce information necessary to fully evaluate the results of proposed courses of action.

At one time, there were many who believed that codetermination was a fair weather system that would collapse in difficult times. There are no longer many who hold that view because the system has functioned very well even during the turbulent 1980s and early 1990s.

Pattern Bargaining

The Legien-Stinnes Accord encouraged the spread of multi-employer bargaining that had begun to develop in a few industries before World War I. After the Nazi hiatus, the pattern was reestablished. Union-management negotiations take place on a regional/industry basis (e.g., the steel industry in the Saar). Although there is no national framework for bargaining, the system maintains coherence largely because of the effective domination of industrial relations by the labor market parties in the metal working industry (Markovits 1986; Thelen

1991; Jacobi et al. 1992; Soskice 1994). Essentially, key agreements reached between the metalworkers union and its employer association counterpart set a pattern for the rest of the economy.

In practice, German labor accepts the basic principle that wage movements must stay within what is possible as a result of productivity increases and must fully acknowledge the necessity of technological advance. These attitudes are natural for a labor movement that considers itself (and is considered by others) to be the general voice of employee interests in the economy. German unions negotiate not only over the sectoral interests of their own members, but instead represent the interests of working people as a whole. Collective agreements reached between unions and employer associations apply to over 90 percent of the labor force.

This broad bargaining coverage is the result primarily of the fact that most employers belong to an employer association and agreements, in effect, apply to all the relevant employees of all of the employers in the association. Confronted with strong national unions, nonassociated employers stand to lose out (to be whipsawed), and thus usually become members of an association. Associated employers are not legally forbidden to pay enterprise rates above the industry norms and indeed, in times of labor market tightness, many do vary the rates upward. However, the national associations have considerable power to sanction members who deviate too far from established standards, and they are not unwilling to use those powers (Soskice 1994). In addition, there is a procedure (similar to one operative in Quebec) whereby agreements may legally be extended to nonassociated employers. It is used rarely these days because the threat of extension is often enough to encourage all employers to associate. As a result of these dynamics, annual wage increases across the economy generally fall within 1–2 percent of the pattern-setting norm (Soskice 1994).

Only 40 percent of German employees are union members, in part because nonmembers get the advantage of bargaining agreements whether they are members or not. In North American terminology, they are free-riders. The right to join a union is sacrosanct in both law and practice. It would be considered highly unethical for an employer to make any effort to sway the opinion of an employee with respect to union membership. On the other hand, compelling reluctant individuals to be union members is considered equally unacceptable. Most workers join unions because of social pressure exerted by coworkers who understand that unions need support if they are effectively to carry out their functions. Workers also join because unions provide conflict insurance—that is, the union is prepared to intervene to help resolve any individual dispute (van de Vall 1970). German unions, however, are generally poorly organized on the shop floor. As a result, they have a difficult time being able to put the case for union membership to the nonunionist.

Collective bargaining is very highly regulated in Germany. For example, unions may strike and employers lock out only under very specific circumstances. All agreements are written. In the last instance, disputes over the application of collective agreements, as well as rights stemming from statute and individual employment contracts, are settled by reference to labor courts.

Because of this structure, as well as the close (albeit informal) consultation between government policy makers and top business and union leaders, wage movements are usually coordinated with economic policy decisions. There is considerable public debate over economic forecasts and what the economy can afford in terms of wage movements in the context of these forecasts. In addition, the central bank stands ready to raise interests rates should wage bargaining produce outcomes threatening to economic performance (Soskice 1994). Since wage negotiations are typically held once each year, the result is a rational and responsive relationship between wage movements and economic policy (Soskice 1990).

The system also allows for the achievement of broad consensus over emerging policy issues. For example, there is broad agreement in Germany over the advisability of restructuring at the level of the workplace in order to allow for more flexibility and worker commitment to continuous improvement in the quality and quantity of production (Turner 1991; Jacobi et al. 1992).

Training and Education

Most Germans, as well as foreign experts, agree that one of the most critical elements in the success of the German economy is the training and education system.[2] German universities and institutes have very high standards, but the centerpiece of German training is the system of apprenticeship known as the dual system.

At about age fifteen, German youngsters choose to pursue academic education or to enter the apprenticeship system (see Streeck et al. 1987). About half take the apprenticeship route. For the next three years (usually), they work in a firm under the close tutelage of skilled workers and trainers. They also spend the equivalent of a few days a week continuing their academic studies, and they attend technical classes during block release periods or during the evening. At the end of the three years, they take a comprehensive exam and, if successful, are declared prepared to accept difficult technical duties.

Many jobs in Germany can only be carried out by craftsworkers who have completed the requirements of the apprenticeship system (Lane 1989). Not only do young people acquire valuable skills, they also acquire mental habits associated with excellence. The system is governed by a complex process (which has evolved piecemeal) in which labor, government (at both the national and provincial levels), and business all have vital roles.

The federal government is responsible for labor market policy, and thus for labor market training. The states, however, have constitutional responsibility for education, and thus for training that takes place as part of overall education policy. Apprentices spend one or two days a week in state-provided classrooms where they study both technical subjects and cultural subjects such as German, history, and religion.

The in-company training is overseen by the Chamber of Commerce. Before 1969, in-company training was entirely under the control of employers, but now there are government imposed regulations with respect to the content and structure of training. Regulations (as well as practically all aspects of labor market training policy) are established by a federal training agency (BIBB) on which labor, management, the states, and the federal government all have an equal number of seats. Qualifying examinations are set by the Chamber. However, trade unions always have representation on the committees that set the exams. Chamber committees on which trade unionists have representation also approve firms to do training within the dual system. Works councils have joint responsibility with management to oversee the training effort at the level of the firm. The number of training places, as well as the specific content of the daily training schedule, are issues for codetermination. The dual system thus requires quadripartite cooperation.

Another major characteristic of the dual system is the broad consensus over the need for employers to hire trainees during both good and bad economic periods. Apprentices are classified as students, not as workers, although they do receive a small salary—smaller than apprentices in most other advanced countries. This has been a key element in maintaining a broad consensus on the importance of full employment.

JAPAN

During the past two decades, Japan's economy has continually grown at rates superior to those in the West, and the productivity of several of its export industries has surpassed Western levels. Fifteen years ago, Westerners wrote off Japanese production practices as a cultural oddity, but they no longer do so. Instead, all over the West, firms today are avidly attempting to emulate those aspects of Japanese practice that are compatible with Western institutions (see, e.g., Adams 1991a; Johnson 1988; Oliver and Wilkinson 1989; Vogel 1979; Womack et al. 1990).

Not only has the Japanese economy grown dramatically, it has also provided full employment, low inflation, and a great deal of flexibility. Companies have been known to completely change product lines and markets in remarkably short periods of time. There is also a low level of strike activity, although it is higher than the rates prevailing in several European countries.

On the negative side, Japanese workers are said to suffer from considerable stress. They work very long hours (much longer than Westerners), under considerable pressure to produce. As well, the social infrastructure of Japan is relatively underdeveloped by international standards. Until the oil crisis of the 1970s, it was explicit government policy to emphasize investment rather than social consumption. Since then, improvements have been made, but not to the level characteristic of Western Europe or North America.

Japan has put most of its energies into developing certain highly efficient and competitive export industries—and successfully so. On the other hand, domestic industries are not so well developed in terms of efficiency and competitiveness.

While workers in competitive, export industries do have high skills and high wages, the skills are very specific and may or may not be portable. They are acquired through continuous training in specific firms. Many of them may be of value only in that particular firm. This approach is almost the antithesis of that followed in Sweden and Germany where the aim is to direct the movement of skills to those parts of the economy where they are most in demand. Because of lifetime employment and the intense enculturation procedures of Japanese corporations, interfirm labor mobility is very limited (Kuwahara 1990, 1993; Shirai 1983).

Although elements of the Japanese system may be traced back for centuries, the system as we know it today took firm shape only in the 1950s and 1960s. After World War II, the occupying powers encouraged unionization and collective bargaining, in part, as insurance against the potential resurgence of a business-military elite like the one that drew Japan into World War II. By the early 1950s, essentially all major corporations were unionized and engaged in collective bargaining. The unions that emerged were enterprise based. All employees of Toyota, white-collar and blue-collar alike, formed a single Toyota employees union. Even though national organizations of employees in different industries were formed, the center of power remained at the local level (Levine 1958; Gordon 1985, 1990).[3]

In the 1950s, there was a good deal of industrial conflict in Japan (Gordon 1985). The unions wanted the continuance of job security and the egalitarian conditions of work for their members that had been established at the end of World War II. Management wanted back the unfettered right to direct the production effort so as to be able to make the decisions necessary to reestablish the competitiveness of Japanese industry. Many companies were hurt by the strife and more than one enterprise union was busted. However, out of that conflict a general labor-management understanding emerged. As had occurred earlier in Germany, a compromise was reached. Management would agree not to dismiss any core (regular, full-time) employees and it would provide egalitarian conditions of employment (e.g., all employees from the highest paid to the lowest paid would be entitled to participate on the same basis in the enterprise bonus scheme). Cafeterias, washrooms, parking lots, and so on would all be used on an equal basis.

In return, the employees were expected to devote their full capacities to the success of the enterprise. This meant that regular employees would be expected continually to improve their performance and that of their work group. They would be evaluated not only on their work, but also on their attitude and their broader contribution to the performance of the enterprise. This agreement did not result in a formal document. It was, and continues to be, very informal and it varies in detail from company to company. Nevertheless, its basic elements are so well known and deeply ingrained that they very nearly have the force of a constitutional principle.

Once this accord was reached, management set about leading Japanese industry on a quest that eventually resulted in its seriously challenging the dominance of the United States. These organizational techniques characteristic of the Japanese system are discussed below.

Group Work

Instead of dividing up the work to be done into specific jobs, Japanese industrial firms typically assign larger chunks of work to groups. Within each group reside all of the skills necessary to complete all of the tasks required by the production cluster, including maintenance and trouble shooting. Because it is not specialized, the group is very flexible. The total pool of talent within the group may be applied widely. When problems arise, they are quickly diagnosed and addressed without the need to draw on specialists.

From the employee perspective, the work is more interesting than it is in traditional Western firms that closely define jobs and worker responsibilities. Each day or week something new is learned and some new challenge addressed. Instead of the mind-numbing drudgery that traditionally has been characteristic of Western factory work, the worker in the ideal Japanese factory is more likely to experience the exhilaration of a member of a competitive sports team.

Continuous Training

Everyone in the group is supposed to be continuously learning new skills as well as teaching skills to less senior employees. Employees are evaluated on both their learning and teaching performance. In many Japanese firms, new employees spend the first several weeks or even months learning about the history, philosophy, structure, and objectives of the firm. Since core employees are expected to spend a lifetime with the organization, employers do not fear that their investment in training will be lost. Managerial experts consider firms with this kind of culture to have a significant advantage over those that are more static with respect to learning.

Continuous Consultation

Before critical decisions are made, including the strategic ones, a great deal of consultation takes place inside the Japanese firm. The object is to reach an internal consensus. Ideally, no decision is taken unless all of those who will be critically affected by it have a chance to consider and comment upon it. Also, ideally, if anyone (e.g., the union) objects strongly to a proposal, no action is taken until the objection is dealt with. In essence, this understanding provides the union with a veto but it is a veto that is very rarely exercised.

The general policy of the unions is that management should be accorded wide latitude to take decisions in accord with the best interests of the whole enterprise community. Because of this attitude, some Western observers consider Japanese unions to be weak and management-dominated (Lincoln and Kalleberg 1990). That is not the opinion of most Japanese and Western experts, however. While there naturally is considerable variation from firm to firm, nevertheless, in general Japanese unions fight hard for the interests of their members and disagreements, some leading to work stoppages, do occur. The apparent high level of cooperation and amicability seems to be due more to the fact that Japanese management has lived up to its negotiated responsibility to take decisions in the best interests of all concerned, instead of because of the weakness or servility of the unions.

Continuous Improvement

As noted above, all employees are expected to contribute suggestions for improving productivity and quality. Often formal quality control circles are established to approach this in a systematic fashion. The ultimate objective is total perfection and total flexibility. For example, in the building of cars, ideally every car would be defect free and unique (Womack et al. 1990).

As productivity improvements are made some workers naturally become redundant. It is for this reason that workers in many countries fear new initiatives and new technology. Few workers anywhere are willing to participate in a process that is likely to result in their dismissal. In Japan, it is the guarantee of lifetime employment that overcomes this reticence to participate in productivity enhancement. From the management point of view, the insistence by the unions on guaranteed lifetime employment compelled great effort to make full use of every employee's inherent capabilities. Not having the luxury of dismissal, Japanese managers were forced to explore creative human resource solutions in order to be competitive.[4]

This train of developments is not well understood in the West where management theorists often assume that Japanese management independently arrived at the principles of empowerment and commitment that are now sweeping the globe. In fact, those principles were born of necessity as the result of labor-imposed constraints. If unconstrained, Japanese managers probably would have emulated U.S. practice which was regarded as by far the most advanced in the 1950s and 1960s.

Lean Production

Continuous improvement applied over several decades has resulted in very lean production systems. For example, Japanese factories carry very little inventory. The object is for each element in the production process to arrive just in time to be assembled. Lean production also implies, as noted above, that as improvements in production are made, employees are removed from the production process. Operating with a minimal crew compels strict attention by crew members to the process and helps to engender quality and continuous improvement. The process has been likened to lowering a river. As the water level is lowered, impediments to progress become apparent. When they are removed, the river is again lowered, repeating the cycle.[5]

Successful lean production requires employees who are highly competent and highly committed to improving the production process. This commitment is forthcoming in part because of job security, but also because employees know that the financial results of productivity improvement will be equitably shared.

Core-Periphery

Employees are prepared continually to contribute ideas for productive improvement because they know that:

they will not be dismissed as a consequence of more efficient practices; and,

they will participate equitably in the financial consequences of improved competitiveness.

However, it is possible for companies to make and keep such promises in part because of their propensity to hire part-time and limited contract employees to whom such promises are not made. During ups and downs in the economy, this periphery may expand and contract. One problem with the Japanese system is that the benefits provided to core employees are not available to those on the periphery—the majority of whom are women. Nevertheless, full employment in the economy provides reasonable insurance that the income stream, even of these less secure workers, will not be severely interrupted. Indeed, the overall dynamics of the corporate system put pressure on the national government to maintain a full employment policy (Levine and Tyson 1990). Without full employment and export growth, corporations would find it very difficult to fulfill their commitments to the workers, and the corporate systems might very well collapse.

One of the odd things about this set of practices is that as late as the 1970s the Japanese did not think of them as particularly effective (Kuwahara 1990). Japanese management longed to emulate American practice and regretted the constraints under which it felt compelled to operate. It was only in the late 1970s and early 1980s that the dynamics of the system began to be understood. Since then it has been widely emulated around the world. Recent research suggests that firms, in any part of the world, that successfully adopt these practices out compete those who continue to operate under older theories of labor management and production organization (Womack et al. 1990). Indeed, some business experts are convinced that these practices—or some close approximation to them—will become the norm by the twenty-first century. According to this school of thought, firms who do not embrace them will fall by the wayside in the global competitive struggle. In practice, there is a very substantial movement among firms in both North America and Europe to emulate what they consider to be the essential aspects of "leanproduction" (Sengenberger 1993).

Policy Consultation

Although the most innovative Japanese practices have taken place at the firm level, there are additional key elements of the total Japanese system. As in Germany, there is substantial consultation at the national level where efforts are made to reach business, labor, and government consensus.[6]

This process dates from the first oil shock of the early 1970s (Taira and Levine 1985; Kume 1988; Armstrong 1990; Shimada 1992). The shock caused negative growth and concern by all parties for the continued progress of the economy. Government convened a series of tripartite meetings that led to an understanding that has held more or less since then.

Following the oil shock unions pushed for large wage increases in order to track inflation, and base rates increased by nearly 30 percent. Labor agreed to modify its wage demands, but only if government agreed to pursue fiscal and monetary policies that would result in price moderation, full employment, and an expansion of the social budget—among the lowest of the developed countries. Business agreed to continue its commitment to lifetime employment for core employees and to adjustment programs where economic conditions made it impossible to honor that promise. Since then, labor-management consultation with respect to various policy issues such as tax reform, working hours, social security, and employment equity has expanded.

The need for effective labor-management relations is clearly understood in Japan. Business, labor, and government do not want to return to the turmoil of the 1950s. Indeed, that experience has produced a Japanese enterprise model that is very different from those operating in the West. Yasua Kuwahara, a highly respected Japanese professor of industrial relations, has suggested that the Japanese enterprise should not be thought of as a vehicle for the achievement of shareholders interests, but rather as a "business community maintained by labor and management" (1990). Becoming a member of the core of a Japanese corporation is more like becoming a citizen of a country, with all the rights and duties that such a status entails. This is opposed to the Western conception of the employment relationship fundamentally thought of as a calculated market transaction in which employers pay for the subservient willingness of the wage earner to obey managerial instructions.

SWEDEN

Like Germany and Japan, Sweden has received considerable attention from economic and industrial relations policy analysts because of its socioeconomic success. As one writer recently put it, "Sweden's achievements are beyond the dreams of most of the world" (Macoby 1991). In the post-World War II period, and until very recently, Sweden was able simultaneously to achieve most of the socioeconomic objectives adopted across the developed liberal democratic world (Hammarström 1993; Peterson 1985; Kjellberg 1992). Unemployment has been continuously low even in the 1980s when rates moved up to high levels in most industrialized countries. A very high standard of living has been achieved, not only in terms of wages, but also in terms of quality of life. Swedish cities, for example, are generally very clean and safe. Sweden has a world-class economy based largely on the production of high quality, high value-added products that are marketed internationally. A very low level of industrial conflict has been a characteristic of the country since the 1930s. Sweden has one of the most extensive social benefit systems in the world. The services provided are regarded to be of very high quality, but they are also very expensive (Meidner 1992). In the 1980s, tax rates in Sweden were among the highest in the world (Bamber and Whitehouse 1992).

Despite their many accomplishments, the Swedes have had a difficult time controlling inflation. In order to keep their products internationally competitive, they have had to devalue the Swedish currency several times (Kjellberg 1992).

The December Compromise of 1906

In the 1890s and in the first decade of the twentieth century, workers began to unionize in large numbers. The official philosophy of the mainstream of the labor movement was a radical one. Like most labor movements on continental Europe, it wanted to replace capitalism with a more egalitarian socialist political economy. This aroused deep concern in the ranks of the business community and the government. Under pressure from the government of the day, in 1902 business leaders formed a national association—the SAF—and opened up discussions with the major trade union federation, the LO (Johnston 1962; Kjellberg 1992).

The result was the December Compromise. In essence, the employers agreed to recognize the LO and its constituent unions as the legitimate voice for both their membership and workers in general. They agreed that they no longer would attempt to dissuade their employees from becoming union members. Employers also proposed negotiations with the unions on a multi-employer (industry) basis over wages, hours, and other basic conditions of employment. In turn, the employers insisted that the LO and its constituent unions agree to recognize the right of employers to hire, fire, and direct work as they saw fit in order to organize production in the most efficient and effective manner. From the trade union perspective, the agreement was less than perfect. The unions acquired general legitimacy. No longer would they have to fight for the right to exist and play a constructive role in society. They also acquired a method (multi-employer bargaining) to be of value to large numbers of working people.

Legislation in the 1920s and 1930s

In the 1920s and 1930s, legislation required that collective agreements last for a specific period of time and contain a peace obligation. According to this obligation, unions could not go out on strike during the term of a collective agreement if a dispute arose with respect to issues in the collective agreement. Unlike North America, however, they could legally strike if an impasse was reached over issues not included in the agreement. This system assumed continuous negotiations over new issues as they arose.

As a counterpart to the union's right to strike, the employers were accorded the right to lockout, and that tactic was used often in the early decades of the twentieth century. A labor court was established to settle disputes over the interpretation of collective agreements and other legal and contractual conditions of employment (Johnston 1962).

Since employers did not feel obliged to recognize and negotiate with white-collar unions under the December Compromise, those unions lobbied government to pass a law requiring management to recognize and bargain with them. That law was passed in the mid-1930s. It requires employers, individually or through their association, to meet with and discuss issues in dispute with any legitimately constituted union (Adams 1974). Unlike North America, there is no majority representation principle.

Originally, employers were opposed to the passage of this law, but after it became an established fact they quickly adjusted to it. By the 1950s, the large majority of white-collar employees were covered by multi-employer collective agreements. Among those involved in bargaining were people such as middle-level managers, technicians, and professionals—employees often considered beyond collective bargaining elsewhere.

Today, almost everyone in Sweden is covered by a collective agreement—including about 70–80 percent of white-collar workers in private industry. In addition, unlike Germany, almost all of those covered by collective agreements also belong to trade unions; although, like Germany, mandatory union membership is all but nonexistent.[7] The difference is due to the fact that the Swedes, unlike the Germans, have developed strong shop-floor union networks, and thus are able easily to approach the nonunionist (Adams 1981; Kjellberg 1992). Moreover, the unions have secured the agreement of employers to permit union organizing on company premises and in the context of processing in new employees (Adams 1975a, 1975b). The unions also manage the unemployment insurance system. Instead of a national, state operated scheme, the Swedish government subsidizes (and regulates) union-operated plans.[8] One does not have to be a union member to access the system, but one does have to go to a union office to fill out the paperwork (Kjellberg 1992).

The Saltsjöbaden Agreement

Despite the mutual recognition embodied in the December Compromise, Sweden witnessed much overt conflict during the first three decades of the twentieth century. Recognition provided a means for channelling conflict, but it had not put an end to confrontation. From the mid-1920s, successive governments attempted to find a solution to the high levels of economic disruption. In the 1930s, a government commission recommended that unless the unions and the employers could find a way to resolve their disputes without continual resort to conflict (that was hurting not only the economy as a whole but also third parties who had no direct interest in the dispute), new restrictive legislation would be introduced.

Neither labor nor business wanted to see new legislation. To avoid that development they held a series of meetings that eventually produced a national conflict prevention scheme. It was named after the seaside resort near Stockholm where most of the meetings were held—Saltsjöbaden. Even more importantly, it produced an informal business-labor consensus to work together in the best interests of the economy as a whole and to respect the interests of each other. Subsequent to the Saltsjöbaden Agreement, Sweden had one of the lowest rates of overt industrial conflict in the world. In the past decade, however, conflict has again been on the increase.

Centralization of Bargaining

During World War II, even though Sweden was not a combatant, it went on a war footing. One result was pressure towards centralization of wage setting. After the war, bargaining returned temporarily to the industry level. However, in the 1950s what might be called articulated bargaining developed.

In essence, bargaining took place at several levels. Periodically (usually every one or two years), a national level agreement on labor costs would be worked out. The deal would then be articulated at the industry level and then at the local (company, plant, workshop, and even, in the case of white-collar employees in the private sector, at the individual) level (Forsebäck 1980; Kjellberg 1992). There was general agreement that wage movements should be closely correlated to the productive capacity of the economy. To a large extent, national bargaining became an exercise in which consensus was sought over how much the economy could afford in the coming period. Even more so than in Germany, this structure and process allowed for the achievement of national agreement on the direction of economic policy and on the relationship between government administered fiscal and monetary policies and wage movements.

The Rehn-Meidner Model

Gösta Rehn and Rudolf Meidner were economists employed by the LO who set about developing a policy framework for the labor movement in the years after World War II (Meidner 1992). The main elements included:

A System of Solidarity Wages. Under this system, workers doing equivalent jobs (e.g., tool and die maker) should be paid the same whatever the economic situation of the employer. Employers who could not pay the requisite wages should not be subsidized with substandard conditions but should instead free up capital to be invested more profitably and efficiently elsewhere; and,

Unions should not oppose the introduction of new technology but should instead actively advocate its adoption. The successful pursuit of these two objects would necessarily result in people being laid off thereby threatening the union objective of stable employment and income. This problem would be solved by using active labor-market policy. Laid-off workers would be guaranteed significant retraining and assistance in finding alternative work. In addition, the government would pursue fiscal and monetary policies resulting in full employment.

There would be very little public ownership of productive organizations, but a fairly dense network of statutes and collective agreements would be put in place to ensure that business would conduct itself in a manner deemed to be in the public interest.

There would also be a highly developed welfare state to provide economic and social security on a universal basis from cradle to grave. To win the support of the middle class, it would have to be of very high quality and thus would have to be expensive (Meidner 1992).

As well, a network of agencies directed by representatives from labor and business (and other constituencies as relevant) would be created to manage the various aspects of social policy. For example, there would be a Labor Market Board that would have the responsibility for managing the active labor market policy. The unemployment insurance system would be administered by the trade unions.

While this plan was proposed by the unions, it had considerable appeal for employers. It meant that:

Wages would be standardized and therefore be taken out of domestic competition;

General wage movements would be largely predictable (Contrary to expectations, however, they tended to drift upward between wage rounds. See Flanagan et al. 1983).

Technological innovation would be vigorously pursued with little concern for resistance to change;

Profitable companies would have a high level of retained earnings available for reinvestment.

Because it had considerable advantages, not only for labor and business, but also for government and the citizenry as a whole, this scheme won very broad support. It functioned remarkably well for about three decades during which Sweden attracted international acclaim for its middle way.

Contemporary Sweden

While these key elements of the Swedish system contributed to growth, stability, and equity for most of the post-World War II period, the system ran into trouble from about the middle to late 1970s, and is currently in the midst of a crisis (Ahlén 1989; Rehn and Viklund 1990; Martin 1987; Kjellberg 1992). Several key factors seem to have caused problems for the operation of the system.

Despite the December Compromise, unions continually attempted to achieve influence over the organization and management of the production process. By the 1950s, the unions had been successful in establishing local organizations responsible for overseeing and implementing collective agreements at the firm level, and for working with management jointly to develop policy with respect to specific issues. For example, national collective agreements had been signed during the 1940s calling for the joint regulation of health and safety and training (Johnston 1962). After World War II, LO and SAF negotiated an agreement calling for the establishment of works councils that would receive information on the economic status of the firm and would jointly seek ways of achieving greater productivity.

Despite progress in expanding joint regulations at the enterprise level the unions were not satisfied. The SAF continued to insist that the clause giving management the right to hire, fire, and direct work be included in every collective agreement. In the 1970s, the unions abandoned bargaining over the issue and were successful, working with the government, to push through a law requiring employers to negotiate about all issues of concern to workers. This law did away with the reserved right to hire, fire, and organize work. It specified that management could no longer insist that the clause be included in collective agreements. All corporate issues were negotiable.

Employers considered this broad ranging act to be a betrayal of the spirit of the understanding, going back to the December Compromise, that they had the function of organizing and directing production. It also went against the implicit understanding under the Saltsjöbaden Agreement that labor and management should solve their problems without resorting to government intervention. On the other hand, trade unions felt compelled to seek legislation on these issues because negotiation had not produced acceptable results (Kjellberg 1992).

Business also opposed the development of more detailed agreements at the central level (Myrdal 1991). Initially, central bargaining led to agreement on the percentage increase in the employer wage bill for the ensuing period. This frame agreement would be further articulated at the industrial and local levels. Thus, it seemingly provided both for national coordination of economic and wage policy and for sectoral and local flexibility. As bargaining rounds progressed, however, the LO began to press for special increases at the national level for women and low-paid workers. Thus, the central agreement became more complex. All employers in the SAF were required to put into effect a national formula.

In addition, the LO bargained successfully for decreasing differentials between higher-paid and lower-paid employees. It resulted in a more equal distribution of income, but it also made it more difficult for employers to reward exceptional performance. It was these types of constraints to which employers were increasingly unwilling to be bound.

From its perspective, labor felt that, despite considerable achievements on behalf of workers, industrial democracy had not yet been achieved. As a result, the LO proposed in the mid-1970s (in addition to enhanced worker rights in the firm), the establishment of a wage earner fund. In essence, it was proposed that companies with excess profits should pay a percentage of those profits into a fund that would be controlled by worker representatives. Since payments would be made in shares rather than in cash, capital would remain with firms and not be available for consumption.

While similar schemes designed to generate investment capital are relatively uncontroversial, the Swedish plan led to a great furor in the business community because it would pay no dividends and would not distribute its earnings or trade its shares. In short, whatever entered the fund would not leave. As a result, in the long run the fund would inevitably own the entire Swedish economy (Myrdal 1981).

Employers considered this proposal to be an act of bad faith and were able to delay its introduction. A much watered down version of the scheme was finally initiated, but with a time limit that expired in 1990 (Pontusson and Kuruvilla 1992).

The Swedish system was also seen to be increasingly problematic from the perspective of white-collar workers, particularly government employees. Until the 1980s, these employees generally deferred to the initiatives of the blue-collar federation. An economic strategy worked out by the chief economists of the blue-collar federation, the LO; the major white-collar federation, the TCO; and the employer federation, the SAF, specified that the wage agreements worked out in the internationally exposed goods sector should set the pace for the economy. This meant that white-collar and especially government workers were wage takers and that public sector incomes would not easily be able to react appropriately to changes in the market (Martin 1987). In the 1980s, public sector workers became increasingly less willing to accept these constraints. As a result, internecine conflict between unions increased.

The solidarity wages scheme also became problematic. It implied not only equal pay for equal work, but also the gradual narrowing of wage differentials. This meant that workers with strong bargaining power had to agree voluntarily to accept wages and benefits below what their market power could achieve so that weaker groups might improve their situation. Over time, that forbearance became increasingly troublesome to maintain. In 1983, when the Engineering Industry Employer's Association sought negotiations separate from the national framework, the Metalworkers Union was not too difficult to convince.

In 1991, a conservative government dedicated to the construction of institutionally unconstrained markets replaced the Social Democrats, and in January 1992 employers affiliated with the SAF withdrew from all bipartite and tripartite corporatist agencies. As a result, the future for labor-management cooperation in Sweden looks very bleak.

LESSONS FROM THE EXPERIENCE OF THE THREE COUNTRIES

We are living in an area of rapid globalization. The world is truly becoming a global village. If it was ever warranted to ignore what was happening elsewhere, that is no longer a serious option. Socioeconomic success in the twenty-first century is likely to go to those who carefully study and learn from their major competitors.

The experience of the countries discussed here suggests that the separate interests of labor and management, under liberal democracy, cannot be simultaneously maximized. If one of the parties achieves all that it desires, then the other one is likely to oppose it vigorously resulting in instability and conflict. In turn, instability and conflict are negative influences on economic and social performance. To optimize socioeconomic goals, compromise has been necessary.

In Sweden, Germany, and Japan, agreements that in retrospect had very positive effects were initially entered into only grudgingly. For example, in the December Compromise in Sweden, management conceded the right of workers to join or form unions without fear of reprisal or intimidation, and the right of unions to bargain on behalf of workers generally. These were concessions that many individual employers felt to be improper given the long tradition in which employers had maintained a unilateral right to operate their enterprises as they saw fit. In return, the SAF was able to secure union agreement that management had the right to organize and manage the production process without continual interference. Unions that previously had been considered only quasi legitimate won respect and recognition. They also acquired a method (collective bargaining) to be of real and immediate value to workers. The German Legien-Stinnes Accord had similar qualities.

As a consequence of the Swedish Saltsjöbaden Agreement of the 1930s, individual employers gave up a considerable amount of enterprise autonomy to industry associations and to the national employer federation in return for an expectation (later borne out by experience) of stable, uninterrupted production. Local and national unions also gave up a substantial amount of autonomy to the LO.

In Japan, management from the 1960s gave up (de facto) its right to dismiss core employees, and it agreed to an egalitarian system of remuneration. In a nation characterized by authoritarian rule and ruthless repression of opposition, it is remarkable that this standard should have been achieved and maintained. In retrospect, it certainly has paid dividends.

Another example is the milieu surrounding the advent of works councils in Germany. The unions were afraid that the councils would act as a competitive institution and thus were opposed to them. The employers considered the councils (and the placement of worker representatives on boards of directors) to be a violation of their historic rights to be "master in their own house." But unions considered the councils to be preferable to no employee representation within the firm, and employers saw the formation of statutory councils elected by all enterprise employees as preferable to dealing daily with militant local unions infused with ideological fervor.

The experience of these countries also suggests that agreements once reached cannot be considered safely done. Agreements have to be worked out continually and fundamental understandings must be respected or the overall structure can collapse. Sweden provides a good example of a case in which understandings disintegrated because they were not continually renewed. The collapse of the U.S. post-World War II accord is another example.

The experience reviewed here indicates that it is possible for labor, management, and the state to reach accord over a wide variety of issues and under a wide variety of circumstances. Agreement has been reached on ways to deal with inflation, job security and full employment, union recognition for the purposes of collective bargaining and the broader representation of worker interests, wage movements, training, technological change, and more (see, e.g., Muthuchidambaram 1986). Agreement has been reached under both governments of the left (Sweden in 1938) and governments of the right (Japan in 1973).

There may be cultural constraints on the achievement of such agreements, but the experience reviewed here suggests that the primary constraint is the unwillingness of one party or the other to compromise in order to achieve a solution superior to continual conflict. Indeed the international experience suggests that institutional accord can be a powerful factor in overcoming deeply ingrained cultural traits. Codetermination has clearly helped to modify German managerial style from authoritarian to something more akin to humanitarian, without, it should be noted, altering its capacity for efficiency and effectiveness. The broad understandings reached in Sweden in the 1930s and Japan in the 1960s also helped to bring about significant changes in what must have seemed to contemporary observers to be sharply etched cultural proclivities. During the first three decades of the twentieth century, the Swedes, for example, were among the most quarrelsome of peoples, but by the 1970s the world was acclaiming their propensity to find mutually acceptable solutions to difficult socioeconomic problems. In short, attitudes and behavior embraced for decades or even centuries can be changed. The evidence reviewed here suggests that human societies are quite malleable.

The multinational experience also suggests that the relationship between regulation and competitiveness is far from simple. In the United States and Canada, companies operating under collective bargaining are as economically viable as those operating with no collective agreement. In Japan, Germany, and Sweden, companies function under a variety of constraints that, in total, are at least as considerable if not more so than those operative in much less successful economies. No doubt, some forms of constraint hinder management in its pursuit of its duty to lead the enterprise in the most efficient and effective manner. However, the regulatory institutions developed in these countries have, not only not hindered business, but they have been a positive force for competitiveness. They have compelled management to conduct the business in a manner conducive not only to the best interests of the shareholders, but also in the interests of working people and of society as a whole. The lesson would seem to be that the form of regulation is more relevant to socioeconomic performance than the amount of regulation.[9]

In Germany, the necessity of building employee concerns into strategic plans (rather than addressing reaction to such plans) resulted in enormous restructuring with a minimum of disruption. In Japan, the challenge of being competitive without being able to dismiss or layoff employees led to creative solutions that are now being widely emulated in the West. In Sweden, the inability of less profitable firms to be subsidized by below market wages contributed to a dynamic economy in which the most vital and competitive companies were encouraged and rewarded.

The experience of these countries clearly indicates that institutions make a difference. Governments may have the primary responsibility in liberal democratic society to deliver both economic and social performance to the citizenry. However, without effective labor-management institutions, they are unlikely effectively to live up to their responsibilities.

Combined with the broader data presented in chapter 6, these cases are strongly supportive of the proposition that concertation, based on mutual recognition and acceptance of the validity of the interests of all three actors, is highly superior to confrontation. Adversarialism is a loser's game; social partnership is the way of champions.

Chapter 8

TRANSCENDING ADVERSARIAL INDUSTRIAL RELATIONS

HOW WE GOT THIS WAY: A THEORY

The analysis presented in the first three chapters of this book suggests a theory regarding the development of industrial relations systems in Europe and North America. The most fundamental proposition in the theory is that the broad characteristics of the industrial relations systems in place today in Europe and North America may be traced back to labor's choice of ideology (and the strategy associated with it) which took shape between about 1880 and 1920.

Prior to the middle of the nineteenth century, the labor movements in Europe and North America developed in very similar ways. As far as industrial relations go, America in 1880 was not all that unique or exceptional. With the collapse of medieval institutions, local, craftbased unions began to appear. They were strongly opposed both by employers and by governments. Despite that opposition, they survived and in the second half of the nineteenth century they began to unite into national unions and national federations. Whereas the activity of the early unions was nostalgic in that many of the symbols and traditions of the medieval guilds were emulated and pragmatic in that it was not informed by any clear ideology, in the second half of the nineteenth century labor movements began to think self-consciously about their nature and purpose. It was in this period that the paths of European and American movements went in different directions.

European Developments

On continental Europe, the mainstream of the labor movements in all of the major nations adopted a philosophy which called for the establishment of a new socioeconomic system. Even though the rhetoric of these movements was often more radical than their actual behavior, nevertheless, they attracted a wide following and frightened the parties in power into compromising with them. Governments addressed many of labor's grievances by taking the first steps towards today's welfare states. Employers and governments both extended recognition to union federations as legitimate agencies to speak for the interests of working people as a whole. On granting that general recognition, employers insisted that their rights to manage (and thus their legitimacy to direct modern industry) be honored in return. Specifically, they agreed to bargain over wages, hours, and other basic conditions of work but insisted on the maintenance of control within the enterprise. In particular, the employers refused to bargain with ideological local unions who, they were sure, had no commitment to the welfare of the enterprise. This strategy was most clearly in evidence in Scandinavia and thus might be called the Scandinavian strategy. It was not, however, limited to Scandinavia, but may also be seen in broad outline in many European countries.

In Germany and Austria, the strong employer defense of managerial rights at the level of the enterprise led to a compromise. Instead of local unions, worker interests inside the enterprise would be looked after by councils with a statutory mandate to represent all enterprise employees. The councils were also required by statute to be concerned with the prospects of the enterprise. The German solution was later emulated by several other European countries, either through legislation or through national bargaining.

The Scandinavian strategy led to the institutionalization of multi-employer bargaining. In the middle of the nineteenth century, what bargaining there was in Continental Europe was mostly local and ad hoc. By the 1930s, it was mostly multi-employer and regularized. Negotiations took place at regular intervals over a mutually acceptable range of issues centered on wages and hours of work. Multi-employer bargaining appealed both to employers who wanted to minimize union influence at the level of the shop and to socialist unions who wanted to raise the overall standards of the working class.

The socialist government, which came to power in Germany towards the end of World War I, also instituted the concept of worker representatives on corporate boards of directors over the muted objections of a weakened business class. The Nazis did away with that innovation, but after the demise of that regime it was reinstituted. The German experiment was watched closely by other European countries and, in the 1960s and 1970s, was widely adopted throughout Europe in a weaker form.

The basic agreements which led to the recognition of the legitimacy of the labor movement meant that employers would no longer attempt to dissuade individual employees from becoming union members. In return, however, they insisted that they must have the ability to select the most capable employees regardless of their affiliation (or not) with trade unions. They also insisted that no employee should be compelled to be a union member against his/her wishes and that argument was generally accepted by the unions. As a result, today in continental Europe, the decision to join or not to join a union generally may be made freely without fear of retribution. The other side of the coin is that mandatory union membership is rare and in several countries it is illegal. Another result is that union membership is widespread across the work force, but it is fairly unusual to find situations were everyone is a member. Another consequence is that more people are covered by collective agreements than are union members.

Mutual recognition by central organizations of employers and trade unions also meant that discussions at the national level of major socioeconomic policies became feasible. Such discussions, often with the government as a formal or informal party, had already begun to occur in some countries before World War II, but the practice became especially common in the inflationary 1960s and 1970s. Since then, formal political bargaining has waned in some countries, but has continued strongly in others. The basic principle of engaging in social dialogue with a view towards the achievement of consensus over a broad range of issues, however, has been widely and firmly established in Europe (Soskice 1990; Treu 1992).

The United States

The American trajectory was much different from the European one after 1880. Several ideologies struggled for dominance and, as in Europe, leftist movements appeared. Union membership and militancy increased and a socialist political party attracted a growing number of adherents. This left-militant form of labor ideology and strategy was, however, strongly challenged by a more politically conservative movement. Business unionism competed with and defeated both radical and reform socialism to achieve dominance in the mainstream of the American labor movement.

The implicit choice by the U.S. movement of business unionism set in motion a train of events that produced the exceptional industrial relations system that exists today. Although aroused to some concern by the swell of leftist militancy, American employers were not sufficiently alarmed to overcome their natural propensity to individualism and competitiveness—a propensity common to employers everywhere (Windmuller and Gladstone 1984). As a result, contrary to developments on continental Europe, they generally did not form associations nor a national federation; they did not reach a national recognition agreement with the labor movement in the first decades of the twentieth century. Some business leaders decided to work with the conservative unions to fight radical tendencies; some (the same people usually) also counselled employers to recognize and deal with the pure and simple unions in order to weaken any attraction that individual workers might have to radicalism. For the most part, however, that counsel was ignored. Instead of welcoming labor leaders who affirmed the principles of capitalism, individual companies, by and large, did all they could to keep the unions out.

This American strategy of fighting unions on a company-by-company, plant-by-plant, basis was generally successful. By the mid-1930s, less than 15 percent of the American labor force was represented by trade unions. Where they were compelled by threat of disruption to grant local recognition, American employer strategy was almost identical to that in Europe. The object became to retain as much control as possible. Towards that end, employers negotiated for written agreements containing management's rights clauses that gave them the right unilaterally to decide any issue not included in the collective agreement.

Despite opposition, where they were strong American unions were able to develop shop steward organizations at the level of production to oversee the application of the collective agreement. In many cases, those organizations were able to place significant constraints on managerial discretion at the shop floor. Also, by judiciously using the strike threat, American unions were able, little by little, to expand collective agreements to a point where organized employers in the 1980s would be complaining bitterly about constraints on their ability to manage effectively.

From the employer perspective, the American strategy carried a higher risk and promised a greater reward than the Scandinavian strategy. In the United States, where the union "got in," it likely would have a more significant impact on the organization and direction of work than would the typical European union. On the other hand, in the United States, employers maintained good prospects of remaining entirely free from labor interference in the operation of the enterprise. This aspect of the American strategy prolonged and exacerbated the adversarial attitudes common everywhere during most of the nineteenth century. Since American employers stood to lose more control over the production process as a result of unionization than did their European counterparts, they had a stronger motivation to avoid it.

In the nineteenth and the first part of the twentieth century, U.S. governments did not have to worry nearly as much as their continental European counterparts about the potential of the labor movement to bring about radical change. The left-radical movement was small. The primary means chosen to deal with it was suppression rather than compromise, and by the 1920s it had been all but destroyed.

In the 1930s, however, the labor movement began to stir once again. The apparent failure of capitalism during the Great Depression gave new hope to left movements. Unions began to form among the unskilled and semiskilled workers in the mass-production industries. From the outset, these unions were more politically oriented than had been their craft union predecessors. They fully supported active government intervention in the economy and the New Deal administration, experimented to find ways out of the depression, and passed a considerable amount of social and labor legislation.

A keystone piece of New Deal legislation was the Wagner Act which, formally, was designed to encourage collective bargaining. Employers were supposed to recognize and deal with unions freely chosen by their employees. Intransigent employers would be compelled to negotiate. This legislation is generally credited with stimulating union growth and the spread of collective bargaining, but from the perspective of the 1990s that interpretation looks doubtful (Adams 1993b). Unions did grow and collective bargaining did spread, and no doubt the firm support given to those developments by the government was helpful. The law itself was, however, a two-edged sword. While it provided the unions with a way to bring intransigent employers to the bargaining table, it also provided unorganized employers with a means and a justification for keeping the union out. Unionization and collective bargaining was depicted as the resort of dissatisfied malcontents. A battle was entered into for the hearts and minds of the unorganized.

Because of the victory of the theory that unionization was only necessary where management failed to do right willingly, instead of stimulating labor-management cooperation, the Wagner Act had the opposite effect. It further embedded adversarialism. Not wanting to be branded as having failed, staying unorganized became a managerial priority. Unions came to be considered not as social partners, as they were defined in Europe, but instead as a kind of punishment for managerial sins.

Even though coercion and intimidation of potential unionists was forbidden, unorganized employers argued successfully that they had a right to state their views (almost universally negative) about unions and collective bargaining. Not wanting to anger their employers, and not necessarily dissatisfied with their substantive conditions, many unorganized employees decided—contrary to the formal policy of the government—to forego the steps necessary to establish a collective bargaining regime. The Wagner Act gave unorganized employers the right to refuse to recognize and meet with any union that failed to win the support of more than 50 percent of the relevant employees (Adams 1994). Even if it clearly represented a substantial number of employees, the law permitted the employer to refuse to grant it any status whatsoever. This aspect of the law focused the attention of the unions on certification. They made little effort to attempt to represent the interests of minority groups of employees because of the almost certain opposition of employers.[1] As a result, the American labor force split into two parts laboring under two very different industrial relations regimes. In Europe, basic agreements produced unitary systems of industrial relations with the result that basic conditions of employment are fairly evenly spread across the economy.

In the unorganized and unrepresented sphere in the United States, the employees could negotiate perhaps their starting salary and a few other individual conditions of employment, but for the most part they were on the receiving end of rules formulated unilaterally by their employers. Market forces, of course, did constrain managerial decision making but, in most cases, those forces were sufficiently weak to allow management considerable discretion. Contrary to standards generally in place across the liberal democratic world, the unorganized in the United States were provided with no objective mechanism for the settlement of disputes over the interpretation or implementation of the rules of work; they could be fired at any time for any or no reason. The conditions under which they worked could be radically changed at any time without their consent or participation.

Very few people working for unorganized employers were union members because there was little or nothing the unions could or would do for them. In organized enterprises, however, union density was very high, in part because U.S. law and practice tolerated mandatory union membership. It did so on the theory that since the certified union was legally required to represent the interests of all bargaining unit employees, it was not unreasonable that it should be supported by all of those who received the benefit of the negotiated conditions. It seems indisputable that this stipulation infringes the globally accepted principle of freedom of association, but it is one of the many unfortunate natural side effects of the Wagner-Act model.

From the point of view of American management, certification came to be thought of as a humiliation, but not a total disaster. Because of the weight of public opinion and government policy, large, unionized employers reached an informal understanding with the unions after World War II to bargain fairly with them over basic terms and conditions of employment. Unions, however, would be expected to recognize management's reserved right unilaterally to make the decisions necessary to operate the enterprise in an effective manner. Management's rights clauses in collective agreements made the business side of the deal operative. As a result, the industrial relations practices which emerged under the terms of the post-World War II accord prompted management not to seek cooperation with labor over the broad range of issues of mutual concern to shareholders and employees alike, but instead to limit labor's influence to as small a range of issues as possible. By and large, the U.S. courts accepted and supported this employer structuring of the situation (see Summers 1990b).

By providing for bargaining rights on a plant-by-plant basis, the act practically ensured that strong multi-employer organizations would not emerge. Decentralization was perpetuated, thereby precluding the evolution of the institutions essential for social partnership. Instead of a national employer organization similar to those which emerged in most European countries, a number of specific associations were formed, but the great majority of them addressed a broad range of business issues (Derber 1984). Few of these organizations had as their major function negotiations with labor representatives. When, from time to time, national forums were established for the purpose of encouraging policy consensus, businesspeople and labor leaders were appointed as individuals rather than as agents of larger organizations designed to aggregate interests. They could not effectively commit their organizations to action on any point of consensus that might emerge. As a result, these exercises had little impact (see, e.g., Shuster 1990).

In the 1980s and 1990s, even the mild American Labor-Management Accord went by the wayside. Organized labor's influence on conservative Republican Party governments was minimal and those governments did nothing to dissuade organized employers from violating the spirit of the Wagner Act by actively attempting to escape from the confines of collective bargaining. Those governments also looked the other way when unorganized employers blatantly broke the law by making it clearly known that adverse consequences would be the lot of any employee who took the initiative to establish collective bargaining. Because of its continuing legacy of business unionism with its self-centered motto of "more, more, more," the labor movement attracted little public sympathy for its worsening plight.

Britain and Canada

Britain and Canada form a kind of bridge between continental Europe and the United States. In the 1870s, the British labor movement was as pure and simple as the movement in the United States. Indeed the strategies and the philosophies that motivated the British new model unionists and the U.S. craft unionists were essentially identical. Many U.S. unions looked to their British counterparts for inspiration and guidance. From the 1890s on, however, Britain moved in the direction of the continental norm. The unskilled and semiskilled workers who organized en masse in the 1890s were more political by nature than were the skilled craftsworkers. At the turn of the century, political problems arose that called for political strategies. The result was the formation of the Labour Party by the trade unions. Initially the party was more pragmatic than ideological, but by the 1920s it had firmly embraced the philosophy of reform socialism.

Between the 1880s and the 1950s, the Canadian labor movement was pulled between the magnets of Europe and the United States—between socialism and business unionism. In the end, reform socialism won out when in 1960 a firm link was established between the New Democratic Party (a political party that fits neatly into the mold of social democratic parties throughout Europe) and the Canadian Congress of Labor.

Other aspects of industrial relations followed these ideological choices. In Britain, from the 1930s until the advent of the Thatcher regime in 1979, an unbroken succession of British governments of both the left and right recognized the legitimacy of the trade unions to speak for the interests of working people and pressured private sector employers to do the same. As a result, by the mid-1970s over 70 percent of the British labor force was covered by collective agreements (ILO 1985). When the era of corporatism hit Europe in the 1960s and 1970s, Britain was drawn along. Indeed the British social contract of the 1970s is one of the clearest examples of political bargaining that one may find.

On the other hand, there was no formal, national basic agreement in Britain, and as a result there was more leeway for interpretation of the existing informal understanding. In this milieu, employer opposition to unions and collective bargaining has been more in evidence than it has been in many continental European countries. Also, contrary to the common situation on the continent, British unions have traditionally sought to establish mandatory union membership, and until recently British law has tolerated it. In the 1980s, Britain took an unexpected turn when the highly ideological Thatcher regime rejected the policy of labor-management conciliation and actively sought to weaken and exclude the unions (Crouch 1990). The permanency of this turn and its long-range consequences are still to be determined.

Developments in Canada followed a direction influenced by both the United States and Britain. It began as pragmatic, was dominated by pure and simple philosophy during the first part of the twentieth century, but moved left when large numbers of unskilled and semiskilled workers in the mass-production industries organized from the 1930s onward. By the 1960s, the mainstream had embraced reform socialism. Since the adoption of a strong principled political stance by the labor movement, and the relative success of social democratic parties at both the federal level and in several provinces, Canadian governments have found it necessary to negotiate with labor representatives. As a result, both federal and provincial governments have generally recognized the right of their own employees to engage in collective bargaining and have insisted that private sector employers act in accordance with the letter of the Wagner-Act model laws that all Canadian provinces adopted. There also have been more attempts to reach tripartite consensus in Canada than in the United States. But those efforts have borne considerably less fruit than have similar efforts in the more consensual European countries (Waldie 1986). As in the United States, the Wagner-Act model framework continues to elicit confrontation and conflict making the achievement of cooperation difficult.

Japan

Japan developed late and does not fit as neatly within the conceptual framework developed above. There are, however, some continuities that one may identify. Prior to World War II, Japanese developments were not all that dissimilar to nineteenth century developments in the West. In essence, governments and employers suppressed labor movements, especially those that embraced leftist creeds. As a result, the unions were compelled to focus most of their energies on survival. After World War II, however, the occupying forces dominated by the United States decided to encourage collective bargaining as a democratizing force. The result was a great growth in unionism and labor-management negotiation over conditions of work. However, contrary to the wishes of the occupying powers, the mainstream labor movement adopted a radical socialist philosophy which by the late 1940s threatened the operation of government.

As a result, government policy turned against the encouragement of unionism and joint regulation. For civil servants, bargaining was outlawed. In the private sector, employers attempted to win back control that they had lost. The consequence was a series of struggles which by the mid-1970s had produced an implicit basic agreement with some aspects similar to the accords found in Europe, and others like the U.S. understandings that held sway in the decades after World War II. As in Europe, employers agreed to recognize and bargain with unions, but (as in the U.S.) only where they had already become established. The existence of a Wagner-Act model labor policy framework, imposed by the occupying powers in the 1940s, limited the coverage of collective bargaining and worked against the emergence of a strong and confident labor movement capable of making positive contributions to the public welfare. Nevertheless, in the midst of the economic turmoil wrought by the first oil crisis of the 1970s, the government reached out to the unions and to employers in an effort to achieve national consensus on the appropriate strategy for dealing with the disaster. Tripartite socioeconomic cooperation has slowly increased since that time (Kume 1988; Sugeno 1993).

The Japanese Accord had special features not found in the West. Unlike the Scandinavian and American strategies, the strategy of Japanese management was to agree to the union demand for lifetime employment, egalitarian conditions of work, and a commitment to operate the enterprise in the best interests not only of the shareholders but also of the employees in return for agreement by the employees to put their full physical and intellectual capacities behind the efforts of the enterprise to compete. That accord has produced a tremendous explosion of innovation and productivity.

CONSEQUENCES

The industrial relations systems that we have in place in Europe, North America, and Japan today are not the result of uncontrollable forces of nature. Nor are they the result of immutable cultural propensities. They certainly have been shaped by history and culture, but more than anything they are the result of choices made by labor, management, and governments. The choices have had significant political and economic consequences.

The economic success of the United States is uncontestable, but there is little reason to believe that the institutions of industrial relations have contributed to that success. The United States has been successful economically in spite of, rather than because of, its industrial relations practices. In the past, adversarial industrial relations did not severely restrict the implementation of the Taylorist system of production organization. While that system of production was dominant, the United States could succeed despite labor-management confrontation and despite the potential squandered by a human resource system that created compliant wage slaves whose primary function was to obey rather than to think.[2] It is very unlikely that the same level of economic performance will be sustained in the future under the new principles of production and high involvement human resource management that are replacing outmoded forms of work organization. Labor-management cooperation seems to be an essential ingredient for the successful operation of the new systems of industrial production.

At the macroeconomic level, also, the evidence seems to be clear that, at this point in history, countries that are able to achieve labor-management-government consensus rather than continual confrontation are the ones that are likely to be the most successful economically. Articulated cooperation produces an economic synergy that is absent in confrontational societies.

Industrial relations also has significant political implications. Under liberal democracy working people are also citizens. They have a fundamental right to participate in the making of decisions that critically effect their interests.[3] Few decisions are more critical than those made in the context of employment, and thus for democracy to be complete, citizens must have the means to participate in the making of the rules of work. Through some combination of collective bargaining, works councils, and worker representation on corporate boards of directors most continental European countries have constructed institutions that honor that essential necessity. Countries under the Wagner-Act model, however, do not honor it. In the United States, the large majority of working people have no means to participate in the making of most of the critical rules under which they work. Politically, their situation is closely analogous to that of the common people under the authoritarian regimes of predemocratic eighteenth-century Europe. They are being subject to regulation without representation. The Canadian situation is only marginally better.

THE ROAD FROM ADVERSARIAL TO
COOPERATIVE INDUSTRIAL RELATIONS

Adversarialism is not in the economic interests of any society. Confrontational industrial relations systems are a drag on economic performance. Thus, it is in the clear economic interests of any nation to pursue policies designed to elicit consensus. Neither is adversarialism as it exhibits itself in North America consistent with the basic principles of democracy. It results in the majority of citizens being excluded from participation in the making of rules critical to their welfare. North American industrial relations are exceptional in the degree to which they are confrontational and exclusionist, and that exceptionalism is to our economic and political disadvantage.

How may we move from a confrontational, exclusionist system to a consensual, inclusive system? The experience reviewed here suggests that the burden of achieving change most likely must be shouldered primarily by government. Labor unions have rarely been strong enough to bring about fundamental socioeconomic change on their own. Neither does the story told here suggest that it is in their interests to take the initiative to cooperate. The willingness of the American labor movement to accept the basic principles of capitalism in return for recognition by business of its legitimacy to negotiate over terms and conditions of employment has not been successful. Instead of general recognition, American labor's acceptance has been met, for the most part, by contempt and exclusion. On the other hand, the challenge posed by European labor to the viability of capitalism was the catalyst that led to its acceptance and recognition by business. In North America, also, as Canadian unions have become more demanding, business has been more willing to deal with them on an equitable basis.

Neither is business likely to take the initiative to establish a productive, cooperative relationship. Even though the overall result of moving from confrontation to consensus is likely to be in the best interests of business, arriving at that state requires surrendering some control, learning new modes of interaction, and facing a period of uncertainty. The historical and comparative record suggests that in its dealings with labor, business is often not a good judge of its true long-term interests. Few business leaders anywhere have ever been willing without pressure to relinquish control; few have been willing with equanimity to accept uncertainty. On the other hand, once compelled to share power and decision making, employers often have been content with the results and, after the change, have been willing to accept and defend social concertation.

Two aspects of North American labor policy, in particular, stimulate adversarial behavior and thus are prime enemies of social partnership—certification and management's rights. In order to move from confrontation to cooperation, both need to be discarded.

Certification seemed like a good idea when it was first embraced in the 1930s, and if it had materialized as envisioned it might have been a useful policy instrument. It has, however, evolved into a force that stimulates confrontation and perpetuates labor exclusion. As elaborated above, by requiring unorganized employees to take the initiative to certify it ensures that a large number of workers will be without representation if for no other reason than the nuisance of exerting the effort to change the nature of the employment relationship (Adams 1992a, 1992b, 1994). It also supports the theory that unorganized is the natural state to be disturbed only if there is some difficulty with it—a theory diametrically opposed to the proposition that all citizens of a democratic society must have the means to influence the making of decisions critical to their interests. By requiring employees to take the initiative to establish participative decision making, and by supporting the theory that unorganized is the natural state, certification grants legitimacy to employer efforts to avoid employee participation and sets up a situation in which to become unionized is to fail as an effective manager of human resources. Thus, a spiral of labor-management confrontation is perpetuated.

What might be proposed in the place of certification? The international experience offers an extensive menu of policy choices. Statutory works councils might be legislated in order to provide workers universally with a say in the making of critical employment decisions. The concept already exists in Canada with respect to health and safety, and it has been recommended by various commissions and task forces for use as a means to bring about the codetermination of many issues considered to be critical to labor and management alike (Adams 1986). There is extensive experience with the concept in Europe, and all of it suggests that properly designed councils could play a constructive role in North American society (Sturmthal 1964; Summers 1979; Rogers and Streeck 1994). For a council strategy to be successful it would have to include an effective impasse resolution method such as binding arbitration. Without such a mechanism, councils might be manipulated to perpetuate unilateral managerial control at the enterprise level, thus continuing labor exclusion behind a false veil of participation.[4]

There is no limit to the range of issues that could be placed within the mandate of the statutory works councils. They might be given a limited mandate to look at specific issues such as health and safety, the implementation of legislated labor standards, the introduction of new technology, and enterprise training policy. Alternatively, they could be used as a replacement for enterprise level collective bargaining. Because of union objections, no nation has adopted the later strategy. Instead, typically union-management bargaining is designated as the appropriate method for the establishment of wages, hours, and other basic conditions of employment, while the councils are used to address specific issues that might not be dealt with effectively and universally via collective bargaining. Although I have always accepted the latter logic, perhaps it is time to look carefully at the total replacement strategy. Such a policy would leave no doubt about the commitment of the state to the democratic imperative of providing employees universally with a say over the most critical of their employment conditions.

Assuming that the European selected issues approach was adopted, then the problem of how to ensure labor inclusion with respect to wages and hours would still remain. The French government in the 1980s mandated collective bargaining on an annual basis over wages and hours and on a five-year basis over the wage system (Goetschy and Jobert 1993). Instead of finding ways to avoid collective bargaining, the French approach required employers to take the initiative to open negotiations with unions. The result was a great increase in the practice of collective bargaining.

Observers of the French note that although the number of collective agreements greatly expanded as a result of this legislation, union membership fell significantly in the same period. If we were to pass legislation based on the French example, should we expect similar results? Very probably not. North American unions are much better organized internally than French unions. In France the unions have historically considered their primary function to be agitation for change, rather than engaging in hard technical bargaining and contract administration. As a result, North American unions would be much better placed to take advantage of French-like legislation than were the French unions.

Management's rights is the other North American doctrine that perpetuates adversarialism. It incites management to focus on the exclusion of labor from decision making rather than on the achievement of consensus. Technically, it would be a simple matter to introduce legislation requiring that all industrial decision making must be available for discussion and potentially codecision. Such legislation would put an end not only to management's rights clauses in collective agreements, but also to the legal distinction in the United States between mandatory and permissive issues of negotiation under which strikes may not be undertaken in pursuit of certain strategic issues. The experience of European countries as well as Japan suggests that employee representatives would for the most part defer to managerial judgement on matters of strategic importance to the firm. However, in order to avoid future disputes, management would be compelled to explain the logic of the proposed courses of action. The result would be more trust and more commitment to decisions taken. Instead of suspicious resistance to change, employees, knowing that their interests were being represented with respect to the full range of employment relevant issues, could be expected to more easily accept and support needed changes. That certainly has been the experience of Germany, Japan, and Sweden.

A critically important initiative supportive of the objective of improved labor-management trust would be the granting of seats on corporate boards of directors to worker representatives.[5] There is broad experience in Europe with this mechanism. In no case has it been seriously detrimental to corporate performance. Instead, there is considerable evidence of positive competitive consequences. It would ensure workers that their interests were being represented at the highest levels. Moreover, German experience suggests that worker input at the high corporate policy level would improve the quality of the decisions taken. Often worker representatives have a perspective that typical directors are lacking.

Even if fully successful in stimulating universal collective bargaining, bargaining policy modelled on the recent French initiative would perpetuate decentralized negotiations insensitive to the public interest. The parties to negotiations would have no reason to concern themselves with the cumulative impact of their decisions. To bring about bargaining more responsive to the needs of society as a whole, additional initiatives would be required. The Japanese system suggests a way in which decentralized bargaining may be molded into a vehicle more sensitive to the economic environment (Soskice 1990). In Japan, wage agreements typically last for only one year. Each spring they are renegotiated. Although each enterprise union and each company is responsible for arriving at its own deal, on both the union and employer side bargaining is coordinated. Moreover negotiations take place in public. In the bargaining season, negotiations are front-page news. The result is that the parties may not ignore the overall impact of their actions. Economic forecasts and the impact of a given wage increase on inflation, exchange rates, and other economic indicators is part of the grist of bargaining. More economically responsive and responsible agreements are the result.

Although wage increases vary from company to company, the band of variation is narrow. In its economic effect, Japanese bargaining is not that much different than the centralized bargaining that took place in Sweden for several decades or the multi-employer pattern bargaining that is characteristic of Germany. A vast body of research carried out during the past few decades suggests that this pattern of coordinated wage regulation is much superior to the fragmented system that we have in place at present (Soskice 1990, 1994; Pekkarinen et al. 1992; Crouch 1993).

It would not be that difficult to emulate the Japanese experience in North America. Although there would have to be exceptions, a federal law in the United States (and similar laws at the provincial and federal levels in Canada) specifying that the wage clauses in all collective agreements expire at a certain date each year would go a long way towards initiating a Japanese-like system of responsible wage bargaining.[6]

Labor could also be more thoroughly included in the making and administration of the policies in the province of the many government or quasi governmental agencies. The Swedes with their Labor Market Board and the Germans with their quadripartite approach to training are models worth investigating. This is one area in which Canadian practice is further advanced than American. The blatantly partisan appointments made to the National Labor Relations Board in the United States have added significantly to confrontation and exclusionism, whereas the tripartite nature of the Canadian boards helped to foster a belief in the potential efficacy of labor-management cooperation.

With all of these steps, there would still be a need for the establishment of a forum or fora at the national and provincial/state level to deal with policy issues of tripartite relevance. The Dutch Social Economic Council is one model worthy of consideration. In that country, all draft legislation of relevance to labor and management is submitted to the council for its comments (Windmuller 1969; Visser 1992b). Often the legislation is altered to take labor and business views into consideration. If the representatives on the council are able to come up with a consensus position, the government is prone to make that position law. As a result, both labor and management have a strong input into critical policy decisions and, once a piece of legislation is in place, they are committed to make it work.

Other systems for labor-management consultation (such as those in Germany and Japan) are much less formal. The key ingredient seems to be that the parties are consulted about issues critical to their interests and there is a concerted attempt to achieve consensus before any action is taken. Being on the inside and acquiring experience that their interests are not treated cavalierly, labor and management become more willing to commit themselves to positions that in confrontational circumstances both would automatically oppose.

A major problem with the establishment of national and provincial/state fora for the achievement of policy consensus is the absence, especially on the business side, of organizations capable of effectively aggregating interests and committing constituents to decisions taken (Wilson 1982; Adams 1982). If universal labor representation were achieved, this organizational problem likely would disappear. There would be little reason for business not to form national and state/provincial organizations designed to deal with employment issues and positive reasons for them to do so. If government made it clear that it would be pleased regularly to meet with authoritative labor and business organizations in order to attempt the achievement of policy consensus, it would be in the interests of business to organize in order to participate.

Business organization in many countries has been stimulated by government initiatives (Wilson 1982). The formation of national employer organizations at the turn of the twentieth century was in part the result of pressure exerted on employers by governments to come to grips with the labor challenge. The Confederation of British Industry came into being in the 1960s in order to allow British business to deal effectively with an increasingly interventionist government (Palmer 1983, 58). In the decades after World War II, British governments imposed wage and price controls several times, thus removing wage setting from the control of individual employers or even of industrial employer associations. Increasing intervention in the economy by the U.S. government was the major cause for the establishment of the U.S. Business Roundtable— an organization of chief executive officers of top U.S. companies (Wilson 1982). Wage and price controls brought forth a similar organization in Canada in 1976 (Adams 1982).

A comprehensive strategy, consistent with the above discussion, might have the following elements:

1. Mandatory recognition by management of any employee-appointed representative and mandatory bargaining with a view toward achieving mutually acceptable positions on all issues of joint concern.
2. Establishment of statutory works councils with the objectives of:
   a. Ensuring the effective implementation of all relevant social and labor legislation.
   b. Codetermining specified aspects of work critical to employee welfare such as training, technological change, and health and safety.
   c. Cooperating with management to improve the efficiency and competitiveness of the enterprise with special emphasis on the development of a high security, high commitment labor process.
3. Employer initiated annual wage bargaining to be commenced on a specified date each year with either a local union or with a committee to be elected by the relevant employees.
4. Several seats on corporate boards to be set aside for employee-elected representatives.
5. The appointment of labor and management representatives (and representatives of other groups as appropriate) to the controlling boards of all agencies responsible for social and labor market issues.
6. A public commitment by government to seek tripartite consensus on all issues critical to the interests of labor and management.

REALITY AND THE OUTLOOK FOR CHANGE

The steps outlined above are all technically feasible. None of them would lead to institutions radically different from ones that have been tried and have been proven to be effective in achieving better political and economic performance in countries that are very similar to Canada and the United States in terms of their socioeconomic and political characteristics. Their adoption would merely bring us in line with normal practice in the contemporary liberal democratic world. I have been told, however, that such propositions are unrealistic. Our history and our institutions compel us to consider only marginal change—

change that would almost certainly have very little effect. Maybe we can liber-
alize the labor laws to some extent; maybe we can encourage labor-management cooperation by offering financial incentives for that behavior, but major
change cannot be achieved and thus is unworthy of discussion. That position is,
it seems to me, defeatist. Culture and history are being used as excuses for
muddling along with the discredited status quo.

The events in East and Central Europe during the past decade illustrate that
social institutions once considered to be immutable can change fundamentally
in a short period of time. We are not insects helplessly enmeshed in a web
created by our history and institutions. We are capable human beings responsible for our actions. If we do not change, we are likely to continue our relative
economic decline. We are also likely to rot in hell for continuing to sin so
egregiously against principles of democracy that we hold to be basic to our
way of life.

NOTES

Preface

1. These projects are regularly reviewed in *Comparative Industrial Relations Newsletter,* an informal publication that I began to distribute in 1990.

Chapter 1:
The Emergence of Modern Industrial Relations

1. Owned is placed in quotes because ownership did not have the same meaning then as it does today. The rights and duties accruing to ownership have changed over time and continue to change today. (See especially Abrahamsson 1980.)

2. The Statute of Artificers (1563) required agricultural workers between ages of twelve and sixty to remain on the land and not enter another occupation. Those with no fixed employment could be conscripted by justices of the peace during the harvest. Unmarried persons or those under thirty years should not leave their calling (Duby 1968).

3. Note that there were village councils and that the villagers were often quite independent to work out their own affairs. Disputes between villagers were in the last resort settled by judges appointed by the lord. Later in the middle ages, in Britain especially, judges appointed by the king could settle disputes between lord and villagers. At least some of the time the judges found in favor of the villagers (see Coulton 1925; Ault 1952; Duby 1968).

4. "Journeyman," as used throughout this volume, should be understood as referring to a skilled worker of either sex.

5. The reasons for the appearance of trade unions has drawn a good deal of inquiry over the years. Sydney and Beatrice Webb, writing in the 1890s, proposed that the essential condition for the appearance of unions was the emergence of a large class of wage earners who had little realistic possibility of owning and controlling their own enterprise. Given this condition, several theorists have suggested that the insecurity brought about by the demise of medieval regulations was a key factor. Unions were an attempt to re-regulate labor markets and conditions so as to recreate some security in employment. One theorist, Frank Tannenbaum (1951), has proposed that in at least some cases, unions were a means to reestablish the sense of community that was destroyed when strangers congregated in the growing urban areas.

6. Thanks to Ron Bean for bringing this observation to my attention.

7. The Chartist movement reached its peak in the 1830s and 1840s but faded away in recessionary times. A similar movement, known as the Thraneite movement, occurred

at about the same time in Norway (see Lafferty 1971), but it too was shortlived and accomplished little.

8. Prior to the passage of the Combination Acts, some forty laws had been passed outlawing combinations in particular industries (Leeson 1979).

9. Cordwainer is an archaic term for shoemaker.

10. For a somewhat different framework see Sturmthal 1972.

11. Ironically, the scenario put forth by the syndicalists did come to pass almost precisely. It did not lead to the downfall of capitalism, however, instead the regimes that collapsed when society no longer continued to accept their authority were the communist governments of Eastern and Central Europe.

12. This variant of unionism was first identified and studied by Robert Hoxie (1917, 45–46).

Chapter 2:
The European Mainstream

1. The works council already had a history in Germany before World War I. It was first suggested in 1848 and an 1891 law required that it be established in factories with more than twenty workers. The early statutory councils had only consultative power and were generally regarded to be ineffective. Councils were often supported by employers as a means to avoid having to deal with independent unions. (See Taft 1952; Sturmthal 1964; Havlovic 1990). Teuteberg (1961) has written a history of the councils in German.

2. The first basic agreement between central organizations of labor and business was signed in Denmark and thus the Danes should be given credit as the initial source of the Scandinavian strategy (see, e.g., Galenson 1952; Due, Madsen, and Jensen 1993). Swedish developments are related here, however, because subsequently they became more widely known and because they very clearly illustrate a nearly ideal version of the strategy. It is also true that there was an industry-wide labor-management agreement in the British engineering industry in the late 1880s that had many of the characteristics of the Scandinavian strategy and may have influenced subsequent developments in Scandinavia, but those links require additional investigation (see, e.g., Crouch 1993).

3. For an interesting British case study which reaches the same conclusion, see Bean (1976).

4. The term "outsider," used to refer to independent unions, was also part of the rhetoric of American employers at this time. (See Adams 1994.)

5. The term "pure and simple" unionism is generally used as a synonym for business unionism.

6. In some countries, trade associations for dealing with competition, tax, tariffs, and other matters were formed before the unions had posed a serious challenge. In such cases, they were generally utilized to meet the union threat. Over time, in many continental countries, two organizations—one for social (e.g., labor) matters and one for economic affairs—were set up. One object of the dual organizational strategy was, as Windmuller (1984, 3) notes, to make it "easier for employers to confine their joint dealings with unions to the area administered by the 'social' (that is, labor relations) associa-

tions and to prevent matters of economic policy from becoming subjects of bargaining or joint consultation." Over the long run, this strategy was less than maximally effective as labor organizations in many countries gained substantial influence over both social and economic policy. Today, where there are two central organizations, companies generally belong to both of them and policy commonly is coordinated. Unlike labor organizations, central business organizations rarely represent widely divergent views.

7. In Germany, the main central union organization, the DGB, officially decided to remain neutral after World War II in order to encourage labor unity. However, most of its key leaders were strong supporters of social democracy and thus many people considered the organization to be socialist.

8. The major exception is Denmark. (See Scheuer 1992.)

Chapter 3:
American Exceptionalism

1. The scenario in the United States is very similar to developments in Britain in several trades about a century earlier. Journeymen's clubs were among the major bulwarks defending guild rules against the rising tide of capitalist production. They were equally unsuccessful. (See Leeson 1979.)

2. In several European countries, instead of setting up national compulsory unemployment insurance, the governments provided subsidies to union-operated schemes (Gordon 1988). These schemes provided an incentive to membership, and over time had a significant positive impact on union density (Visser 1990). There seems to be little evidence, however, that the AFL wanted to take on such a general function in the United States.

3. In the last national elections before the outbreak of World War I, mainstream socialist parties attracted the following percent of votes cast: Austria 25.4 percent, Denmark 29.6 percent, Finland 43.1 percent, France 16.8 percent, Germany 34.8 percent, Italy, 17.6 percent, Netherlands 18.5 percent, Norway 26.3 percent, Sweden 31.1 percent, Switzerland 10.1 percent, and United Kingdom 6.4 percent. Figures reported in Hanagan 1984.

4. Job-conscious unionism is another synonym for business unionism.

5. Union membership increased from under a half million in 1897 to about five million in 1920. (See Derber 1970, 173.)

6. There has been a significant growth of revisionist historical writing in the last few decades that argues against the Perlman thesis. Sean Wilentz (1984), for example, argues that American workers were as class conscious as European workers, but that socialism and syndicalism (e.g., the IWW) were more ruthlessly suppressed in the United States than they had been in Europe.

7. According to Chamberlain and Kuhn (1965, 44), "It has been estimated that in 1932 only about 10 to 12 percent of industrial workers were employed under collective agreements; from 7 to 8 percent came under employee-representation plans; and approximately 80 percent of all industrial workers were employed under individual contracts."

8. Although the passage of the Wagner Act added force to a generally pro-union and collective bargaining environment, it is not as clear as generally proposed that the enforcement powers of the NLRB played a significant role in encouraging union growth. Even though no agency with powers similar to those of the NLRB existed in Canada, union membership expanded during this period at a similar rate. (See Adams 1993b.)

9. Late in 1993, the Ontario Federation of Labor, the provincial arm of the CLC, withdrew its support of the provincial NDP because of unilateral public sector wage-cutting by the provincial NDP government in the face of a very large and increasing budget deficit. The public and private sector unions were deeply split over the issue.

10. In their study of employer associations in liberal democratic countries, Windmuller and Gladstone (1984) found that these organizations were "for the most part committed to the support of classic liberalist ideas"—the central tenets of which were "an abiding belief in the vital force of the basic ideas: free enterprise, private ownership, competitive markets, and individual initiative." Commonly these organizations direct "some of their sharpest attacks against perceived impediments to the free enterprise system: government intervention, nationalization, regulated markets, and collectivism" (6).

Chapter 4:
Contemporary Collective Bargaining

1. This typology was first put forth by Kerr and Siegel (1955) and later developed by Dunlop (1958 1993).

2. The Canadian industrial relations system is somewhat more articulated. There are, for example, mandatory health and safety committees in several jurisdictions that must be established in both unionized and nonunionized companies. In recent years, also, several bipartite union-management agencies have been created to allow for labor-management cooperation at the industry level. At the national level a Canadian Labor Market and Productivity Center (CLMPC) has been in existence since the early 1980s. Both the industry committees and the CLMPC are bipartite but backed by government funding.

3. Paul Malles (1973) stated the issue this way: "once the individual in his relations to the State changed from being a 'subject' to a 'citizen', demands for economic or industrial democracy began to be seen as a corollary to political democracy" (162). Malles quotes a "social-liberal member of the German parliament in 1910" as saying: "The basic question is: how can the monarchically organized industry be permeated with parliamentary institutions? This question which has occupied us for ten to twenty years is really the old liberal question applied to the organization of enterprise" (162).

4. For a particularly vivid and unrestrained use of this imagery, see Farber and Krueger 1993.

5. My first attempt at sketching this notion was in Adams 1986.

6. There has been considerable controversy over the impact of employer campaigns. For a review of studies, see Lawler 1990.

7. For other versions of this argument, see Adams 1990, 1992a, 1992b.

8. Secrecy is considered to be necessary because, as in the United States, when a Canadian private sector employer finds that a campaign to establish collective representation is underway, he/she almost always takes steps to counter it. In Canada, however, employer opposition is more commonly within the law than is the case in the United States.

9. Two examples will illustrate this pattern. In the late 1970s, there was a very nasty, protracted strike over compulsory union membership. To forestall similar strikes in the future, the conservative government passed a law saying that the union was entitled to receive financial support from all employees in a bargaining unit whether or not they were union members. This action effectively ended mandatory membership strikes. In the early 1980s, a Toronto firm hired a spy to infiltrate a union on strike and to report back the strategy of the union. When this was discovered, a law was quickly passed outlawing such practices (see, e.g., Meltz 1985).

10. The public sector labor force is more thoroughly involved in collective bargaining in most countries than the private sector. Public sector coverage rates in Europe are commonly 80–95 percent; in Canada, public sector coverage is about 70–75 percent; in the United States it is about 40–45 percent. For data on Canada and the United States see Kumar 1993 and Riddell 1993.

11. In the 1970s, a labour government attempted to put a procedure in place that was somewhat like that in the United States. If a union had substantial (but not necessarily majority) support and the employer would not negotiate with it in good faith, it could take issues in dispute to arbitration for binding judgement. Margaret Thatcher's government did away with that system after she was elected in the late 1970s.

12. To the best of my knowledge, the term "articulated bargaining" was first used to refer to developments in the bargaining structure of Italy during the 1960s (see Guigni 1965).

13. There are no definitive statistics on either union density or bargaining coverage. Union membership is recorded by trade unions and collected by various governmental and private agencies. However, some unions have retired, unemployed, and self-employed individuals as members and others do not. Moreover, it is known that for political reasons some unions report more (or fewer) members than they actually have. As a result, it is necessary to estimate membership. The most concerted effort to take account of these sources of variation is Visser 1992. As a result of various exclusions, he reports density levels that are lower than those generally believed to prevail.

14. Unassociated employers are, for the most part, of two types. Some very large companies, whose bargaining power is equivalent to that the unions, prefer to bargain tailor-made agreements. Very small employers, on the other hand, with special circumstances remain independent in hopes either of avoiding the attention of the unions altogether or of persuading the unions to take their special situation into account.

15. *NLRB v. Wooster Division of Borg-Warner Corporation,* 356 U.S. 342 (1958).

16. For evidence in support of this proposition in Canada, see Adams 1986.

17. For some North American workers, notably those is the arts (musicians, actors) the contract establishes only minimum terms from which the individual may negotiate upward.

18. In the early 1980s, the arbitration system was dismantled in New Zealand based on the theory that a deregulated market would produce greater efficiency. For the same reason, the system was under pressure in Australia. (See Harbridge 1993.)

19. If the strikebreaker quits the job and the job continues, the striker is supposed to be given the first opportunity to fill the position.

20. In some jurisdictions, only those that break new ground are published.

21. Some of these issues are less settled in Canada than in the United States. For example, if the collective agreement is silent on disciplinary process, the duty of the employer to conduct an equitable investigation is not firmly established. (See e.g., Brown and Beatty 1988.)

22. As a result of crisis bargaining in the 1980s, some American unions were offered board seats in return for concessions considered by management to be critical to enterprise survival. In the airline industry, the auto industry, and a few others union leaders accepted these offers. On the other hand, few North American unions have made the acquisition of board seats a priority union goal. The United Steelworkers of America is a notable exception.

Chapter 5:
The Organized and the Unorganized

1. Union membership estimates vary considerably because there are no standardized collection methods. Unions and federations have their own methods of accounting for membership and the resulting data are collected by various public and private sources. Some unions count retired, unemployed, and self-employed individuals as members and others do not. Some unions keep good records and others do not. Some over or under report the actual membership for their own reasons. The Chang and Sorrentino data are consistent over the period and consistent with many other reports, and thus are suitable for my purpose here—that is to illustrate the scope of variation and change over recent decades. Visser (1992) has attempted to adjust data to remove the sources of unwanted variation. His density estimates are lower than those of Chang and Sorrentino, and below those more generally reported. For 1989, Visser's estimates are as follows: United Kingdom 39, United States 15, Canada 30, Australia 45, Japan 26, Denmark 76, France 10, Germany 32, Italy 34, Netherlands 24, Sweden 81, and Switzerland 28.

2. Absenteeism is a big problem in Sweden. (See, e.g., Kennedy 1980.)

3. A good review of the debates about union growth in that era is included in Ginsburg 1971.

4. Statistical research in the United States has found a correlation between lagged proportion of potential members unionized and union growth, and this has been interpreted as support for the saturation hypothesis (Stepina and Fiorito 1986). It is also consistent with a theory that the particular U.S. institutional configuration has the result of making it increasingly difficult for unions to recruit the next potential member on the margin. Although plausible in the abstract when placed in comparative perspective, the saturation hypothesis is doubtful. Since there are other plausible explanations for the statistical association, a more adequate theory needs to be sought.

5. It would be more accurate to say that they have made little effort to make use of the capacity that the law gives them to be of service where certification has not been achieved. In recent years, some American law scholars have been urging unions to make use of provisions of the American National Labor Relations Act which permits them to act for noncertified employees. (See, e.g., Summers 1990a, 1992.)

6. Although debate continues over the propriety of stipulations requiring workers to be union members as a condition of employment, there is a justification in North America that does not exist in most other countries. Under the Wagner-Act model, certified unions are required to represent all employees in the bargaining unit whether or not they are union members. As a result, it is argued that they should receive support from all of those whom they represent. In essence, in Europe the right of association is a right possessed by individuals whereas in North America the institutional system makes it a right that can only be made fully effective by the action of groups.

7. Although the statement is generally true, three Canadian jurisdictions—federal, Quebec, and Nova Scotia—have instituted laws making it illegal to dismiss unorganized employees for reasons other than just cause and allowing adjudicators the right to reinstitute wrongfully discharged employees. Whereas under collective bargaining reinstatement is the standard remedy, in the three jurisdictions with unjust dismissal provisions the victim may be awarded either reinstatement or a financial settlement—the latter remedy has been used a great deal. For a brief review, see Adams, Adell, and Wheeler 1990.

8. In turn, the greater political involvement of Canadian labor may be the result of social values different from those in the United States, but that proposition is very abstract and speculative. The argument has been made by Seymour Martin Lipset (1986).

9. Under these conditions, membership may also go down during periods of full employment when fear of job loss is very low. (See, e.g., Kjellberg 1992.)

Chapter 6:
Industrial Relations and Socioeconomic Performance

1. A severe recession hit both Canada and the United States in 1990 and, as generally happens, strike incidence decreased. During recessions there is not much to be gained by striking. This normal cyclical variation is largely irrelevant to the discussion in this section. On the other hand, if conflict remains at very low levels after economic activity picks up, that will be data in need of explanation.

2. Despite this exclusionary policy at the company level, during the past fifteen years, a few institutions for labor-management cooperation have appeared at the industry and national level. The most notable organizations are the Canadian Labor Market and Productivity Center and the Canadian Steel Trades and Employment Congress. On the sectoral initiatives, see CLMPC 1991.

3. Although this is the dominant historical outlook of union activists in France, there is of course variation from pure and simple to very radical. (See, e.g., Meyers 1981.)

4. In Canada, some business leaders do participate with top union leaders in attempts to reach accord with respect to some issues at the national and sectoral level (see CLMPC 1992; Waldie 1986). On the other hand employers in both British Columbia and Ontario vehemently resisted the passage of mild labor law reform bills in the early 1990s.

5. The comparison is also problematic technically. As Clarke (1990) points out, "in the case of sickness absence, a fairly small proportion of workers are normally absent at any one time and their colleagues try to ensure that all essential work is carried out. The net effect on production is usually small. In the case of a strike, every effort is made by the strikers to ensure that the cessation of work is complete" (183–84).

6. In 1993, the United States and Canada did better than the OECD average outside of North America largely because the economic cycle in Europe and North America was somewhat out of synchronization. In 1991, the economies of the United States and Canada shrunk while those of most European countries were continuing to expand. By 1992, however, the German, Italian, and Swedish economies had begun to contract and those of other countries slowed significantly. By 1993, the United States and Canada were expanding at a much faster rate than were the economies of Europe. One result of this development was that unemployment rates outside of North America uncharacteristically moved to levels higher than those in the United States. Whether this is a permanent change or a temporary abberation is yet to be established. (See "OECD Economic Outlook—Highlights," *OECD Observer,* February/March, 1993.)

7. A recent study by Card and Riddell (1993) puts empirical flesh on this theoretical skeleton. They compared unemployment rates in Canada and the United States over the past several decades. Until the early 1970s, rates in the two countries were about the same. From that point in time, however, they have diverged significantly and now the Canadian rate is much higher. The main reason for the divergence, they found, was that the Canadian system of unemployment insurance was liberalized in the early 1970s. Not that, in comparison to Europe, the Canadian system is generous. It is not. As of the mid-1980s, the income replacement ratio in Canada was about 60 percent (50 percent in the United States) whereas in Denmark it was 90 percent, in Sweden 80 percent, and in Finland 75 percent. In Canada, about 50–55 percent of the unemployed were eligible for benefits (U.S. figures are 34–42 percent), whereas in Belgium 85 percent qualified, 73 percent in Denmark, and between 85–90 percent in Sweden. In Canada, benefits normally expired after six months (the same for the United States), but in every major European country benefits continued for at least one year and in many they were paid indefinitely (Layard, Nickell, and Jackman 1991, annex 1; Card and Riddell 1993). In short, we achieve the rates that we do only by a niggardly distribution of income to job seekers. Because of our miserliness, we force people quickly to take jobs for which they are overqualified, and in the process undermine the efficiency of our labor market (Rowthorn 1992).

8. It is true that more jobs came into existence in Canada and the United States during the past twenty years than in any of the other advanced, market economy countries. However, as Wilensky (1992) has convincingly shown, that was the result almost entirely of demographic factors. Public policy had essentially nothing to do with that job

growth. Moreover, in comparison to other countries, the jobs that were created by the "Great American Job Machine" were inordinately low wage, low skill jobs. Dispersion around the wage mean is much greater in North America than it is in Europe. As a result, "in the European core, the greatest inequality in the potential work-force is between those with jobs and those without. Those fortunate enough to have jobs are, for the most part, moderately well off. This is not the case, however in the United States, where there is a large underclass of what might be called the "working poor" (Rowthorn 1992, 104). One result of the restructuring which took place in the 1980s and 1990s was an increase in wage and income inequality between the rich and the poor in North America. Especially in the United States, the rich got richer and the poor got poorer. These issues are discussed in Card and Freeman, eds. 1993, Pekkarinen, et al. 1992, and Layard, Nickell, and Jackman, et al. 1991.

9. On this theme see the useful monograph by Gorham 1986.

10. This classification is similar to, but not exactly the same as, the corporatist/ pluralist spectrum utilized extensively by economists and political scientists. In that literature, countries are ranked more or less corporatist/pluralist on the basis of attributes such as the degree of organization and centralization of labor and management and the degree of centralization of bargaining. In my classification, the emphasis is more on the extent to which organized labor is recognized and integrated into the network of socioeconomic institutions (and the extent to which there is commitment on the part of all three major actors to recognize as valid the interests of the others), as well as a commitment to achieve consensus with respect to socioeconomic decisions. In the countries classified as cooperative, labor during most or all of the twenty-year period between 1970 and 1990 was highly integrated into both political and industrial decision making. In those countries classified as adversarial, labor was either excluded from or only very weakly involved in most critical, political, and industrial decisions made during the period covered. The terms social concertation and tripartism are often applied to the cooperative countries in my classification (see Treu 1993). Although there is a good deal of overlap between the cooperative/adversarial and corporatist/pluralist concepts, they are not synonymous. Thus, Japan is generally rated low on corporatist scales but it is clearly high on attributes of cooperation. For a review of the concept of corporatism, as well as efforts to quantify it, see Dell'Aringa and Lodovici 1993. Details of arrangements in the countries included in table 6.9 are included in Ferner and Hyman 1992, Frenkel 1993, Bamber and Lansbury 1993, and Hartog and Theeuwes 1993.

Chapter 7:
From Confrontation to Cooperation

1. Technological changes, however, must not be instituted "in obvious contradiction to the established findings of ergonomics." Disputes over this issue are arbitrable. (See Federal Minister of Labour and Social Affairs 1980, 153).

2. Much of the material for this section was acquired from interviews carried out in Germany on behalf of the International Labour Office in 1991.

3. The national organizations are known as federations but, despite the name, they are equivalent not to national federations in other countries, but rather to national unions.

4. The willingness of Japanese employers to provide lifetime employment was contingent on a commitment by the workforce to work diligently in the interests of the enterprise. One part of the union-management understanding was the implicit agreement on the part of the union that it would not defend individual employees who failed to live up to the labor part of the bargain. As a result, slackers are often harassed by management (and sometimes by the employees themselves) until they willingly leave the company. This is a major difference between Japanese lifetime employment and that provided in the Communist countries. In the latter, not only could management not fire the worker, but also the workers frequently were not permitted to quit of their own accord.

5. I am indebted to John Miltenburg for bringing this analogy to my attention.

6. Early works by Johnson (1982) and by Pempel and Tsunekawa (1979) suggested that labor had little influence on political decision making in Japan. Those efforts, however, focused largely on the left-wing, primarily public sector federation Sohyo. More recent research has uncovered a substantial jump in the political influence of the private sector unions following the oil crisis of 1973. (See especially Levine and Taira 1985; Kume 1988; Shimada 1992; Sugeno 1993.)

7. There are some exceptions, for example, the unions do have understandings with cooperatively owned organizations that all employees should be union members.

8. This approach was first developed in Belgium and is known as the Ghent System. (See Gordon 1988.)

9. This proposition is strongly supported by research on the relationship between unemployment and regulation. (See especially Buechtemann 1993.)

Chapter 8:
Transcending Adversarial Industrial Relations

1. The case for a union initiative to represent workers even where they have no members has been well put by Clyde Summers (1990a, 1992).

2. The term "wage slave," although very strong and archaic is technically a good description of the status of the unorganized employee. A slave is "one whose person and services are under the control of another." According to the legal and economic interpretation of the modern employment relationship, the employer purchases the right to control the activities of the employee over a certain range. In a manner similar to the slave, the role of the employee is to obey all reasonable instructions.

3. In its Green Paper on employee participation published in 1975, the Commission of the European Communities put it this way. There is a "democratic imperative" which insists that "those who will be substantially affected by decisions made by social and political institutions must be involved in the making of those decisions" (9).

4. Prominent labor experts such as Paul Weiler (1990) and Richard Freeman (1990) have also suggested the use of works councils, but as advisory mechanisms without

clear codecision rights. Councils of that nature are much more akin to those in France which have been much less successful than those in, for example, Germany where true codetermination exists. For management to fully cooperate with labor representatives, it must have no option to continue to pursue exclusion. Advisory systems do not meet that standard. This argument is elaborated to some extent in Adams 1992.

5. For the application of the concept in the United States and Canada, see Summers 1982, McKersie 1990, and George Adams 1990.

6. Although it would be preferable if all Canadian jurisdictions had the same policy, that probably would not be necessary in order for the strategy to be successful. Because they contain such a large part of the total working population, it would probably be sufficient if Ontario and Quebec had such common expiry laws in effect.

BIBLIOGRAPHY

Aaron, Benjamin. 1990. "Settlement of Disputes over Rights." In R. Blanpain, ed. *Comparative Labour Law and Industrial Relations in Industrialised Market Economies.* Deventer, Netherlands: Kluwer.

Aaron, Benjamin, Joyce M. Najita, and James L. Stern. 1988. *Public-Sector Bargaining.* 2nd ed. Madison, Wis.: Industrial Relations Research Association.

Abella, Irving, ed. 1974. *On Strike: Six Key Labour Struggles in Canada.* Toronto.

Abrahamsson, B., and A. Brostrom. 1980. *The Rights of Labor.* Beverly Hills, Calif.: Sage.

Adams, George W. 1990. *Worker Participation in Corporate Decision-Making: Canada's Future.* Kingston: Queens University Industrial Relations Center.

Adams, R. J. 1974. "Solidarity, Self-Interest and the Unionization Differential Between Europe and North America." *Relations Industrielles* 29, no. 3: 497–512.

———. 1975a. "White-Collar Union Growth: The Case of Sweden." *Industrial Relations* 13, no. 2: 164–76.

———. 1975b. *The Growth of White-Collar Unionism in Britain and Sweden: A Comparative Investigation.* Madison, Wis.: Industrial Relations Research Institute.

———. 1981. "A Theory of Employer Attitudes and Behaviour Towards Trade Unions in Western Europe and North America." In G. Dlugos and K. Weiermair, eds. *Management Under Differing Value Systems.* Berlin: deGruyter.

———. 1982. "The Federal Government and Tripartism." *Relations Industrielles* 37, no. 3: 606–17.

———. 1986. "Two Policy Approaches to Labour-Management Decision Making at the Level of the Enterprise." In W. C. Riddell, ed. *Labour Management Cooperation in Canada.* Toronto: University of Toronto Press.

———. 1987. "Employment Standards in Ontario, An Industrial Relations System Analysis." *Relations Industrielles* 42, no. 1: 46–64.

———. "North American industrial relations: Divergent trends in Canada and the United States." *International Labour Review.* 128, no. 1: 47–64.

———. 1990. "Universal Participation, a moral imperative." *Industrial Relations Research Association.* Annual Meeting, Washington, D.C., 319–27.

———. 1991a. "Employment Relations in an Era of Lean Production." McMaster University Faculty of Business Working Paper No. 361. Hamilton, Ont.

———, ed. 1991b. *Comparative Industrial Relations, Contemporary Research and Theory.* London: Harper Collins.

———. 1992a. "Efficiency is not enough." *Labor Studies Journal* 17, no. 1: 18–28.

———. 1992b. "The Right to Participate." *Employee Responsibilities and Rights Journal* 5, no. 2: 91–99.

———. 1992c. "The Role of the State in Industrial Relations." In D. Lewin, O. Mitchell, and P. Sherer, eds. *Research Frontiers in Industrial Relations and Human Resources.* Madison, Wis.: Industrial Relations Research Association.

———. 1993a. "Regulating Unions and Collective Bargaining: A global, historical analysis of determinants and consequences." *Comparative Labor Law Journal* 14, no. 4.

———. 1993b. "Did the Passage of the Wagner Act Encourage U.S., Union Membership Growth? A Canadian Perspective." Paper presented at the Fifteenth Annual North American Labor History Conference, Wayne State University, Detroit, Mich.

———. 1994. "Union certification as an instrument of labor policy, a comparative perspective." In R. Seeber et al. *Labor Law Reform.* Ithaca, N.Y.: ILR Press.

———, and C. H. Rummel. 1977. "Workers' Participation in Management in West Germany: Impact on the Worker, the Enterprise and the Trade Union." *Industrial Relations Journal* 8, no. 1: 4–22.

———, B. Adell, and H. Wheeler. 1990. "Discipline and Discharge in Canada and the United States." *Labor Law Journal* (August): 596–601.

———, and Bernard Adell. 1992. "Canada." In H. Wheeler and J. Rojot, eds. *Workplace Justice, Employment Obligations in International Perspective.* Columbia: University of South Carolina Press.

Adell, Bernard, and Roy J. Adams. 1993. "Discipline and Discharge for Theft in Ten Countries." *Industrial Relations Research Association.* Proceedings of the annual meeting. Anaheim, Calif. January 5–7. Madison, Wis.: IRRA.

Ahlén, Kristina. 1989. "Swedish Collective Bargaining Under Pressure: Inter-union Rivalry and Incomes Policy." *British Journal of Industrial Relations* 27, no. 3: 330–46.

Aldir, Laura. 1989. "The American Model Unrealized: A Reevaluation of Plant Bargaining in France." *Comparative Labor Law Journal* (Winter).

Armstrong, Tim. 1990. "Industrial Relations-Japanese Style." *Challenges* (Winter).

Arthurs, H. W., D. D. Carter, H. J. Glasbeek, and J. Fudge. 1988. "Canada." In R. Blanpain, ed. *International Encyclopedia of Labour Law and Industrial Relations.* Deventer, Netherlands: Kluwer.

Ashenfelter, O., and R. Smith. 1979. "Compliance With Minimum Wage Laws." *Journal of Political Economy* (April): 330–50.

———, and J. H. Pencavel. 1969. "American trade union growth 1900–1960." *Quarterly Journal of Economics* 133 (August): 434–48.

Ashton, T. S. 1964. *The Industrial Revolution 1766–1830.* New York: Oxford University Press.

Atiyah, P. S. 1979. *The Rise and Fall of Freedom of Contract.* Oxford: Clarendon Press.

Atleson, James B. 1983. *Values and Assumptions in American Labor Law.* Amherst: University of Massachussetts Press.

Ault, W. O. 1952. *The Self-Directing Activities of Village Communities in Medieval England.* Boston.

Baglioni, Guido, and Colin Crouch, eds. 1990. *European Industrial Relations, the Challenge of Flexibility.* London: Sage.

Bain, G. S., and F. Elsheik. 1976. *Union Growth and the Business Cycle.* Oxford: Blackwell.

Bain, Trevor. 1992. *Banking the Furnace, Restructuring the Steel Industry in Eight Countries.* Kalamazoo, Mich.: W. E. Upjohn.

Bamber, G., and G. Whitehouse. 1992. "International data on economic, employment and human resource issues." *International Journal of Human Resource Management* 3, no. 2 (September).

———, and R. Lansbury, eds. 1993. *International and Comparative Industrial Relations.* St. Leonards, Australia: Allen and Unwin.

Banks, A., and J. Metzgar. 1989. "Participating in Management: Union Organizing on a New Terrain." *Labor Research Review* 8, no. 2.

Banting, K., ed. 1986. *The State and Economic Interests.* Toronto: University of Toronto Press.

Barbash, Jack. 1972. *Trade Unions and National Economic Policy.* Baltimore: Johns Hopkins University Press.

———. 1988. "The New Industrial Relations in the US, Phase II." *Relations Industrielles* 43, no. 1: 32–42.

Barkin, Solomon, ed. 1975. *Worker Militancy and Its Consequences, 1965–1975.* New York: Praeger.

Bean, R. "Employers' Associations in the Port of Liverpool, 1890–1914." *International Review of Social History* 21, pt. 3: 358–82.

———. 1985. *Comparative Industrial Relations, An Introduction to Cross-National Perspectives.* London: Croom-Helm.

———, and K. Holden. 1989. "Economic and Political Determinants of Trade Union Growth in Selected OECD Countries: An Update." *Journal of Industrial Relations* (September): 402–6.

Beatty, D. 1987. *Putting the Charter to Work, Designing a Constitutional Labour Code.* Kingston and Montreal: McGill-Queen's University Press.

Begin, James P., and Edwin F. Beal. 1985. *The Practice of Collective Bargaining.* 7th ed. Homewood, Ill.: Irwin.

Bell, Daniel. 1961. *The End of Ideology.* New York: Collier Books.

Berggren, Christian. 1992. *Alternatives to Lean Production.* Ithaca: ILR Press.

Berghahn, Volker R., and Detlev Karsten. 1987. *Industrial Relations in West Germany.* Oxford: Berg.

Berle, A., and G. Means. 1932. *The Modern Corporation and Private Property.* New York: Macmillan.

Bird, Derek. 1991. "International Comparisons of Industrial Disputes in 1989 and 1990." *Employment Gazette* (December).

Blain, Nick, John Goodman, and Joseph Loewenberg. 1987. "Mediation, conciliation and arbitration: An international comparison of Australia, Great Britain and the United States." *International Labour Review* 126, no. 2 (March–April): 179–98.

Blanpain, R., ed. 1990. *Comparative Labour Law and Industrial Relations in Industrialised Market Economies.* 4th ed. Deventer, Netherlands: Kluwer.

Bok, Derek. 1971. "Reflections on the Distinctive Character of American Labor Laws." *Harvard Law Review* (April): 1394–463.

Brewster, C., A. Hegewisch, L. Holden, and T. Lockhart. 1992. *The European Human Resource Mangement Guide.* London: Academic Press.

Bridgford, Jeff. 1990. "French trade unions: crisis in the 1980s." *Industrial Relations Journal* 21, no. 2.

Britt, David, and Omer R. Gallie. 1974. "Structural antecedents of the shape of strikes: a comparative analysis." *American Sociological Review* 39: 642–51.

———. 1972. "Industrial Conflict and Unionization." *American Sociological Review* 37: 46–56.

Brooks, Brian. 1992. *Contract of Employment, Principles of Australian Employment Law.* 4th ed. Sydney: CCH Australia Ltd.

Brown, D., and D. Beatty. 1988. *Canadian Labour Arbitration.* 3rd ed. Aurora, Ont.: Canada Law Book.

Brown, William. 1993. "The Contraction of Collective Bargaining in Britain." *British Journal of Industrial Relations* 32, no. 1 (June): 189–200.

Bruce, Peter G. 1989. "Political Parties and Labor Legislation in Canada and the U.S." *Industrial Relations* 28 (Spring): 115–41.

Buechtemann, Christoph, ed. 1993. *Employment Security and Labor Market Behavior.* Ithaca, N.Y.: ILR Press.

Bunel, Jean, and Jean Saglio. 1984. "Employers Associations in France." In J. P. Windmuller and A. Gladstone, eds. *Employers Associations and Industrial Relations, A Comparative Study.* Oxford: Clarendon Press.

Card, David, and W. Craig Riddell. 1993. "A Comparative Analysis of Unemployment in Canada and the United States." In David Card and Richard B. Freeman, eds. *Small Differences That Matter.* Chicago: University of Chicago Press.

Carlson, Bo. 1969. *Trade Unions in Sweden.* Stockholm: Tidens förlag.

Chaison, Gary N., and Joseph B. Rose. 1990. "Continental Divide: The Direction and Fate of North American Unions." In D. Lewin, D. Lipsky, and D. Sockell, eds. *Advances in Industrial and Labor Relations.* Greenwich, Conn.: JAI Press.

———. "The Macrodeterminants of Union Growth and Decline." In G. Strauss, D. Gallagher, and J. Fiorito, eds. *The State of the Unions.* Madison, Wis.: Industrial Relations Research Association.

Chamberlain, Neil, and James Kuhn. 1965. *Collective Bargaining.* 2nd ed. New York: McGraw-Hill.

Chang, Clara, and Constance Sorrentino. 1991. "Union membership statistics in 12 countries." *Monthly Labor Review* (December).

Clarke, R. O. 1990. "Industrial Conflict: Perspectives and Trends." In R. Blanpain, ed. *Comparative Labour and Industrial Relations in Industrialised Market Economies.* 4th and rev. ed. Deventer, Netherlands: Kluwer.

———. 1993. "Conclusions: Towards a synthesis of international and comparative experience of nine countries." In G. Bamber and R. Lansbury, eds. *International and Comparative Industrial Relations.* 2nd ed. Allen and Unwin.

Clegg, H. A. 1972. *The System of Industrial Relations in Great Britain.* Oxford: Basil Blackwell.

———. 1976. *Trade Unionism Under Collective Bargaining.* Oxford: Basil Blackwell.

CLMPC. 1992. "The Role of Business/Labour Sectoral Initiatives in Economic Restructuring." *Quarterly Labour Market and Productivity Review* no. 1–2: 26–37.

Commission of the European Communities. 1975. "Employee Participation and Company Structure." *Bulletin of the European Communities* no. 8.

Commons, J. R. et al. 1918. *History of Labor in the United States.* New York: Macmillan.

Commons, John R. 1909. "American Shoemakers, 1648–1895." *Quarterly Journal of Economics* 24. Reprinted in Larson, Simeon and Bruce Nissen, 1987. *Theories of the Labor Movement.* Detroit, Mich.: Wayne State University, 140–155.

Conner, Valerie Jean. 1983. *The National War Labor Board, Stability, Social Justice, and the Voluntary State in World War I.* Chapel Hill: University of North Carolina Press.

Córdova, E. 1985. "Strikes in the public service: some determinants and trends." *International Labour Review* 124, no. (March–April): 163–80.

———. 1990. "Collective Bargaining." In R. Blanpain, ed. *Comparative Labour Law and Industrial Relations in Industrialised Market Economies.* 4th ed. Deventer, the Netherlands: Kluwer.

Coulton, G. G. 1925. *The Medieval Village.* London: Cambridge University Press.

Craig, Alton W. J. 1986. *The System of Industrial Relations in Canada.* 2nd ed. Scarborough, Ont.: Prentice-Hall.

———, and Norman Solomon. 1993. *The System of Industrial Relations in Canada.* 4th ed. Scarborough, Ont.: Prentice-Hall.

Creighton, B. 1990. "Freedom of Association." In R. Blanpain, ed. *Comparative Labour Law and Industrial Relations in Industrialised Market Economies.* 4th ed. Deventer, the Netherlands: Kluwer.

Crouch, Colin, and Alessandro Pizzorno, eds. 1978. *The Resurgence of Class Conflict in Western Europe Since 1968.* London: Macmillan.

Crouch, Colin. 1990. "United Kingdom, the Rejection of Compromise." In Guido Baglioni and C. Crouch, eds. *European Industrial Relations, the Challenge of Flexibility.* London: Sage.

———. 1993. *Industrial Relations and European State Traditions.* Oxford: Clarendon Press.

Curme, Michael A., Barry T. Hirsch, and David A. Macpherson. 1990. *Industrial and Labor Relations Review* 44, no. 1: 5–33.

Dahl, Robert. 1984. "Democracy in the Workplace: Is it a Right or a Privilege?" *Dissent* 31, no. 1: 54–60.

Daley, Anthony. 1992. "The Steel Crisis and Labor Politics in France and the United States." In Miriam Golden and Jonas Pontusson, eds. *Bargaining for Change.* Ithaca: Cornell University Press.

Davies, Paul. 1993. "Employee Representational Participation in Britain." Paper presented at an International Colloquium on "Models of Employee Representational Participation." Philadelphia, Penn.: Wharton School, 26 March.

Davis, H. B. 1941. "The theory of union growth." *Quarterly Journal of Economics* 55, August, 611–37.

Deane, Phyllis. 1969. *The First Industrial Revolution.* Cambridge: Cambridge University Press.

Delamotte, Yves. 1988. "Workers' participation and personnel policies in France." *International Labour Review* 127, no. 2: 221–41.

Dell'Aringa, Carlo, and Manuela Lodovici. 1993. "Industrial Relations and Economic Performance." In T. Treu, ed. *Participation in Public Policy-Making.* Berlin: deGruyter.

Derber, Milton. 1970. *The American Idea of Industrial Democracy, 1865–1965.* Urbana: University of Illinois Press.

———. 1984. "Employers Associations in the United States." In J. Windmuller and A. Gladstone, eds. *Employers Associations and Industrial Relations, a Comparative Study.* Oxford: Clarendon Press.

Douglas, Paul. 1921. "Shop Committees: Substitute for, or Supplement to, Trades-unions?" *Journal of Political Economy* February.

Duby, G. 1968. *Rural Economy and Country Life in the Medieval West.* London: Edward Arnold.

Due, J., J. Madsen, and C. Jensen. 1993. *Labour Market Consensus, the Main Pillar of the Danish Model.* Copenhagen: Danish Ministry of Labour.

Dulles, Foster Rhea, and Melvyn Dubofsky. 1984. *Labor in America, a History.* 4th ed. Arlington Heights, Ill.: Harlan Davidson.

Dunlop, John T., and Walter Galenson, eds. 1978. *Labor in the Twentieth Century.* New York: Academic Press.

———. 1958. *Industrial Relations Systems.* New York: Holt.

———. 1993. *Industrial Relations Systems.* rev. ed. Boston: Harvard Business School Press.

Eden, Genevieve. 1993–94. "Unjust Dismissal and the Remedy of Reinstatement." *Journal of Individual Employment Rights* 2, no. 3: 183–98.

Edwards, Paul, Mark Hall, Richard Hyman, Paul Marginson, Keith Sisson, Jeremy Waddington, and David Winchester. 1992. "Great Britain: Still Muddling Through." In A. Ferner, and R. Hyman, *Industrial Relations in the New Europe.* Cambridge: Basil Blackwell.

Esenwein, George. 1992. "Spain." In J. Campbell, ed. *European Labor Unions.* Westport, Conn.: Greenwood.

Esping-Anderson. Gosta. 1990. *The Three Worlds of Welfare Capitalism.* Princeton: Princeton University Press.

Farber H., and A. Krueger. 1993. "Union Membership in the United States: The Decline Continues." In B. Kaufman and M. Kleiner, eds. *Employee Representation, Alternatives and Future Directions.* Madison, Wis.: Industrial Relations Research Association.

Federal Minister of Labour and Social Affairs. 1980. *Co-determination in the Federal Republic of Germany.* Geneva: International Labour Organisation.

Ferner, A., and R. Hyman. 1992a. "Italy: Between Political Exchange and Micro-Corporatism." In A. Ferner and R. Hyman, eds. *Industrial Relations in the New Europe.* Oxford: Basil Blackwell.

———. 1992b. "Industrial Relations in the New Europe: Seventeen Types of Ambiguity." In A. Ferner and R. Hyman, eds. *Industrial Relations in the New Europe.* Oxford: Basil Blackwell.

———, eds. 1992c. *Industrial Relations in the New Europe.* Oxford: Basil Blackwell.

Finkelman, J., and S. Goldenberg. 1983. *Collective Bargaining in the Public Service, the Federal Experience in Canada.* Montreal: Institute for Research on Public Policy.

Filtzer, D. 1986. *Soviet Workers and Stalinist Industrialization.* Armonk, N.Y.: M. E. Sharpe.

Flanagan, Robert J. 1987. *Labor Relations and the Litigation Explosion.* Washington, D.C.: Brookings Institution.

Flanagan, Robert J., David W. Soskice, and Lloyd Ulman. 1983. *Unionism, Economic Stabilization, and Incomes Policies: European Experience.* Washington, D.C.: Brookings Institution.

Flanders, Allen. 1968. *Trade Unions.* 7th rev. ed. London: Hutchinson University Library.

Fogarty, Michael. 1957. *Christian Democracy in Western Europe, 1820–1953.* London: Routledge and Kegan Paul.

Forbath, William E. 1991. *Law and the Shaping of the American Labor Movement.* Cambridge: Harvard University Press.

Form, William. 1973. "Job Vs. Political Unionism: A Cross-National Comparison." *Industrial Relations* 12, no. 2.

Forsebäck, Lennart. 1980. *Industrial Relations and Employment in Sweden.* Uppsals: Almquist and Wiksell.

Fox, A. 1985. *History and Heritage: The Social Origins of the British Industrial Relations System.* London: Allen and Unwin.

Freeman, Richard. 1990a. "On the divergence of unionism among developed countries." In R. Brunetta and C. Dell'Aringa, eds. *Labour Relations and Economic Performance.* London: Macmillan.

———. 1990b. "Employee Councils, Worker Participation and Other Squishy Stuff." *Proceedings of the Forty-Third Annual Meeting of the Industrial Relations Research Association.* Madison, Wis.: Industrial Relations Research Association.

———, and James Medoff. 1984. *What Do Unions Do?* New York: Basic Books.

———, and M. Rebick. 1989. "Crumbling Pillar? Declining Union Density in Japan." *Journal of Japanese and International Economies* 3, 578–605.

———, and M. Kleiner. 1990. "Employer behavior in the face of union organizing drives." *Industrial and Labor Relations Review* 43, no. 4: 351–73.

———, and J. Rogers. 1993. "Who Speaks for Us? Employee Representation in a Nonunion Labor Market." In B. Kaufman and M. Kleiner, eds. *Employee Representation, Alternatives and Future Directions.* Madison, Wis.: Industrial Relations Research Institute.

Frenkel, Stephen, ed. 1993. *Organized Labor in the Asia-Pacific Region.* Ithaca, N.Y.: ILR Press.

Fuerstenberg, Friedrich. 1993. "The Federal Republic of Germany." In G. Bamber and R. Lansbury, eds. *International and Comparative Industrial Relations.* St. Leonards, Australia: Allen and Unwin.

Galenson, Walter. 1961. "Why the American Labor Movement Is Not Socialist." *The American Review* (reprinted in Ray Marshall and Richard Perlman, eds. 1972. *An Anthology of Labor Economics.* New York: Wiley, 61–74.

———, ed. 1952. *Comparative Labor Movements.* New York: Prentice-Hall.

Gardner, Margaret, and Gill Palmer. 1992. *Employment Relations, Industrial Relations and Human Resource Management in Australia.* Melbourne: Macmillan.

Gaudier, Maryse. 1988. "Workers' participation within the new industrial order: a review of the literature." *Labour and Society* 13, no. 3: 313–32.

Geary, Dick. 1991. *European Labor Politics From 1900 to the Depression*. Atlantic Highlands, N.J.: Humanities Press International.

Ginsburg, Woodrow. 1971. "Union Growth, Government and Structure." In Gerald G. Somers, ed. *A Review of Industrial Relations Research*. Vol. 1. Madison, Wis.: Industrial Relations Research Association.

Godard, John. 1994. *Industrial Relations, the Economy and Society*. Toronto: McGraw-Hill Ryerson.

Goetschy, Janine, and Patrick Rozenblatt. 1992. "France: The Industrial Relations System at a Turning Point?" In A. Ferner and R. Hyman, eds. *Industrial Relations in the New Europe*. Cambridge: Basil Blackwell.

———, and Annette Jobert. 1993. "France." In G. Bamber and R. Lansbury, eds. *International and Comparative Industrial Relations*. 2nd ed. St Leonards, Australia: Allen and Unwin.

Goldfield, Michael. 1987. *The Decline of Organized Labor in the United States*. Chicago: University of Chicago Press.

Goldthorpe, John H. 1984. *Order and Conflict in Contemporary Capitalism*. Oxford: Clarendon Press.

Gordon, Andrew. 1985. *The Evolution of Labor Relations in Japan: Heavy Industry-1853–1955*. Cambridge: Harvard University Press.

———. 1990. "Japanese Labor Relations During the Twentieth Century." *Journal of Labor Research* 11 (Summer).

Gordon, Margaret S. 1988. *Social Security Policies in Industrial Countries, a Comparative Analysis*. Cambridge: Cambridge University Press.

Gorham, Lucy. 1986. *No Longer Leading: A Scorecard on US Economic Performance and the Role of the Public Sector Compared with Japan, West Germany, and Sweden*. Washington: Ecomonic Policy Institute.

Grancelli, B. 1988. *Soviet Management and Labor Relations*. Boston: Allen and Unwin.

———. 1992. "Soviet Union." In J. Campbell, ed. *European Labor Unions*. Westport, Conn.: Greenwood.

Grebing, Helga. 1969. *The History of the German Labour Movement*. London: Oswald Wolff.

Gregg, Pauline. 1971. *A Social and Economic History of Britain, 1760–1970*. 6th ed. London: Harrop.

———. 1976. *Black Death to the Industrial Revolution*. London: Harrop.

Gross, J. A. 1981. *The Reshaping of the National Labor Relations Board*. Albany: State University of New York Press.

———. 1985. "Conflicting statutory purposes: another look at fifty years of NLRB lawmaking." *Industrial and Labor Relations Review* 39, no. 1: 7–18.

Guigni, G. 1965. "Recent Developments in Collective Bargaining in Italy." *International Labour Review* 273–91.

Gulick, Charles A. 1948. *Austria From Habsburg to Hitler*. Vol. 1. *Labor's Workshop of Democracy*. Berkeley: University of California Press.

Gunderson, Morley. 1989. "Union Impact on Compensation, Productivity, and Management of the Organization." *Union-Management Relations in Canada*. 2nd ed. Don Mills, Ont.: Addison-Wesley.

Haas, Ain, and Steven Stack. 1983. "Economic Development and Strikes: A Comparative Analysis." *The Sociological Quarterly* 24 (Winter): 43–58.

Hammarström, Olle. 1993. "Sweden." In G. Bamber and R. Lansbury, *International and Comparative Industrial Relations*. St. Leonards, Australia: Allen and Unwin.

Hanagan, Michael. 1984. "Response to Sean Wilentz, 'Against Exceptionalism: Class Consciousness and the American Labor Movement, 1790–1920.'" *International Labor and Working Class History* no. 26 (Fall): 31–36.

Hanson, C., S. Jackson, and D. Miller. 1982. *The Closed Shop*. Aldershot, England: Gower.

Harbridge, Raymond, ed. 1993. *Employment Contracts: New Zealand Experiences*. Wellington: Victoria University Press.

Hartog, Joop, and Jules Theeuwes, eds. 1993. *Labour Market Contracts and Institutions, A Cross-National Comparison*. Amsterdam: North-Holland.

Hattam, Victoria. 1993. *Labor Visions and State Power: The Origins of Business Unionism in the United States*. Princeton: Princeton University Press.

Havlovic, Stephen J. 1990. "German Works' Councils: A Highly Evolved Institution of Industrial Democracy." *Labor Studies Journal* 15, 2: 62–73.

Helm, Jutta A. 1986. "Codetermination in West Germany: What Difference Has It Made?" *West European Politics* 9, no. 1 (January).

Hepple, Bob. 1986a. "Welfare Legislation and Wage-Labour." In Bob Hepple, ed. *The Making of Labour Law in Europe: A Comparative Study of Nine Countries up to 1945*. London: Mansell.

———. 1986b. *The Making of Labour Law in Europe: A Comparative Study of Nine Countries up to 1945*. London: Mansell.

———. 1990. "Flexibility and Security of Employment." In Blanpain, ed. *Comparative Labour Law and Industrial Relations in Industrialized Market Economies*. 4th and rev. ed. Deventer, Netherlands: Kluwer.

Héthy, Lajos. 1991. "Industrial Relations in Eastern Europe, Recent Developments and Trends." In R. J. Adams, ed. *Comparative Industrial Relations, Contemporary Research and Theory*. London: Harper Collins.

Hibbert, Francis A. 1970. *The Influence and Development of English Gilds*. Augustus M. Kelley (originally published in 1891).

Hibbs, D. A. 1976. "Industrial Conflict in Advanced Industrial Societies." *American Political Science Review* 70: 1033–58.

———. 1978. "On the Political Economy of Long-Run Trends in Strike Activity." *British Journal of Political Science* 8: 153–75.

Hince, Kevin. 1993. "Is Euro-American Theory Universally Applicable? An Australasian Perspective." In R. J. Adams and Noah Meltz, eds. *Industrial Relations Theory, Its Nature, Scope and Pedagogy*. Methuen, N.J.: Scarecrow.

Hirsh, B. and D. Macpherson. 1993. "Union Membership and Coverage Files From the Current Population Surveys: Note." *Industrial and Labor Relations Review* 46, no. 3: 574–78.

Horowitz, Gad. 1968. *Canadian Labor in Politics*. Toronto: University of Toronto Press.

Hoxie, Robert. 1917. *Trade Unionism in the United States*. New York: Appleton.

International Labour Office. 1985. *World Labour Report—2*. Geneva.

Jackson, Andrew. 1993. "Unions, Competitiveness, and Productivity: Towards a Labour Perspective." Kingston, Ontario, Queen's University Papers in Industrial Relations, 38.

Jackson, Michael P. 1987. *Strikes.* New York: St. Martin's Press.

———. 1991. *An Introduction to Industrial Relations.* London: Routledge.

Jacobi, O., B. Keller, and W. Müller-Jentsch. 1992. "Germany, Codetermining the Future?" In A. Ferner and R. Hyman, *Industrial Relations in the New Europe.* Oxford: Basil Blackwell.

Jacobs, Antoine. 1986. "Collective Self-Regulation." In Bob Hepple, ed. *The Making of Labour Law in Europe.* London: Mansell.

Jarman, T. L. 1951. *Landmarks in the History of Education.* London: Cresset.

Johnson, Chalmers. 1982. *MITI and the Japanese Miracle.* Stanford: Stanford University Press.

———. 1988. "Japanese-Style Management in America." *California Management Review* (Summer).

Johnston, T. L. 1962. *Collective Bargaining in Sweden.* Cambridge: Harvard University Press.

Juris, Hervey, Mark Thompson, and Wilbur Daniels, eds. 1985. *Industrial Relations in a Decade of Economic Change.* Madison, Wis.: Industrial Relations Research Institute.

Kassalow, Everett M. 1969. *Trade Unions and Industrial Relations: An International Comparison.* New York: Random House.

Katz, Harry, and Thomas A. Kochan. 1992. *An Introduction to Collective Bargaining and Industrial Relations.* New York: McGraw-Hill.

Kaufman, Bruce E. 1991. *The Economics of Labor Markets.* Chicago: Dryden Press.

Keller, Bernd. 1981. "Determinants of the Wage Rate in the Public Sector. The Case of Civil Servants in the Federal Republic of Germany." *British Journal of Industrial Relations* 19, no. 3: 345–60.

———. 1991. "The Role of the State as Corporate Actor in Industrial Relations Systems." In In R. J. Adams, ed. *Comparative Industrial Relations, Contemporary Research and Theory.* London: Harper Collins.

Kendall, Walter. 1975. *The Labour Movement in Europe.* London: Allen Lane.

Kennedy, Thomas. 1980. *European Labor Relations.* Lexington, Mass.: Lexington Books.

Kerr, Clark, and Abraham Siegel. 1955. "The Structuring of the Labor Force in Industrial Society: New Dimensions and New Questions." *Industrial and Labor Relations Review* (January).

———, J. Dunlop, F. H. Harbison, and C. A. Myers. 1960. *Industrialism and Industrial Man.* Cambridge: Harvard University Press.

Kjellberg, Anders. 1992. "Sweden: Can the Model Survive?" In A. Ferner and R. Hyman, *Industrial Relations in the New Europe.* Cambridge: Basil Blackwell.

Klare, Karl. 1978. "Judicial Deradicalization of the Wagner Act and the Origins of Modern Legal Consciousness, 1937–1941." *Minnesota Law Review* no. 62: 265–339.

Knapton, Ernest, and Thomas Derry. 1966. *Europe and the World Since 1914.* New York: Charles Scribner's Sons.

Knight, Thomas, and Donna Sockell. 1988. "Public Policy and the Scope of Collective Bargaining in Canada and the United States." *Proceedings of the Forty-First Annual Meeting of the Industrial Relations Research Association.* Madison, Wis.: IRRA, 279–87.

Kochan, T. A., and T. A. Barocci. 1985. *Human Resource Management and Industrial Relations.* Boston: Little, Brown, and Co.

———, H. C. Katz, and R. B. McKersie. 1986. *The Transformation of American Industrial Relations.* New York: Basic Books.

Kochan, T. A., and K. Wever. 1991. "American Unions and the Future of Worker Representation." In G. Strauss, D. Gallagher, and J. Fiorito, eds. *The State of the Unions.* Madison, Wis.: Industrial Relations Research Association.

Köhler, Peter A., F. Zacher, and Martin Partington, eds. 1982. *The Evolution of Social Insurance 1881–1981.* London: Pinter.

Kumar, Pradeep. 1988. "Estimates of Unionism and Collective Bargaining Coverage in Canada." *Relations Industrielles* 43, no. 4: 757–79.

———. 1993. *From Uniformity to Divergence, Industrial Relations in Canada and the United States.* Kingston, Ont.: IRC Press.

Kume, Ikuo. 1988. "Changing relations among the government, labor, and business in Japan after the oil crisis." *International Organization* 42: 659–87.

Kuwahara, Yasuo. 1993. "Japan." In G. Bamber and R. Lansbury, eds. *International and Comparative Industrial Relations.* 2nd ed. St. Leonards, Australia: Allen and Unwin.

———. 1990. "Changing Industrial Relations in the Context of Industrial Restructuring: The Case of Japan." *Bulletin of Comparative Labour Relations* 20.

Labour Canada. various years. *Collective Bargaining Review.* Ottawa.

Lacroix, R. 1986. "Strike Activity in Canada." In C. Riddell, ed. *Canadian Labour Relations.* Toronto: University of Toronto Press.

Lafferty, William M. 1971. *Economic Development and the Response of Labor in Scandinavia.* Oslo: Universitetsforlaget.

Landauer, Carl. 1959. *European Socialism.* Vol. 1. *From the Industrial Revolution to the First World War and Its Aftermath.* Berkeley: University of California Press.

Landes, David S. 1969. *The Unbound Prometheus.* Cambridge: Cambridge University Press.

Lane, Christel. 1989. *Management and Labour in Europe.* Brookfield, Vt.: Gower.

Larson, Simeon, and Bruce Nissen, eds. 1987. *Theories of the Labor Movement.* Detroit: Wayne State University Press.

Laslett, J. H. M. 1970. *Labor and the Left: A Study of Socialist and Radical Influences in the American Labor Movement, 1881–1924.* New York: Basic Books.

———, and S. M. Lipset. 1974. *Failure of a Dream? Essays in the History of American Socialism.* Garden City, N.Y.: Anchor.

Layard, Richard, Stephen Nickell, and Richard Jackman. 1991. *Unemployment, Macroeconomic Performance and the Labour Market.* Oxford: Oxford University Press.

Lawler, John J. 1990. *Unionization and Deunionization.* Columbia: University of South Carolina Press.

Leeson, R. A. 1979. *Travelling Brothers.* London: George Allen and Unwin.

Levine, David I., and Laura D'Andrea Tyson. 1990. "Participation, Productivity and the Firm's Environment." In Alan S. Blinder, ed. *Paying for Productivity.* Washington, D.C.: Brookings Institution.

Levine, S. 1958. *Industrial Relations in Postwar Japan.* Urbana: University of Illinois Press.

Lewin, David. 1978. "The Impact of Unionism on American Business: Evidence for an Assessment." *Columbia Journal of World Business* no. 13: 89–103.

———, and Richard B. Peterson. 1988. *The Modern Grievance Procedure in the United States.* New York: Quorum Books.

Lewis, P., and D. Spiers. 1990. "Six Years of the Accord: An Assessment." *Journal of Industrial Relations* 32, no. 1 (March): 53–68.

Lincoln, James R., and Arne L. Kalleberg. 1990. *Culture, Control, and Commitment, A Study of Work Organization and Work Attitudes in the United States and Japan.* Cambridge: Cambridge University Press.

Lindblom, C. E. 1977. *Politics and Markets.* New York: Basic Books.

Lipset, Seymour Martin. 1986. "North American Labor Movements: A Comparative Perspective." In S. M. Lipset, ed. *Unions in Transition.* San Francisco: Institute for Contemporary Studies, 421–52.

Lorwin, Val. 1954. *The French Labor Movement.* Cambridge: Harvard University Press.

Lucio, M. 1992. "Spain: Constructing Institutions and Actors in a Context of Change." In A. Ferner and R. Hyman, eds. *Industrial Relations in the New Europe.* Oxford: Basil Blackwell.

Macoby, Michael. 1991. "Introduction: Why American Management Should be Interested in Sweden." In M. Macoby, ed. *Sweden at the Edge, Lessons for American and Swedish Managers.* Philadelphia: University of Pennsylvania Press.

Mahoney, T., and M. Watson. 1993. "Evolving Modes of Work Force Governance: An Evaluation." In B. Kaufman and M. Kleiner, eds. *Employee Representation, Alternatives and Future Directions.* Madison, Wis.: Industrial Relations Research Association.

Malles, Paul. 1973. *The Institutions of Industrial Relations in Continental Europe.* Ottawa: Labour Canada.

Malles, Paul. 1977. *Canadian Industrial Conflict in International Perspective.* Ottawa: Informetrica.

Markovits, Andrei S. 1986. *The Politics of the West German Trade Unions.* Cambridge: Cambridge University Press.

Martin, Andrew. 1987. "The End of the 'Swedish Model?' Recent Developments in Swedish Industrial Relations." *Bulletin of Comparative Labour Relations* 16: 93–128.

McKersie, Robert B. 1990. "Governance: A Framework for Our Field." *Proceedings of the Forty-Third Annual Meeting of the Industrial Relations Research Association.* Madison, Wis.: Industrial Relations Research Association.

McNaught, Kenneth, and David Bercuson. 1974. *The Winnipeg Strike: 1919.* Don Mills, Ont.: Longman Canada.

Meidner, Rudolph. 1992. *The Swedish Model: Concept, Experiences, Perspectives.* York University Center for Research on Work and Society, Working Paper No. 1. Toronto.

Meltz, Noah. 1985. "Labor Movements in Canada and the United States." In T. Kochan, ed. *Challenges and Choices Facing American Labor.* Cambridge, Mass.: MIT Press.

———. 1989. "Interstate and Interprovincial Differences in Union Density." *Industrial Relations* 28, no. 2: 142–58.

Meyer, Adolphe E. 1965. *An Educational History of the Western World.* New York: McGraw-Hill.

Meyers, Frederic. 1981. "France." In A. Blum, ed. *International Handbook of Industrial Relations.* Westport, Conn.: Greenwood Press.

Mills, C. W. 1948. *New Men of Power.* New York: Harcourt, Brace.

Mitchnick, M. 1987. *Union Security and the Charter.* Toronto: Butterworths.

Murphy, William P. 1987. "Establishment and Disestablishment of Union Representation." In C. Morris, ed. *American Labor Policy.* Washington, D.C.: Bureau of National Affairs.

Muthuchidambaram, S. 1986. *New Technology and Industrial Relations: Policy and Practices in Selected Countries.* Ottawa: Report Prepared for the Canadian Labour Market and Productivity Centre.

Myrdal, Hans-Göran. 1981. "Collective wage-earner funds in Sweden, A road to socialism and the end of freedom of association." *International Labour Review* 120, no. 3 (May–June): 319–34.

———. 1991. "The hard way from a centralized to a decentralized industrial relations system, the case of Sweden and SAF." In O. Jacobi and D. Sadowski, eds. *Employers' Associations in Europe: Policy and Organization.* Baden-Baden: Nomos Verlag.

Neef, Arthur, and Christopher Kask. 1991. "Manufacturing Productivity and Labor Costs in 14 Countries." *Monthly Labor Review* 114, no. 12 (December).

Ng, Ignace. 1987. "The Economic and Political Determinants of Trade Union Growth in Selected OECD Countries." *Journal of Industrial Relations* (June): 233–41.

Noël, Alain, and Keith Gardner. 1990. "The Gainers Strike: Capitalist Offensive, Militancy, and the Politics of Industrial Relations in Canada." *Studies in Political Economy* 31 (Spring): 31–72.

OECD. 1993. "OECD Economic Outlook—Highlights." *OECD Observer* (February/March).

Oliver, Nick, and Barry Wilkinson. 1989. "Japanese Manufacturing Techniques and Personnel and Industrial Relations Practice in Britain: Evidence and Implications." *British Journal of Industrial Relations* (March).

Olson, Craig. 1988. "Dispute Resolution in the Public Sector." In Benjamin Aaron, Joyce M. Najita, and James L. Stern, eds. *Public-Sector Bargaining.* 2nd ed. Madison, Wis.: Industrial Relations Research Association.

Ozaki, M. 1987a. "Labour Relations in the Public Sector, 1. Methods of determining employment conditions." *International Labour Review* 126, no. 3 (May–June): 277–99.

———. 1987b. "Labour Relations in the Public Sector, 2. Labour disputes and their resolution." *International Labour Review* 126, no. 4 (July–August): 405–22.

———. 1990. "Labour Relations in the Public Sector." In R. Blanpain, ed. *Comparative Labour Law and Industrial Relations in Industrialised Market Economies.* 4th and rev. ed. Deventer, Netherlands: Kluwer.

Paldam, Martin, and Peder J. Pederson. 1984. "The Large Pattern of Industrial Conflict—A Comparative Study of 18 Countries, 1919–1979." *International Journal of Social Economics* 11, no. 5: 3–28.

———. 1982. "The Macroeconomic Strike Model: A Study of Seventeen Countries, 1948–1975." *Industrial and Labor Relations Review* 35, no. 4: 504–21.

Palmer, Gill. 1983. *British Industrial Relations.* London: George Allen and Unwin.

Panitch, Leo. 1977. "The development of corporatism in liberal democracies." *Comparative Political Studies* 10.

———, and Donald Swartz. 1984. "Towards Permanent Exceptionalism: Coercion and Consent in Canadian Industrial Relations." *Labour/Le Travail* no. 13 (Spring).

Parker, Mike, and Jane Slaughter. 1988. *Choosing Sides: Unions and the Team Concept.* Detroit: Labor Notes Books.

Pekkarinen, Jukka, Matti Pohjola, and Bob Rowthorn. eds. 1992. *Social Corporatism: A Superior Economic System?* Oxford: Clarendon Press.

Pelling, Henry. 1973. *A History of British Trade Unionism.* Harmondsworth, Middlesex, England: Penguin.

Pempel, T. J., and Keiichi Tsunekawa. 1979. "Corporatism without Labor?" In P. Schmitter and C. Lehmbruch, eds. *Trends Toward Corporatist Intermediation.* New York: Sage.

Perlman, Selig. 1928 [1970]. *A Theory of the Labor Movement.* New York: A. M. Kelley.

Peterson, Richard B. 1985. "Economic and Political Impacts on the Swedish Model of Industrial Relations." In Hervey Juris, Mark Thompson, and Wilbur Daniels, eds. *Industrial Relations in a Decade of Economic Change.* Madison, Wis.: Industrial Relations Research Institute.

Pinson, Koppel S. 1954. *Modern Germany, It's History and Civilization.* New York: Macmillan.

Pirenne, Henri. 1937. *Economic and Social History of Medieval Europe.* New York: Harcourt, Brace and World.

Plowman, David. 1989. *Holding the Line: Compulsory Arbitration and National Employer Co-ordination in Australia.* Melbourne: Cambridge University Press.

Ponak, Allen and Mark Thompson. 1989. "Public Sector Collective Bargaining." In Anderson, John, Morley Gunderson, and Allen Ponak. eds. *Union-Management Relations in Canada.* 2nd ed. Don Mills, Ont.: Addison-Wesley.

Pontusson, J., and S. Kuruvilla. 1992. "Swedish Wage-Earner Funds: An Experiment in Economic Democracy." *Industrial and Labor Relations Review* 45, no. 4: 779–91.

Poole, Michael. 1993. "Industrial Relations: Theorizing for a Global Perspective." In R. J. Adams and N. M. Meltz, eds. *Industrial Relations Theory: Its Nature, Scope and Pedagogy.* Metuchen, N.J.: Scarecrow.

Price, Robert. 1991. "The Comparative Analysis of Union Growth." In Roy J. Adams, ed. *Comparative Industrial Relations, Contemporary Research and Theory.* London: HarperCollins.

Raby, D. 1992. "Portugal." In J. Campbell, ed. *European Labor Unions.* Westport, Conn.: Greenwood.

Rehn, Gösta, and Birger Viklund. 1990. "Changes in the Swedish Model." In Guido Baglioni and C. Crouch, eds. *European Industrial Relations, the Challenge of Flexibility.* London: Sage.

Reynolds, Lloyd G. 1988. "Labor Economics Then and Now." In Bruce Kaufman, ed. *How Labor Markets Work.* Lexington: Lexington Books.

Riddell, W. Craig. 1993. "Unionization in Canada and the United States: A Tale of Two Countries." Kingston, Ontario, Queen's University Papers in Industrial Relations.

Rogers, Joel, and Wolfgang Streeck, eds. 1994. *Employee Participation and Works Councils.* Chicago: University of Chicago Press.

Rose, Joseph B. 1983. "Some Notes on the Building Trades-Canadian Labor Congress Dispute." *Industrial Relations* 22, no. 1: 87–93.

———. 1984. "Growth Patterns of Public Sector Unions." In M. Thompson and G. Swimmer, eds. *Conflict or Compromise, The Future of Public Sector Industrial Relations.* Montreal: Institute for Research on Public Policy.

Ross, A. M., and P. T. Hartman. 1960. *Changing Patters of Industrial Conflict.* New York: Wiley.

Rostow, W. W. 1960. *The Stages of Economic Growth.* Cambridge: Cambridge University Press.

Rowthorn, Bob. 1992. "Corporatism and Labour Market Performance." In Pekkarinen, J., M. Pohjola, and B. Rowthorn, eds. *Social Corporatism: A Superior Economic System?* Oxford: Clarendon Press.

Saxe, Stewart D. 1992. *Ontario Employment Law Handbook.* 3rd ed. Toronto: Butterworths.

Scheuer, Steen. 1992. "Denmark: Return to Decentralization." In A Ferner and R. Hyman, *Industrial Relations in the New Europe.* Oxford: Blackwell.

Segrestin, Denis. 1990. "Recent Changes in France." In G. Baglioni and C. Crouch, eds. *European Industrial Relations, the Challenge of Flexibility.* London: Sage.

Sellier, F. 1978. "France." In J. Dunlop and W. Galenson, eds. *Labor in the Twentieth Century.* New York: Academic Press.

Sengenberger, Werner, ed. 1993. *Lean Production and Beyond, Labour Aspects of a New Production Concept.* Geneva: International Institute of Labour Studies.

Sexton, Jean. 1987. "First Contract Arbitration in Canada." *Labor Law Journal* (August).

Sherman, Herbert L. 1981. "Reinstatement as a Remedy for Unfair Dismissal in Common Market Countries." *American Journal of Comparative Law* 29: 467–511.

Shimada, Haruo. 1992. "Structural Adaptation of the Japanese Economy and Labour Market." In T. Treu, ed. *Participation in Public Policy-Making.* Berlin: de Gruyter, 250–78.

Shirai, Tashiro, ed. 1983. *Contemporary Industrial Relations in Japan.* Madison, Wis.: University of Wisconsin Press.

———, and H. Shimada. 1978. "Japan." In John T. Dunlop and Walter Galenson, eds, *Labor in the Twentieth Century.* New York: Academic Press.

Shorter, E., and C. Tilly. 1971. "The shape of strikes in France, 1830–1960." *Comparative Studies in Society and History* 13: 60–86.

Shuster, Michael. 1990. "Union-Management Cooperation." In J. A. Fossum, ed. *Employee and Labor Relations.* Washington, D.C.: Bureau of National Affairs.

Skogh, Göran. 1984. "Employers Associations in Sweden." In John P. Windmuller and Alan Gladstone, eds. *Employers Associations and Industrial Relations.* Oxford: Clarendon Press.

Slomp, Hans. 1990. *Labor Relations in Europe, A history of issues and developments.* New York: Greenwood.

Snyder, David. 1977. "Early North American Strikes: a reinterpretation." *Industrial and Labor Relations Review* 30: 324–41.

———. 1975. "Institutional Setting and Industrial Conflict: Comparative Analyses of France, Italy and the United States." *American Sociological Review* 40: 259–78.

Sombart, Werner. 1976. *Why Is There No Socialism in the United States?* White Plains, N.Y.: International Arts and Science Press.

Soskice, David. 1990. "Wage Determination: The Changing Role of Institutions in Advanced Industrialized Countries." *Oxford Review of Economic Policy* 6, no. 4 (Winter): 36–61.

———. 1994. "The German Wage Bargaining System." Paper presented at the Annual Meeting of the Industrial Relations Research Association, Boston, January. Madison, Wis.: Industrial Relations Research Association.

Stepina, Lee, and Jack Fiorito. 1986. "Toward A Comprehensive Theory of Union Growth and Decline." *Industrial Relations* 25 (Fall): 248–64.

Streeck, Wolfgang. 1984a. "Co-determination: the fourth decade." In W. Wilpert, ed. *International yearbook of organizational democracy.* Norfolk: John Wiley.

———. 1984b. *Industrial Relations in West Germany, A case study of the car industry.* London: Heineman.

———, Josef Hilbert, Karl-Heinz van Kevelaer, Frederike Maier, and Hajo Weber. 1987. *The Role of the Social Partners in Vocational Training in the Federal Republic of Germany.* Berlin: CEDEFOP.

Sturmthal, Adolf. 1944. *The Tragedy of European Labour.* London.

———. 1964. *Workers Councils.* Cambridge: Harvard University Press.

———. 1966a. "Economic Development and the Labor Movement." In A. M. Ross, ed. *Industrial Relations and Economic Development.* London: Macmillan.

———, ed. 1966b. *White-Collar Trade Unions, Contemporary Developments in Industrialized Societies.* Urbana: University of Illinois Press.

———. 1972. *Comparative Labor Movements, Ideological Roots and Institutional Development.* Belmont, Calif.: Wadsworth.

———. 1973. "Industrial Relations Strategies." In A. Sturmthal and J. Scoville, eds. *The International Labor Movement in Transition.* Urbana: University of Illinois Press.

Sugeno, Kazuo. 1993. "Japan: The State's Guiding Role in Socioeconomic Development." *Comparative Labor Law Journal* 14, no. 3 (Spring): 302–20.

Summers, Clyde. 1979. "Industrial Democracy: America's Unfulfilled Promise." *Cleveland State Law Review* 28: 29–49.

———. 1982. "Codetermination in the United States: A Projection of Problems and Potentials." *Journal of Comparative Corporate Law and Securities Regulation* 4: 155–91.

———. 1984. "The Usefulness of Unions in a Major Industrial Society—A Comparative Sketch." *Tulane Law Review* 58, no. 6 (June): 1409–40.

———. 1990a. "Unions without Majorities: The Potentials of the NLRA." *Proceedings of the Forty-Third Annual Meeting.* Madison, Wis.: Industrial Relations Research Association.

————. 1990b. "The Supreme Court and Industrial Democracy." In H. Willenreuther, ed. *German and American Constitutional Law.*

————. 1992. "Unions without majority—a black hole?" *Chicago-Kent Law Review* 66, no. 3: 531–48.

Taft, Philip. 1952 "Germany." In W. Galenson, ed. *Comparative Labor Movements.* New York: Russel and Russel.

————. 1964. *Organized Labor in American History.* New York: Harper and Row.

Taira, Koji, and Solomon B. Levine. 1985. "Japan's Industrial Relations: A Social Compact Emerges." In Hervey Juris, Mark Thompson, and Wilbur Daniels, eds. *Industrial Relations in a Decade of Economic Change.* Madison, Wis.: Industrial Relations Research Association.

Tannenbaum, Frank. 1951. *A Philosophy of Labor.* New York: Knopf.

Taylor, Benjamin, and Fred Witney. 1987. *Labor Relations Law.* 5th ed. Englewood Cliffs, N.J.: Prentice-Hall.

Teuteberg, Hans. 1961. *Geshickte der Industriellen Mitbestimmung in Deutschland.* Tübingen: J. C. Mohr-Paul Siebeck.

Thelen, Kathleen. 1987. "Codetermination and Industrial Adjustment in the German Steel Industry: A Comparative Interpretation." *California Management Review* 29, no. 3 (Spring).

————. 1991. *Union of Parts, Labor Politics in Postwar Germany.* Ithaca: Cornell University Press.

Therborn, G. 1977. "The Rule of Capital and the Rise of Democracy." *New Left Review* 103: 3–41.

Thompson, Mark. 1991. "Union-management Relations: Recent Research and Theory." In Roy J. Adams, ed. *Comparative Industrial Relations, Contemporary Research and Theory.* London: HarperCollins.

Tomlins, C. 1985. *The State and the Unions.* Cambridge: Cambridge University Press.

Towers, Brian. 1989. "Running the gauntlet: British trade unions under Thatcher." *Industrial and Labor Relations Review* 42, no. 2: 163–88.

Treu, Tiziano, ed. 1992a. *Participation in Public Policy-Making, the Role of Trade Unions and Employers' Associations.* Berlin: deGruyter.

————. 1992b. "Tripartite Social Policy-Making: An Overview." In Treu, ed. *Participation in Public Policy-Making, the Role of Trade Unions and Employers' Associations.* Berlin: deGruyter.

Turner, Lowell. 1991. *Democracy at Work, Changing World Markets and the Future of Labor Unions.* Ithaca: Cornell University Press.

Unwin, George. 1957. *Industrial Organisation in the 16th and 17th Centuries.* London: Cass.

van de Vall, Mark. 1970. *Labor Organizations.* Cambridge: Cambridge University Press.

van der Linden, M. 1990. *Revolutionary Syndicalism: an International Perspective.* Brookfield, Vt.: Gower.

Veneziani, Bruno. 1986. "The Evolution of the Contract of Employment." In B. Hepple, ed. *The Making of Labour Law in Europe.* London: Mansell.

————, ed. 1993. *Economic and Political Changes in Europe: Implications on Industrial Relations.* Proceedings of the Third Regional Congress of the International Industrial Relations Association. Bari: Cacucci Editore.

Visser, Jelle. 1990. "In Search of Inclusive Unionism." *Bulletin of Comparative Labour Relations* no. 18: 1–278.

———. 1992a. "Union Organization: Why Countries Differ." *Proceedings of the Ninth World Congress of the International Industrial Relations Association.* Geneva: International Industrial Relations Association.

———. 1992b. "The Netherlands: The End of an Era and the End of a System." In A. Ferner and R. Hyman, eds. *Industrial Relations in the New Europe.* Cambridge: Basil Blackwell.

———. 1993. "Employee Representation in Western European Workplaces (structure, scale, scope and strategy)." In B. Veneziani, *Economic and Political Change in Europe: Implications on Industrial Relations.* Bari: Cacucci Editore.

Vogel, E. 1979. *Japan As Number One.* Tokyo: Charles Tuttle.

von Beyme, Klaus. 1980. *Challenge to Power, Trade Unions and Industrial Relations in Capitalist Countries.* London: Sage.

von Prondzynski, Ferdinand. 1987. *Freedom of Association and Industrial Relations: a comparative study.* London: Mansell.

Wachtel, Howard M. 1992. *Labor and the Economy.* 3rd ed. New York: Dryden Press.

Waldie, K. G. 1986. "The Evolution of Labour-Government Consultation on Economic Policy." In W. Craig Riddell, ed. *Labour-Management Cooperation in Canada.* Toronto: University of Toronto Press.

Wallerstein, Michael. 1989. "Union Organization in Advanced Industrial Democracies." *American Political Science Review* 83, no. 2: 481–501.

Webb, Sidney, and Beatrice Webb. 1894. *History of Trade Unionism.* New York: Longmans, Green, and Co.

Webb, Beatrice, and Sydney Webb. 1902. *Industrial Democracy.* London: Longmans.

Weber, Max. 1958. *The Protestant Ethic and the Spirit of Capitalism.* Trans. Talcott Parsons. New York: Scribner.

———. 1966. *General Economy History.* New York: Collier Books.

Weiler, Paul C. 1980. *Reconcilable Differences.* Toronto: Carswell.

———. 1990. *Governing the Workplace, the Future of Labor and Employment Law.* Cambridge: Harvard University Press.

Weiss, M., S. Simitis, and W. Rydzy. 1984. "The Settlement of Labour Disputes in the Federal Republic of Germany." In T. Hanami and R. Blanpain, eds. *Industrial Conflict Resolution in Market Economies, A Study of Australia, the Federal Republic of Germany, Italy, Japan and the USA.* Deventer, the Netherlands: Kluwer.

Wells, Don. 1987. *Empty Promises.* New York: Monthly Review Books.

Wever, Kirstin. 1992. "Political Determinants of Strategic Choice: German Employers' Views of Labour Representation." Northeastern University School of Business Working Paper. Boston.

Wheeler, Hoyt N., and John A. McClendon. 1991. "The Individual Decision to Unionize." In G. Strauss, D. Gallagher, and J. Fiorito, eds. *The State of the Unions.* Madison, Wis.: Industrial Relations Research Association.

————, and Dennis R. Nolan. 1992. "The United States." In H. Wheeler and J. Rojot, eds. *Workplace Justice, Employment Obligations in International Perspective.* Columbia: University of South Carolina Press.

————, and Jacques Rojot, eds. 1992. *Workplace Justice, Employment Obligations In International Perspective.* Columbia: University of South Carolina Press.

Wilensky. 1992. "The Great American Job Machine in Comparative Perspective." *Industrial Relations* 31, no. 3: 473–88.

Wilentz, Sean. 1984. "Against Exceptionalism: Class Consciousness and the American Labor Movement, 1790–1920." *International Labor and Working Class History* no. 26 (Fall): 1–24.

Wilson, G. K. 1982. "Why is There No Corporatism in the United States?" In G. Lehmbruch and P. Schmitter, eds. *Patterns of Corporatist Policy-Making.* London: Sage.

Windmuller, John P. 1969. *Labor Relations in the Netherlands.* Ithaca: Cornell University Press.

————, ed. 1977. "Industrial Democracy in International Perspective." *Annals of the American Academy of Political and Social Science* 431 (May).

————. 1987a. *The International Trade Union Movement.* Deventer, Netherlands: Kluwer.

———— et al. 1987b. *Collective Bargaining in Industrialised Market Economies: a Reappraisal.* Geneva: International Labour Office.

————. 1984. "Employers Associations in Comparative Perspective: Organization, Structure, Administration." In John P. Windmuller and Alan Gladstone, eds. *Employers Associations and Industrial Relations, A Comparative Study.* Oxford: Clarendon Press.

————, and Alan Gladstone, eds. 1984. *Employers Associations and Industrial Relations, A Comparative Study.* Oxford: Clarendon Press.

Womack, James P., Daniel T. Jones, and Daniel Roos. 1990. *The Machine the Changed the World.* New York: Maxwell Macmillan International.

Woods, H. D. 1973. *Labour Policy in Canada.* Toronto: Macmillan.

Yamaguchi, K. 1983. "The Public Sector: Civil Servants." In T. Shirai, ed. *Contemporary Industrial Relations in Japan.* Madison, Wis.: University of Wisconsin Press.

INDEX